To Johnnie

and Gregory

with love

from

Jackie.

18.5,79

MILESTONES

MILESTONES

Sir John Smyth
V.C.

SIDGWICK & JACKSON

LONDON

OTHER BOOKS BY THE SAME AUTHOR

Defence Is Our Business (1944)
The Western Defences (ed.) (1950)
Lawn Tennis – A History of the Game (1953)
The Game's the Same (1957)
Before the Dawn (Dunkirk and Burma) (1957)
The Only Enemy (autobiography) (1959)
Sandhurst (1961)
The Story of the Victoria Cross (1962; Cadet edition, 1963)
Beloved Cats (1963)
Blue Magnolia (1964)
Behind the Scenes at Wimbledon (with Colonel Duncan Macaulay)
(1965)
Ming – The Story of a Cat Family (1966)
The Rebellious Rani (1966)
Bolo Whistler – The Life of Sir Lashmer Whistler (1967)
The Story of the George Cross (1968)
In This Sign Conquer – The Story of the Army Chaplains (1968)
The Valiant (1970)
The Will to Live (1970)
Percival and the Tragedy of Singapore (1971)
Jean Borotra – The Bounding Basque (1974)
Leadership in War, 1939–45 (1974)
Leadership in Battle, 1914–18 (1975)
Great Stories of the Victoria Cross (1977)

CHILDREN'S BOOKS
Paradise Island (1952)
Trouble in Paradise (1959)
Ann Goes Hunting (1960)

PLAYS
Burma Road (with Ian Hay) (1945)
Until the Morning (with Ian Hay) (1950)

First published in Great Britain in 1979 by
Sidgwick and Jackson Limited

Copyright © 1979 by Brigadier The Rt. Hon. Sir John Smyth, BT., V.C., M.C.

ISBN 0 283 98522 4

Printed in Great Britain by The Anchor Press Ltd and bound by
Wm Brendon & Son Ltd both of Tiptree, Essex, for Sidgwick and Jackson Limited
1 Tavistock Chambers, Bloomsbury Way, London WC1A 2SG

To my most beloved wife and companion

FRANCES

this book is dedicated

How many miles to Babylon?
Threescore years and ten.
Can I get there by candlelight?
Yes, there and back again.

The Smyth family motto

NEC TIMEO, NEC SPERNO

(I neither fear my enemy, nor do I despise him)

Acknowledgements

First and foremost I am grateful to my good friend, Sir Charles Forte and his highly reputed publishers, Sidgwick and Jackson, for agreeing to produce this book. Sir Charles has been most helpful to my V.C. and G.C. Association ever since I founded it in 1956 and the Café Royal has been a home away from home for our members.

The part of my book dealing with the Burma Campaign of early 1942 is still the subject of considerable controversy, though, with the passage of time and the publication of several other books, the true facts are coming to light – as they generally do in the end. And in getting these facts established I am particularly grateful for the support I received from two great field-marshals, Sir Claude Auchinleck and Viscount Bill Slim.

But most of all I am grateful for the invaluable support of the late Major-General H. L. (Taffy) Davies, Major-General (Punch) Cowan, Major-General Roger Ekin and Brigadier W. G. N. Thompson. At the time these operations took place Taffy Davies was, first, Chief General Staff Officer to General Hutton, the Burma Army Commander, and then, during the second part of the 1942 Burma Campaign, served in the same capacity to General Bill Slim. Cowan was my Brigadier General Staff and succeeded me in command of the 17th Division. Ekin was commanding the 46th Infantry Brigade and Thompson was my Chief Administrative Staff Officer. No other officers who took part in the so-called 'Sittang Disaster' knew more about this much discussed operation than these four distinguished soldiers. And they made an important contribution to me and to the correctness, or otherwise, of the official history sixteen years later, when the controversial part of the history was being discussed. Had it not been for their invaluable expressions of support, which are recorded in this book, I and my troops would have continued to be regarded as the villains of the piece.

ACKNOWLEDGEMENTS

In the writing of the book I am, as always, extremely grateful to the Chief Librarian of the Ministry of Defence Library (Central & Army) for the provision of such books and documents as I required.

I am also greatly indebted to my Sidgwick and Jackson editor, Jane Heller, for her quite invaluable help and efficiency in the production of the book; Frances and I have found her a great pleasure to work with.

And last, but by no means least, I am for ever grateful to my wife, Frances, who has not only typed (and re-typed) the thirty-two books I have written, but has acted throughout as my invaluable sub-editor and adviser.

J.G.S.

Contents

9

List of Illustrations

Introduction

———————————➤⊂———————————

Most people looking back at their lives realize that there were certain milestones by the way, which may not have been noticed at the time, but which marked radical turning points in their careers. At some of these there may have been turnings to right or to left which could have been taken if it had been so desired, and such turnings could have altered the whole of the rest of their lives. On the other hand it may have been that whatever they had desired, force of circumstance gave them no option.

On looking back at one's life it is interesting to note the important milestones and to differentiate those at which a choice was within one's power. Naturally one cannot say where turnings which could have been taken and were not might have led one. But with hindsight they are generally easy to recognize.

The first fifty years of my life ran along the lines of a successful regular soldier, with service in both world wars and seven Indian Frontier campaigns, a V.C., M.C., Brevet-majority, Brevet-lieut.-colonelcy and six mentions in despatches. But then, in 1942, having commanded a brigade at Dunkirk with distinction and a mention in despatches (the only Indian Army officer to have had a fighting command there), I was given the unenviable task of commanding a very ramshackle division in Burma at the time of the Japanese invasion of that country. I was an acting major-general at the time, two years senior to Bill Slim and two years younger.

As Bill Slim said to me afterwards – though he fully supported my action – 'Jackie, you dropped your Field-Marshal's baton into the Sittang River.' There had been considerable controversy, which still continues, as to whether I dropped it or someone else threw it in. Anyway, the Sittang disaster, followed by many years of ill-health, spelt the end of my military career.

The 'milestone' which pointed to 'Burma 1942' was one which no soldier in his senses would have chosen to take in the circumstances which appertained at the time. Although the Japanese capture of Rangoon was inevitable, the disaster which occurred at Sittang was completely avoidable and would not have happened if I had been allowed to fight the battle under the plan of my own making, and under the direction of higher commanders, had they come up to the battle front and established an advanced headquarters in touch with me; instead they tried to direct operations from the map in far away Java and Rangoon and then put the blame for the inevitable disaster which followed on the troops and their commanders. There was nothing wrong with the British and Indian troops under my command except that they were completely untrained and unequipped for defensive jungle warfare and contained a large Burmese element who were incapable of coping with the Japanese in a regular role, but who would have been invaluable in the guerrilla role in which I wanted to use them.

When, after the fall of Rangoon, the reduced BURCORPS, with the addition of a light armoured brigade and without the Burmese, were required to withdraw to the frontiers of India under command of two first-class fighting generals, Alexander and Slim, they did so without any great trouble from the Japanese. The condemnation of me and my subordinate commanders for the Sittang disaster, which General Wavell made in the heat of the moment and of which he repented later, still lingers on, though it has been largely contradicted by subsequent reports and opinions, particularly in the official history of the campaign.

But, as I have so often said, there is no greater autocrat than a commander-in-chief in the field. He can (and on this occasion did) condemn a subordinate commander under cover of the Official Secrets Act, without the accused being given an opportunity of reply, even when the secrecy ban is lifted. The Americans manage these things in a more democratic way.

I had to pick up the pieces and start again from scratch. My friend Field-Marshal Auchinleck, who was my greatest supporter during my military career, said to a friend on his ninetieth birthday (in 1974): 'What I have most admired in Jackie Smyth's life is his last thirty-two years.' And these have certainly been the most exciting and rewarding, and perhaps the most unusual for a regular soldier.

First I became a journalist and broadcaster – Military Correspondent (and later Lawn Tennis Correspondent) to the *Sunday Times* and several other newspapers, and then an author. Since 1944 I have written thirty-two books, children's books, cat books, lawn tennis books and, particularly, military history and biographies. I went into politics, fought the 1945 election against Ernie Bevin in Central Wandsworth, then won back Norwood for the Conservatives in 1950 and remained their M.P. until my retirement from politics in 1966.

During this time I held two ministerial appointments in the Governments of Winston Churchill and Anthony Eden and was awarded a baronetcy and a Privy Councillorship – one of only six people in our history to have been a V.C. and a P.C. I became a Freeman of the City of London in the Farriers' Livery Company, and subsequently Master; and I have been a governor of a number of schools, including seventeen years as Comptroller of the Royal Alexandra and Albert School for Orphan and Necessitous Children.

I have always been tremendously interested in sport, having represented the Army at four different games. In the world of lawn tennis I have been a member of the All England Lawn Tennis Club at Wimbledon for nearly forty years, and Vice-President of the International Lawn Tennis Club of Great Britain and a member of the I.C.s of U.S.A. and France.

I have held leading positions in many of the ex-service associations and perhaps the thing in my life of which I have been most proud is to have been the founder, first Chairman (for fifteen years) and then President, following Sir Winston Churchill's death, of the V.C. and G.C. Association. So one way and another, I have passed a lot of interesting milestones, had a lot of ups and downs, and met many interesting people on the way.

No soldier who has done as much battle fighting as I have done could fail to escape some hard knocks and these affect one more in later life. I was only once hit by a bullet (and that was a glancing wound) but have had several bullets through my clothing and on several occasions was blown up by shells and mines in the early trench warfare days of 1914–15 in France. And the first gas attack at Ypres in April 1915, when we had no gas masks, didn't do me any good either. But the worst war disability I suffered was the aftermath of my anal operation in Quetta in October 1941 and the illness which followed the Burma Campaign of 1942. This complete breakdown in health, accompanied by frequent attacks of paroxysmal tachycardia, made my climb back to a successful career in civil life extremely difficult. But I refused to contemplate an easy life growing cabbages in the country and in this decision I was much encouraged by a first-class Harley Street specialist, alas now deceased, in the whole subject of disorders of the nervous system. I should never have come to the surface at all without the robust support of my wife, Frances, and to her I owe a debt of gratitude which I can never repay.

J.G.S.

CHAPTER ONE

Family Background, the Dragon School, Repton and Sandhurst

T HE Smyths were a well-known Yorkshire family. John Smyth first bought land at Heath, near Halifax, in 1707, afterwards acquiring Heath Hall, the family seat. John Smyth's son, the fourth John Smyth of Heath, who was born in 1748, became the first of the Smyths to enter public life, being a Member of Parliament for the Borough of Pontefract for twenty-five years. He became a Privy Councillor and was successively a Lord of the Admiralty, a Lord of the Treasury and Master of the Mint, and was a member of the Government during the American War of Independence. He married Lady Georgiana Fitzroy, daughter of the third Duke of Grafton. His eldest surviving son, John Henry, married, as his second wife, his cousin, Lady Elizabeth Ann Fitzroy, daughter of the fourth Duke of Grafton, thus further cementing the union of the Smyth and Fitzroy families.

John Henry Smyth was Member of Parliament for Cambridge from 1812 until his death in 1822. Politics and soldiering had by this time become established careers for the Smyths.

John Henry's eldest son, John George, married at the age of twenty-two the Honourable Diana Macdonald, a daughter of Macdonald the Lord of the Isles, and by her had four sons and four daughters. The eldest son, George John Fitzroy Smyth, succeeded his father in 1869 and was the last of the Smyths to live at Heath Hall, but only for a very short time owing to the decline in the family fortunes and the fact that the Hall was right in the centre of a vast coal-mining area. He lived the greater part of his life in the Imperial Hotel in Bournemouth where I often used to stay with him. He never married and died aged ninety-four – a marvellous old Guardsman of whom I was very fond.

Diana Smyth, his eldest sister, married, as his second wife, the fourth Earl of Harewood, whose grandson, the sixth Earl, married H.R.H. The Princess Royal in 1922. I was to see much of the latter in later years when she was the devoted Patron of the 'Not Forgotten' Association and also Patron of the Distinguished Conduct Medal League, of which I was Vice-President and President respectively.

To return to John Henry Smyth. His younger brother, Henry, John George's brother, chose the Army as his profession and became a Lieut.-General in 1876. In 1865 he married Rebecca, the eldest daughter of Thomas Pierce Esq. My father, William John Smyth, born on 2 May 1869 at Sidmouth in Devon, was their third son. Early in 1893 he married my mother, Lillian May Clifford, the daughter of a Captain in the Royal Navy. They were both twenty-three when they married in London. Neither of them had any money so he applied for the Indian Civil Service. He had only just come down from Balliol College where he was a double first and a brilliant scholar. Although the I.C.S. was a fine service, it was rather a waste for such a brilliant man to spend his life in the jungles of Burma, but after four expensive years at Oxford he had to adopt a profession which would be quickly self-supporting. Love wouldn't wait and I was born in October of that year in Teignmouth, Devon, in which county my father had also been born. Devon was a favourite holiday county for the Smyths and later I chose to be a Baronet of Teignmouth rather than of Heath.

My father was tall and handsome, a fine cricketer and keen yachtsman, with a delightful sense of humour. My mother had no intellectual attainments at all. She was small, sturdy and good-looking, with an immense capacity for making friends. Quite early in their married life, having produced three sons, they had to face the critical decision which confronted so many families tied to a job in the East. Should the wife remain with her husband and let other people look after her children in England, or should she go home and let other people look after her husband? As soon as I was of prep school age she chose the former and was thereafter nearly always with me at home during this period of our lives. The three sons were myself, John George, named after my grandfather's distinguished brother; Herbert Edward Fitzroy, my next brother, named after the Fitzroy side of the family and commonly called 'Billy', and the youngest, Henry Malcolm (known to us always as 'Lit', the little one, though he grew to be almost twice my size). He was called Malcolm after my godfather, Malcolm Jardine, who was the father of Douglas Jardine, England's famous cricket captain. Malcolm Jardine and my father were great friends at Oxford and played a lot of cricket together.

From 1901 to 1908 I was educated at that very wonderful and

successful preparatory school, the Dragon, at Oxford. The headmaster, C. C. Lynam, always known as the Skipper, was a most remarkable man. He was an Oxford graduate, scholar, fine rugby football player and well-known amateur yachtsman. To all outward appearances he was everything a schoolmaster ought not to be – unpunctual and untidy to a degree. He was incredibly generous and would give his last penny to some down-and-out he came across and leave himself with no money to get home. But he was the finest leader of small boys I have ever met. His square, sturdy figure was generally clad in an old blue, double-breasted suit, covered in places with daubs of paint. His rubicund, weather-beaten face, flowing grey locks and foul old pipe were redolent of ropes and sails and sea breezes.

Apart from his school the Skipper's passion was for the sea and his stout little yawl, *The Blue Dragon*, in which I had two adventurous voyages as cabin boy. On one of these *The Blue Dragon* sailed up the west coast of Scotland, to Orkney and Shetland and over to Norway. This won the cup given for the most adventurous amateur cruise by a small sailing boat in that particular year. I never knew how well-known the Skipper and *The Blue Dragon* were until I joined the Indian Army and was invited to the Bombay Yacht Club and found the red carpet laid out for me as ex-cabin boy of the bold *B.D.*

The Skipper was a very canny and experienced yachtsman but somewhat unorthodox, and his crew, though eager to learn, were a remarkable collection of old boys and young boys – and girls – mostly from the Dragon School. The Sidgwicks, Frank and Hugh, wrote some wonderful doggerel about life on *The Blue Dragon*, such as the following:

Nimium ne Crede Experto

'This narrow strait,' (the Sailing Directions said)
'Is full of rocks and difficult to enter;
Whirlpools are common here at every tide;
There are uncharted reefs on every side
And currents (twenty knots) along the centre.'

'Come,' said the Skipper, 'We will go in here.'
    (We went in there.)

'There is no sand,' (the Sailing Directions said),
'The anchorage is thoroughly unsafe.
There is no shelter from the frequent squalls
Boats should go on to Lock MacInchmaquaif.'

'Come,' said the Skipper, 'We will anchor here.'
    (We anchored here.)

Another fabulous figure on the *B.D.* was the Mate, Harry 'Jugs' Vassall.

The sun is high on the Scottish Isles,
And the tea is in the cup.
And the Mate and the Skipper, sleepy-eyed,
With a thundering splash go over the side
Get up you brute, get up.
For that is the eight o'clock August gun
And this is the old B.D.
And today, they say, we mustn't delay
To go over the sea, the sea.

H. H. 'Jugs' Vassall was to be my housemaster in the Priory when I went to Repton. He was a vast mountain of a man, one-time captain of England at rugger and also – like the Skipper – a very great leader of boys and men.

I loved my time at the Dragon School, where my two brothers followed me, despite the fact that for two years I was in bed from a combination of dropsy and Bright's disease, from which the doctors of the day said that recovery was almost a miracle. The person who was absolutely certain that I would recover was the Skipper.

This illness came upon me with startling suddenness just before my tenth birthday, up to which time I had shown signs of becoming an outstanding athlete, with quite a good brain. I felt very lethargic one hot summer afternoon and told my mother that my leg appeared swollen and when I pressed it the finger mark remained. Next day I felt no better, a doctor was called and within a week I was completely bed-ridden – and remained so for two long years.

In fact these two years were, from a character-forming point of view, the most important in my life. Doctors came and went and could offer no solution. These were distressing and expensive years for my mother and father; the latter came over from Burma to see me, and this was one of the only times in my life that I saw him. My mother of course remained with me all the time. I had quite a lot of discomfort but very little pain. I lived in a little world of my own – a world of fantasy and make-believe – and became perceptive with an awareness far beyond my years. I didn't mind being alone and, in a way, revelled in the privacy of my own thoughts. I read voraciously and with intense concentration. I was not afraid of death nor did I recognize, as those around me did, that it appeared inevitable.

At last, after every cure and diet had been tried in vain, I heard my nurse say : 'He has very little time to live now, he can have whatever he likes to eat.'

I said in a still, small voice : 'I'll have a steak.'

In due course the steak arrived. I could eat very little of it but, marvellous to relate, from that moment I started to recover. I no longer swelled up like a balloon and had to be 'tapped', as had happened throughout two long years. My skin hung in folds around me. But although I never regained the high athletic promise I had shown at the age of nine, I was one of the leading Dragon games players at cricket, rugger, soccer and hockey before I left.

The Dragon School achieved its century of boys whilst I was there. Later it became enormous for a preparatory school – 450 boys and a long waiting list. But they had the buildings to house the boys, and the playing fields; they also had their pick of masters, and somehow the special Dragon spirit and atmosphere continued.

The Dragon School made a big sacrifice in both world wars : eighty-three old boys killed in the First World War, when the school of course was much smaller in numbers, and 134 in the Second, amongst them my eldest son, John.

On Tuesday, 13 July 1915, having just been invested with my V.C. by King George V at Buckingham Palace, I went down to visit the Dragon School by special request. What a welcome they gave me ! The late Cyril Harvey, who was head boy, did the honours and told me I must certainly ask for a whole holiday. The headmaster not only gave one but made it an annual event for 18 May – the day I won the Cross.

At the time when I visited the Dragon School in July 1915 there were three boys who became Members of Parliament with me after the Second World War, all three on the Labour side, whilst I was a Conservative. These were the two Mallalieus – Per and Lance – and Hugh Gaitskell. The latter was nine years and four months in July 1915. He was in the last form but one; but was already showing considerable promise. When, many years later, the Dragon School became a Trust, Hugh Gaitskell and I became the first Trustees. Although I didn't always agree with Hugh I had a great admiration for him. It was a tragedy that he was struck down with a fatal illness when he was Leader of the Opposition and had so much to offer both to the Labour Party and to his country. He was certainly one of the most talented and brilliant men the Dragon School has ever produced.

The first big milestone of my life, and one which was entirely within the control of myself and my parents, was with regard to my future career and how I should set about it. By family acclaim and my own wish I was destined from childhood to become a regular soldier. I intended to go into the Army via the University of Oxford, which was then a possible and quite popular procedure, but as my father was in the I.C.S. and seldom came home on leave my mother and I had to do the family planning between us. We soon discovered that in the penurious state of the Smyth family fortunes Oxford University was beyond our means. I had therefore to get to Sandhurst, which was not easy at that time, and having got there, to obtain a commission in the Indian Army, where it was possible to live on one's pay. There was very great competition to get Indian Army for this reason and also because there were more opportunities for seeing active service on the North-West Frontier of India. So we decided that I should have a go for the Indian Army, realizing that if I did not get it I should have to adopt some other career.

In my little study at 177 Banbury Road where we then lived in Oxford my mother pasted up on the wall to encourage me: 'It is strange that a man should miss when his life depends on his aim.' My mother was a great one for mottoes.

Number 177 Banbury Road was one of a long row of rather dingy looking dwellings with small front gardens bordering on the main road. At the back there was a long, narrow strip of garden with two apple trees at the far end. These two trees performed an important function in our lives. They were the goal posts for football, the wickets for cricket, the targets for my air gun and bows and arrows. They looked like two trees in the Ypres Salient after a bombardment, since they were literally riddled with bullets; yet each year they bore the most wonderful apples, in recollection the sweetest I have ever tasted. Whatever shortcomings 177 Banbury Road may have had, it had none for us; we were a very happy family.

Just up the road was our rival prep school, Summerfields, where Harold Macmillan (later my Prime Minister and a year younger than me) was a pupil. And still further away, far beyond Summerfields, was Wolvercote cemetery, to which at an unearthly hour in the morning I made my brothers, Bill and Malcolm, run with me. As they used to say in later years, how they never laid their bones there was a miracle. But after my long and debilitating illness I had to toughen myself up again and physical fitness became a *sine qua non* all the days of my life.

In 1907 I went to Repton where, fortunately for my parents' pocket, I had obtained an exhibition scholarship. Like most Dragons I went to the Priory House, of which Jugs Vassall, the mate of *The Blue Dragon*, was the housemaster. Because of my illness, I didn't go to Repton until I was over fourteen and, as the age of admission to Sandhurst had recently been lowered to seventeen, I had very little time to prepare myself for the Sandhurst examination.

Jugs Vassall, the housemaster at the Priory, was a great character. Built on colossal lines, with his cheerful red face and bellowing laugh, he exuded cheerfulness and confidence. I have never forgotten the occasion when, at morning prayers one day, with the boys mumbling and longing to get on with their breakfast, Jugs suddenly stopped, banged on the table with a mighty fist so that all the tea-cups leapt from their saucers, and said : 'Pray up, you chaps,' and we certainly did from that moment onwards.

As a building the Priory was very old and very picturesque; but it was dark and cramped, and a lot of the studies were below ground level. A few years after I left it was converted into a library and then made into a very lovely school war memorial. Just after the war I was invited to unveil it, which I would like very much to have done; but the ship in which I was sailing from India was delayed and I couldn't get there in time.

My first headmaster at Repton was Lionel Ford, who left to become headmaster at Harrow. He was succeeded by Billy Temple who was afterwards Archbishop of Canterbury. He was under thirty when he became headmaster, which was unusually young for those times. Rotund, bespectacled, and benign to look upon, he was indeed a remarkable character and at his untimely death he had become a great churchman and one of the most respected figures in Britain. He was the best preacher I have ever heard and as a mover of hearts he had few equals. The boys of Repton, some of whom did not regard Sunday Chapel as one of their favourite occasions, used to look forward all the week to his sermons.

Though we only met seldom in the years to come we always resumed our friendship where it left off. Towards the end of the Second World War, when I was living in Dolphin Square, quite close to Lambeth Palace, I saw more of him. Shortly before his death, when he was too weak to write, he dictated a letter to me which was full of hope for his recovery. But it was not to be. He was succeeded as Archbishop of Canterbury by Dr Fisher (later Lord Fisher of Lambeth), who had succeeded him as headmaster of Repton. In 1961 Fisher was succeeded by Dr Ramsay, also a Reptonian – though rather after my time. So Repton had made a unique corner in Archbishops of Canterbury. Some envious fellow from another school once described it to me as : 'A disgraceful example of ecclesiastical nepotism !'

In 1960 I was invited to become President of the Old Reptonian Society and then, unusually, asked to remain for another year to see out the last period of that very distinguished headmaster, my friend

Lynam Thomas. During his seventeen years as headmaster he had made a great contribution towards the creation of Repton into a fine, forward-looking school with a very high reputation. I was tremendously impressed by the boys and the masters and with the excellent relationship they had with one another.

In 1911, having passed in eighteenth out of a very big field, I was admitted to the Royal Military College Sandhurst. I was then eighteen. In those days there were two military cadet establishments, the Royal Military Academy Woolwich (generally known as 'The Shop'), the object of which was to train officers for the Royal Engineers and the Royal Artillery; and the Royal Military College Sandhurst, which trained officers for all other arms of the Service. The two establishments were amalgamated in 1947 and became known as the Royal Military Academy Sandhurst. The history of the so-called 'Gentleman Cadet', once described by a French professor as 'almost an officer and not quite a gentleman', really began when the Royal Military Academy was founded by Royal Warrant of H.M. King George II on 30 April 1741. The R.M.C. had its beginning some fifty-eight years later.

Shortly after I joined the R.M.C. it had been nearly doubled in size by the addition of the so-called 'New Building', a large red brick structure, not nearly so picturesque as the old college, but far lighter, more sanitary and up-to-date. The new building had its own lecture rooms, dining halls and parade ground, so we were quite independent of the other half of the college and only went there to take part in battalion parades. A, B and C Companies were located in the old building and D, E and F in the new. I was posted to E Company which, for the second year running, had earned the honourable distinction of being 'Champion Company at Arms'. This title of Champion Company had only recently been introduced and was much prized. Every cadet played his part in it by the number of marks he was awarded in all the various activities which went to make up our life at the College. The keenness was intense : as we marched on to a battalion parade, after all the other companies, and took our places on the right of the line, it was quite a thrill and we really did throw a chest. (The Champion Company has now become the Sovereign's Company.)

Soon after we 'juniors' arrived, 250 of us, it was announced that the top hundred cadets at the end of the year would be passed out and given commissions straight away, whilst the remaining 150 would have to stay on for another term to start the new eighteen-month courses. I had therefore two incentives : by passing out in the first hundred I should gain six months' seniority, but it would be no good my doing that unless I passed out high enough to get into the Indian Army – and Indian Army vacancies out of one hundred would be few indeed.

This was a challenge which I fully realized and accepted. When Claude Auchinleck (later Field-Marshal) had been faced with the same problem in 1902 conditions were somewhat different. A cadet then had to pass *into* Sandhurst in the first forty-five to get Indian Army: Auchinleck passed in forty-fifth and obtained the last vacancy. How lucky for the Indian Army! Five or six years later the conditions were again different: by 1907 it was necessary to pass *out* in the first thirty-five to be sure of an Indian Army vacancy. In that year one Bernard Montgomery (later Field-Marshal Viscount) was also trying for the Indian Army. But he only passed out thirty-sixth and so just missed it. He was bitterly disappointed. However, he managed to get posted to a British battalion serving in India, where the pay, though not so good as in the Indian Army, was yet better than in a British battalion at home.

I organized my life accordingly. I allowed myself little time for games. I did play fairly regularly for the College Hockey XI, until I was beguiled into playing for the Soccer XI, with the result that I played against the Shop at neither game. I did get my 'Blue', however, for revolver shooting, and also shot for the Army Eight, purely by chance as one of their crack shots dropped out and they 'requisitioned' me. Cricket and rugger, both of which I loved, took up too much time and, as Repton was a soccer school, I had hardly played rugger since I left the Dragon School.

The regime at Sandhurst at that time, though it would be criticized today as being too 'military', was a good preliminary training for a young officer of that day and age, bearing in mind that the clouds of war were already looming on the European horizon. The life was hard and the discipline strict. Very great importance was attached to drill – rigid barrack-square drill – and the drill and discipline of the cadet battalions at Sandhurst was second to none in the British Army. The drill instructors were nearly all Guardsmen and marvellously smart they were, and no respecters of persons. Any cadet whose stomach stuck out and spoilt the dressing was told to hurry forward his confinement by taking daily runs until his figure improved. No cars were allowed and not much leave. We lived in uniform always, no mufti was allowed in the College. Our ordinary working dress consisted of a khaki serge tunic with a high collar, and full dress (scarlet tunic and blue trousers with a red stripe) for full dress parades. Off duty we were allowed to wear P.T. kit (red and white striped blazer, little pill-box cap and white flannel trousers).

The horse died very hard in the pre-1914 British Army; yet there was so much good in the horse and all that went with it. It cultivated those qualities of nerve, dash and initiative which were assets to the British officer. In my day at Sandhurst it was considered essential that a good officer should be good on a horse. Those of us who were keen on riding, like myself, enjoyed it; but quite a number of my fellow cadets, who had never been used to horses, were completely ruined thereby. In trying to compete with this rigid requirement they lost confidence in themselves, not only as horsemen but as officers.

Among the cadets in my senior term were two who were to play a particular part in my life. One was Alexander (later Field-Marshal); and the other was C. J. R. Turner. Jack Turner was instrumental in getting me into the 15th Sikhs. Later we played hockey together for the Army and the Combined Services, and he for England. We soldiered together and remained lifelong friends.

But it was in my own E Company at Sandhurst that I found a really congenial spirit in an Australian cadet called Chisholm. He was not engaged in the race for Indian Army but was determined to pass out top of the whole lot. Short, square, tough as teak, he had tremendous application and cut out everything that interfered with his work. He started with a great handicap as he had not been to a public school, was not good at games and had a very broad Australian accent. Sandhurst, and of course the British Army generally, was a very snobbish place in those days and lords, honourables and old Etonians seemed to get along rather better than any of them should have done. But, be it said, they died as gallantly and with equal distinction as most of the rest of us when all the chips were down.

Chisholm had a model after his own heart in his cousin, Major-General Robertson, who was Commandant of the Staff College next door. General Robertson (who later became Field-Marshal Sir William Robertson and wrote *From Private to Field-Marshal*, Constable, 1921) had risen from the ranks entirely by his own efforts and ability and became one of the outstanding British soldiers of the First World War. 'Wully' Robertson was a great character. He dropped his aitches all over the place and always said exactly what he thought. Chisholm used to take me along to tea with him at the Staff College and, realizing our keenness to learn, he took trouble in his busy life to expound his philosophy on the art of war.

The fateful examinations approached at last. The subject for the military history paper was the Peninsular Campaign, the textbook for which had been issued to us. Chisholm had actually learnt the whole book by heart – a colossal achievement of application and memory. However the questions were so worded that only half of them required direct answers from the book; and for these he quoted the book verbatim. A few days later he was run in on a charge of cheating as the examiners said he must have had the book in with him. I had to come forward to assure them that he knew the whole book by heart.

I got the military history prize, three calf-bound volumes of *Clausewitz On War*, which I have taken around the world with me ever since, but never read! When the results of the final examinations were announced I had passed out ninth which, even with a reduced allotment for Indian Army, made quite certain of my getting a vacancy. Chisholm was not far behind. He joined a British Line regiment and was killed at Mons. The great majority of my contemporaries at Sandhurst were killed in the early days of the First World War, which took such a heavy toll of 'His Majesty's Second Lieutenants'.

CHAPTER TWO

India

MY 'First Commission', a very impressive parchment docu-
ment, arrived in August 1912 and the following month I
sailed for India in the troopship *Plassey*, to join the 1st
Yorkshire Regiment (the Green Howards), with whom I was to do a
year's attachment preparatory to joining the Indian Army.

What a thrill it was, that first voyage to India – and certainly an
important milestone in my life. It was fitting that someone of my name,
with strong family roots in Yorkshire, should have joined such a regiment as the Green Howards. They were stationed in Sialkot in the
Punjab, with its lovely cold weather climate. In the hot weather the
Regiment left one company in the plains while the other three companies went up to Barian in the Murree Hills. I much enjoyed my year
with them and they did me the honour of inviting me to give up the
Indian Army and stay with them; but I decided that, having worked
so hard to get Indian Army, I should stick to my decision, and I have
never regretted it.

The all-important decision which faced those officers who had been
successful in getting Indian Army, was to choose, or be chosen for,
the regiment or battalion in which they would spend their regimental
lives. Some officers of course had family connections or 'friends at
court'. But even for them the establishment of British officers for an
Indian battalion was only twelve and there was seldom a vacancy.
The 15th Ludhiana Sikhs had a very high reputation and they were
willing to take me, but they hadn't a vacancy. However, it was agreed
that I should put them down as my first choice and hope for the best.
Just then another very fine batallion, the 7th Gurkha Rifles, asked me
to join them and I put them down second. At the last moment the unexpected happened : one of the 15th Sikh officers died and I was therefore posted to the regiment of my first choice.

In October 1913 I left the Green Howards with the greatest regret and joined the 15th Sikhs in Loralai, Baluchistan. They shared this delightful little frontier station with that famous Indian cavalry regiment, Hodson's Horse, who sent a mounted escort to meet me at Harnai on the railway line to Quetta and thence escorted me in my humble horse-drawn tonga for the eighty miles through wild and desolate country, to Loralai. I felt very honoured at being the subject of so much attention, but there was great comradeship between Indian Army units in those days and the life of a subaltern in the 15th Sikhs was just as important to Hodson's Horse as would have been the life of one of their own.

No British officer could expect to become a good leader of Indian troops unless he could speak their language and know all about their religion and their habits. The British and Indian officers of the 15th Ludhiana Sikhs believed that religion was an important factor in the make-up of a good soldier and it was a disciplinary offence for a man to be guilty of breaking one of the tenets of his own religion. Some of the British officers believed that their Christian faith was an asset to their own morale. But they were perhaps more particular that their men should be good Sikhs than that they themselves should be good Christians.

The Sikh religion was founded by Baba Nanak, the first of the Sikh Gurus, who was born in the Lahore District about the year 1500. The religion flourished. Sikhism, like Buddhism, was inspired by a spirit of revolt against the ceremonial and social restrictions of the Hindu religion, as well as against the arrogance of its heriditary priesthood, the Brahmans. It is not always realized that the term Sikh was a religious and not a racial designation and that it belonged only to those who accepted the faith of the Khalsa. The teaching of Nanak, which was essentially non-aggressive, was that there was but one God, who was neither the God of the Hindu nor of the Mohammedan, but the God of the Universe, and all men were equal in his sight. In fact the teaching of Nanak was in many ways very similar to that of Jesus Christ.

During the next 200 years, however, by the time the tenth and last Guru, Govind Singh, held sway, the Sikhs had been transformed, as a result of Mohammedan persecution, into a sect of fanatical and ferocious warriors. Admission to the 'Khalsa' was gained by the baptismal ceremony of the 'pahul' and its military nature was marked by the bestowal of the title of 'Singh' or 'Lion' on all who entered it.

Guru Govind taught his followers that they must practise arms and never show their backs to the foe in battle. His life was spent in a series of wars, sometimes with the Hindu Rajputs but more often with the Mohammedan governors of the Emperor Aurungzeb.

Towards the end of the eighteenth century the Sikhs, under their strong and energetic ruler, Maharajah Ranjit Singh, became the greatest power in the Punjab and subsequently gave the British their strongest opposition in the two Sikh Wars, the second of which was eventually brought to a conclusion with the crushing defeat of the Sikhs at Gujerat in 1949. The Government of India, much impressed by the stubborn valour displayed by the Sikhs, determined to make use of them in their own native army. In 1846 therefore orders were issued for the formation of two Sikh battalions at Ferozepore and Ludhiana and, ten years later, a third. These three regiments became famous as the 14th (Ferozepore), 15th (Ludhiana) and 45th (Rattray's) Sikhs. After the First World War they became the 1/11th, 2/11th and 3/11th Sikhs. (I won my Victoria Cross with the 15th Sikhs in 1915 and commanded the 45th from 1936 to 1939.)

When the Indian Mutiny broke out in 1857 the spirit of the Khalsa was aroused at the thought of active service and the Sikhs flocked to join the British cause and supported them with a loyalty that never wavered. When the Indian Army was reorganized after the Mutiny this loyalty was rewarded. These then were the men with whom my life was to be bound up.

Although there was no social life and very few amenities in Loralai it was, to my mind, an ideal station in which to start my new life in the Indian Army. If the British officers could play games with the men so much the better, but that was not so easy as the Sikhs were superlative athletes. No British officer could have taken them on at wrestling or long distance running; but Jack Turner and I could play hockey with them on level terms, as could several of the British officers, and I could beat the Sikh officers at revolver shooting and sabre fighting. Other sports available for the officers included polo of a not too professional sort, good tennis courts and some rough shooting.

Half the battalion was away on outposts and one officer was nearly always out there visiting them. This meant something extra in travelling allowance and was also an excellent opportunity for getting to know the men. Though perhaps not so easy to manage as some of the other classes of which the Indian Army was composed, no class responded better to good leadership than the Sikhs. The Sikh soldier throve on strict discipline and hard training and went to seed very quickly in an environment of too much ease and comfort. Given leaders whom he respected and trusted there was no class which could rise to greater heights of courage, endurance and loyalty.

The 15th was a 'class regiment' of Jat (cultivator) Sikhs. When the Indian Army was reorganized after the Mutiny most of the regiments became 'class company' or 'class squadron', the idea being that in a regiment of different classes there was less likelihood of any internal trouble; but there were still a number of 'class regiments' left. The 'class regiment' was of course much simpler to manage and administer, the placing of officers was no problem and it was easier for them to get to know their men than in a 'class company' regiment, where there were several castes and dialects to be mastered.

Just as the 15th had their pick of British officers so they had their pick of Sikhs and they only accepted men of the highest physical standards. The Battalion's average height was not far short of six feet and in their full-dress uniform, with their rolled beards and massive pagris with the quoit on the front, they were a magnificent sight on a ceremonial parade. There were some twenty Viceroy's commissioned officers, Subadars and Jemadars who were the platoon commanders and kept discipline in the Lines.

The Subadar-Major was a very important person. He was the Commanding Officer's confidential adviser on all matters pertaining to the well-being and the discipline of the men, their administration and their morale. The backbone of every Indian battalion however was its British officers and their standard of leadership was high, and very important to the morale of the battalion. In the 15th Sikhs there was a great spirit of comradeship and trust between all ranks.

In the early summer of 1914 I was invited by Colonel Carr-White, the Residency Surgeon in Nepal, to spend my two months' leave with them in Khatmandu. His son, Reggie, then a subaltern in the 31st Lancers, had been my greatest friend at the Dragon School. I had spent my 1913 leave with them in Kotah, an Indian State in Rajputana. This invitation to Nepal was one that everyone envied, particularly British officers in Gurkha regiments, who felt they were lucky to be allowed to spend ten days in the land where their soldiers came from, for at that time Nepal was a country closed to the outside world except by very special permission.

The journey from Loralai was a strenuous one, particularly in the middle of the hot weather, as I had to travel the whole breadth of India, by train for a start; then, from railhead, I was carried by night in a kind of stretcher through the Nepal Terai, perhaps the best jungle for big game in the world, but in the hot weather a deadly malarial region. The coolies pushed through the jungle at a steady jogtrot, with frequent changes. Then followed two days' trek, partly on foot and partly by pony, until the motor road leading to Khatmandu, the capital, was reached.

In addition to renewing my friendship with the Carr-Whites, I formed a lifelong friendship with the Resident, Colonel Jack Manners-Smith V.C., and his delightful family. I also met and made friends with the Prime Minister and Supreme Commander-in-Chief of Nepal, General Sir Shumshere Jung, who presented me with a lovely kukri which hangs in my study to this day.

Whilst I was in Nepal two planters from Assam were invited to Nepal with a string of magnificent polo ponies. A polo match was arranged: Nepal versus India. The former consisted of Colonel Manners-Smith, Colonel Carr-White, Reggie Carr-White and a Duffadar of the Resident's Bodyguard. 'India' consisted of myself, the two Assam planters, who mounted me, and one Sowar of the Bodyguard. The home team won 3–2 and when we challenged them to a return they won by the same score. The ground we played on was like a billiard table and the conditions perfect. I had hardly ever played the game before but I took to it like a duck to water. It was the first polo match ever played in Nepal and was for me the start of a great love of polo, which might have made another milestone in my life.

This polo match in Nepal was remarkable from several points of view. The Nepalese (unlike the Chitralis with whom I played polo twenty-four years later) were not horsey people and so far as I know this was the only polo match which has ever been played in Nepal. The Assam planters were keen on the idea because they wanted to have a look at Nepal, which could only be visited in those days by a special invitation from the Prime Minister. It was a risky business transporting their valuable polo ponies over the mountainous approaches to Katmandu, but they considered it well worth it. It was a curious coincidence that the No. 3 for Nepal was a famous V.C., Jack Manners-Smith, and exactly a year later, on 18 May 1915, the No. 1 in the 'India' team (myself) was also awarded the V.C., perhaps as a consolation prize for being on the losing side.

At the time I joined the 15th Sikhs in Loralai the Battalion was commanded by Johnny Hill, a jovial bon viveur who had many friends in high places and knew the Sikh from A to Z. How lucky that was for us when the First World War started. Stuck out as we were at the back of beyond in the hills of Baluchistan, with half the men on outpost duty, we hadn't a hope of getting to the war. But Johnny, bless him, was immediately up in Simla, pulling all the strings, and within forty-eight hours of war being declared we got a telegram ordering us to mobilize, hand over our outposts and get down to Karachi within fifteen days!

Talk about the 14th Army in Burma in the Second World War and their saying: 'The impossible will take a little longer', we were being asked to do the impossible and do it a little quicker. The outposts were eighty miles from Loralai; there was no motor transport and when we had completed the reliefs we had to mobilize in Loralai and march another eighty miles to railhead, with a longish troop train journey to

As cabin boy on the *Blue Dragon*, 1907

C. C. 'Skipper' Lynam
on board the *Blue Dragon*, 1906

Gentleman cadet J. G. Smyth,
Sandhurst 1911

My Subedar-Major
Kaka Singh Bahadur, O.B.I., I.D.S.M.,
at the Coronation in London, 1937

follow – and all this in the blistering temperature of the hot weather, with all the British officers on leave (some in England) except me and three others.

Hodson's Horse, although terribly disappointed at being left behind, were splendid and helped us in every way possible. Without their assistance and that of the Indian Police and Frontier Militia in taking over our posts with the minimum of red tape and delay, we couldn't have made it. I was despatched with a bag of rupees to hire every donkey and camel I could find, to get the outposts relieved and march them into Loralai. What responsibilities the young Indian Army officer had in those days – but what fun it was! I reckoned we would have to average twenty-eight miles marching a day to get the whole of the outposts back after relief and give us twenty-four hours in Loralai, which was the least possible time we would require to equip and mobilize the men.

The heat was terrific in those stony valleys, the thermometer rising to over 120 degrees fahrenheit in the shade at times. There were a number of sick in the outposts, where malaria was rife, some of whom would obviously have to be left behind. But every single man was desperately keen to go on active service with the Battalion and some were in tears when I refused to take them. There was one man, Harnam Singh, who had been in bed with malaria for ten days and was just a bag of bones. It was clear that he must be left behind, and, despite his pleading, I gave the orders accordingly. Three days later, towards the end of a particularly trying march in great heat, I looked behind me at the men and thought I saw Harnam Singh, stepping out in quite a jaunty way with two other men carrying his rifle and equipment. I thought the heat must be affecting me and that I was 'seeing things'. I did not look round again but when we reached camp I sent for the Indian officer and asked if I had seen aright. With clasped hands he begged for my forgiveness but said that Harnam Singh had managed to fall in with the others and he hadn't the heart to turn him back.

'Never mind about that,' I said, 'but how has he possibly been able to march all this way?'

He replied: 'Oh, opium, Sahib. He is a non-opium eater and the effect of opium on him is therefore very great. We gave him a little opium before the march and put him to bed as soon as we got into camp and then did the same again the next day.'

Harnam Singh managed to get to Karachi with the Battalion, re-covered on the voyage and went through a year of trench warfare in France. The C.O. was so impressed by the way Harnam Singh had managed to march to Loralai in such a debilitated condition that we seriously considered the desirability of officers carrying a small emergency ration of opium in case we were called upon to do something desperate when we were all-in. Eventually we decided against it – wisely I am sure. The danger of once eating opium is that its effect is so magical that it is very difficult to stop. We had a hundred regular opium eaters in the Battalion and they were a very great nuisance as they had to have a regular ration of it every week. In France the opium ration was labelled 'Black Treacle'.

Opium eating in the Indian Army was later completely eradicated, but in May 1915 in France I was once again to see the miraculous effect of opium on a non-opium eater. We had taken over some trenches from a British battalion which had suffered very heavy casualties in an unsuccessful raid. They left behind some fourteen men who were so badly wounded that they couldn't be moved: a couple of hours later I saw some of our Sikh stretcher-bearers preparing to lead them back to the dressing station. The wounded British soldiers were talking and smoking and three of them actually walked back. A little opium had been administered and the effect was magical. Smoking opium of course has quite a different effect.

I had always been interested in the whole question of the effect of drugs and stimulants on the soldier in battle and wrote an article on the subject just after the war, which was published in a Service journal. Many people have sought a drug which would eradicate fear from the soldier without paralysing his brain. The Germans gave far more attention to this matter than the British. The first night we were in action in France the Battalion next to us was suddenly attacked in the middle of the night by a German regiment drugged with what turned out to be a mixture of ether and alcohol. We had no wire to speak of in front of our trenches at that time. A large number of casualties didn't stop these Germans and they went clean through and into some woods at the back. About three hours later the dope started to wear off and was followed by feelings of depression exceeding those of their former exhilaration. Eventually they withdrew just before dawn, for no apparent reason except nerves and a frightful hangover, so much so that some of them gave themselves up.

But to return to August 1914. I got the outpost men to Loralai on time; and, in the single day in which I had to prepare myself, sold or gave away all my belongings and was ready for the road, by that time almost unconscious from fatigue and lack of sleep. I slept all the way to railhead on my pony and my Sikhs saw to it that I didn't fall off! We arrived in Karachi within the time limit set us.

The 15th shared a transport with the 59th Rifles and a great squash it was for the men, who were terribly sea sick for the first few days. We formed part of an enormous convoy of transports. The voyage seemed endless and I kept thinking the war would be over before we arrived, but I spent the time getting fighting fit for the ordeal ahead. With P.T., skipping, boxing and sabres (at which I had become quite an expert) I was really trained like a prize-fighter by the time we reached Marseilles, and it certainly paid me well.

CHAPTER THREE

The First World War

THE 15th Sikhs were among the first Indian troops to arrive in France and the enthusiasm and excitement of the populace were tremendous, and quite unexpected. The men, none of whom had ever been out of India before, were rather dazed as we marched through the streets of Marseilles to our camp. The ranks were soon broken by cheering crowds and one could just see the heads of the Sikhs bobbing about amid an excited sea of French faces. The railings round our camp were thick with people all day long. The Sikh is a cleanly creature and gets under a pump at every opportunity, no matter how cold the weather or the water. After the dusty march they took down their hair, loosened their beards and set about having a good wash. This brought down the house and there were delighted shrieks of: 'Voilà les femmes Indiènnes.' All these attentions were rather embarrassing after a time and we were glad when we moved to Orléans, where we were supposed to undergo a period of training and acclimatization.

It was now October 1914 and starting to get chilly, and we were clad only in our thin Indian drill uniforms, which the men had to wear through most of that bitter winter. There was a serious shortage of uniforms in the British Army owing to the great expansion which was taking place, and the Indian troops had to wait their turn; but the men did receive an early issue of warm underclothes, gloves and comforters. They didn't quite understand the underclothes at first, never having seen such garments before; on the day these were first issued I came out of my tent just in time to prevent the Subadar-Major 'walking out' on the town, clad only in a thick pink vest and a long pair of pink pants!

The 15th were put into the Jullundur Brigade, in the Lahore Division, which was commanded first by General Watkis and then by General Kearey. The Indian Corps, consisting of the Lahore and Meerut

36

Divisions, was commanded by General Willcocks, a well-known Indian frontier soldier. Each infantry brigade was composed of one British and three Indian battalions, and was commanded by a brigadier-general, who was always referred to as 'General' and not 'Brigadier'. Our British battalion in the Jullundur Brigade was the 1st Manchesters, commanded by Lieut.-Colonel Peter Strickland (later General Sir Peter Strickland) – a real tiger both in action and out.

Although the younger officers of the Indian Army compared more than favourably with their British counterparts as regards professional ability, leadership and physical fitness, the more senior officers were mostly suffering from too many years in the tropics, though there were some notable exceptions such as Generals Birdwood, Claude Jacob and Willcocks.

In the Indian Corps in France in 1914–15, where casualties were a good deal higher than in any previous campaign in which Indian troops had been engaged, the Indian battalion had to face two major problems which the British battalion did not have in anything like the same degree. Firstly, reinforcements took a long time coming from India and the strength of an Indian battalion was apt to dwindle far below the level of operational efficiency, so that sometimes an Indian battalion only 300 strong had to take over a line of trenches which was held by a British battalion of over double that number. Secondly, there was the great difficulty of making good the heavy casualties in British officers, and in the Indian battalion the officer was a marked man, if only by reason of the colour of his face and his different head-dress. Officer reinforcements for British battalions came over the Channel from reserve battalions or reinforcement camps in England and could be fitted comparatively easily and quickly into a unit in France. But the British officer for an Indian battalion had to come all the way from India, and he had to be taught the language and habits of the particular class of Indian troops to which he was to be posted. Nothing lowered the morale of the Indian soldier more than to be commanded by British officers he didn't know and couldn't understand. The Indian officers were too old and not well enough educated to replace the British officers, particularly in a Western theatre of war, where foreign maps and foreign speech made added difficulties. This defect was remedied between the wars and the Viceroy's commissioned officers were streamlined and modernized.

The intention in 1914 was that the Indian Corps should gradually be initiated into the totally new conditions of European warfare. By the middle of October, however, the first Battle of Ypres had reached a very critical stage and all available reinforcements had to be flung in. On my twenty-first birthday, 24 October 1914, the 15th were put in to fill a gap in the line in front of the Rue Tilleloi. We had a Scottish battalion on our right and some French cavalry on our left. It was of course very difficult for the Indian soldier at first to distinguish between French and Germans. I appreciated this and borrowed a French soldier and a German prisoner and paraded them slowly round in front of the company. Nevertheless, I regret to say that the first people we shot in the Great War were undoubtedly French – but it was dark and there was a bit of a mix-up going on, so there was some excuse.

As soon as it was light, with our trenches only half dug, we were subjected to some heavy shelling and had a good many casualties. Johnny Hill had gone sick and Jock Gordon, who was commanding, was wounded, though only a 'cushy' one and he was back with us in a month. George Henderson was hit through both legs and, although he rejoined us for a short time, was never really fit again. Both our doctors and our interpreter were hit and we had about eighty men killed and wounded in that one day.

Those first ten days in the trenches, with an enormous front to hold and no reserves behind us, were very trying indeed and we were dead tired at the end of it, particularly the British officers who were constantly on duty. We were much worried throughout this time by snipers in the houses of the Rue Tilleloi to our rear and the spying and general observation work of the Germans at this period of the war were a revelation. Neither the British nor the Indian Army had paid any attention to this type of warfare at all.

During the last week of October 1914 the Battalion casualties were : three British officers and three Indian officers wounded, and 263 other ranks killed, wounded or missing. We were much heartened by a special message from the Commander-in-Chief, Sir John French, warmly commending the manner in which we had clung on to our position. From then on, until the Battle of Neuve Chapelle in the following spring, we had long spells in the trenches with short periods of rest in billets. We were always around Richebourg, Festubert or Givenchy, and had a good deal of close trench fighting in the latter locality, which changed hands several times during the winter.

The Indian soldier learned to use the bomb, the trench mortar, the rifle grenade and all the other weapons of trench warfare. The German missile I disliked most of all was a very heavy bundle of frightfulness called a Minnenwerfer, which we used to call a 'portmanteau'. You could see it turning over and over in the air and could only stare up at it and hope that it would land somewhere far away. I had one of my narrowest escapes from death from one of these things which pitched so close that it threw up a great mound of earth which completely buried me. My Sikhs dug like madmen to get me out alive, and they just did it; but I had certain parts of both ears damaged which for ever prevented me from hearing some kinds of sound, particularly bells. When, many years later, I became a minister in Winston Churchill's Government, I always had to have a division bell in my room in the House of Commons.

In France that winter there were incessant night patrols and wiring parties, days of rain and snow in waterlogged trenches when the morning rum ration, followed by a cup of hot cocoa, was like nectar from heaven. There were good times in billets when one could ride a horse again, visits to Bethune, which was our nearest point of civilization, and above all, the occasional leave home to England. Living with the men in a trench for weeks on end, one got to know them better than one would have done in years of ordinary soldiering. Some of them died with their heads in my lap and, on the day I was nearly buried, I nearly died with my head in theirs.

Of course there were times when one loathed every minute of it and felt its terrible waste; but I was young and healthy and long since reconciled to accepting my bullet when it came. I became quite an expert on the sounds that shells and bullets made; if you could hear a shell all the way it was not going to be a close one; but if you heard one coming and then stopped hearing it you did well to take cover as quickly as possible. The bullet which cracked unpleasantly wasn't a killer for you, although it might be for someone else. It was the bullet which whispered or hissed which was the near one; and the bullet which took the cigarette out of my mouth at 'Windy Corner' I didn't hear at all.

I had somehow gained a reputation for indestructibility which made people seek to be near me when things became unpleasant. I have never claimed to be a fearless sort of person such as other people I have known, like the V.C.s Freyberg, Carton de Wiart and Leonard Cheshire, and men like Churchill, Wavell and Alexander. But when I was on leave in Nepal just before the war I was given a book which helped me enormously to overcome fear. It was called *Right and Wrong Thinking* by an American, Aaron Martin Crane, published in Boston in December 1905 with ten reprints. Briefly, its thesis was that in the make-up of a human being the mind is the motor power which governs everything everywhere and mind action is the absolute ruler of man himself. By control of his thoughts man can become the arbiter of his own destiny. The thoughts which come into the mind and affect the mental and physical well-being are either harmonious or discordant, each affecting the human organism for good or ill. Provided that one is clear as to what thoughts are harmonious and which discordant, it is possible by persistent practice to drop discordant thoughts from the mind and replace them by harmonious ones. What interested me was, in the dangerous atmosphere of battle could the discordant thought of fear be dropped from the mind and be replaced by the thought of courage?

In the months before the 15th Sikhs sailed for France *Right and Wrong Thinking* was my constant companion and I was able to put into practice its theories with most gratifying results. There were of course times when I failed and was frankly petrified; but I was sufficiently imbued with the essential correctness of the thesis that I was always able to make a comeback and create the image of myself I wanted to give both to myself and to those around me.

One Special Correspondent in France sent the following despatch home, and it was published in *The Times* of 7 August 1915:

I remember a road running behind some famous trenches and a few officer companions there. None of us elders were comfortable. Passing overhead was a procession of horrible sounds. On either hand columns of smoke were bursting, and every house we passed was an abandoned ruin.

There was boy with us, a short, ruddy, smiling officer lad with merry grey eyes. He seemed quite out of place there. He was altogether too cherubic, innocent and happy. He glanced up smiling at the passing shells exactly as if he had never heard them before and did not know what they were. Even his tunic was not exactly the regulation pattern. I thought he was a new arrival who would learn much more presently.

Later on I was told, as a huge joke, that that boy was once lighting a cigarette when a bullet swept the match from his fingers. His cap had been blown off five times by explosions. His proper tunic had been torn off his back by machine gun and rifle fire. He had dragged, that lad, a heavy box of bombs over the corpses, a target for every explosive abomination the Germans could shower round him and his men.

In fact, he was Lieutenant Smyth, and he had just got his V.C. I see they have been recording his features in the illustrated papers since I met him, but the pictures are all wrong, they have left out his luminous and innocent merriment.

Innocent it may have been, but my philosophy was quite hard won. I have always believed that courage is expendable and that too much battle fighting can drain the stock of courage of the bravest. I was never again so brave as in those early days of unbelievable horror when my fervent belief in *Right and Wrong Thinking* (and my youth) kept me on top of the dangerous world in which I had to live or die.

I remember our doctor, Major Odlum, said to me one day when we were walking back from a conference and a burst of shelling started: 'Jackie, do you mind if I take your arm because I know nothing will ever hit you.' But he dropped me like a red hot coal a minute later when a piece of shrapnel shrieked past, slightly cutting my neck and almost taking his nose off. You had to be very lucky to remain alive as an officer in the trenches for any length of time in that first year of the war, and indeed in later years too.

One day we had a message to say that the Indian Maharajah of Tikari was coming to spend a few days in our trenches. He rolled up one evening in a smart uniform and beautifully polished boots, with an orderly carrying his kit. I gave him a dugout and he retired to sleep. Early next morning, clad in a pair of blue silk pyjamas, he came to me and asked if he could have a place to snipe from. I gave him a little cul-de-sac where he would be in no one's way and told him to be careful as the German trenches were only eighty yards away and their snipers were very active. I then started off on my rounds and forgot about him. Shortly afterwards I heard some dull clangs, followed by roars of rage from the German trenches. I peeped over the top and saw that six of their steel loopholes had been flattened. This seemed very queer as the .303 bullet generally used to ping off them with a sort of frustrated whining sound.

I suddenly thought of the Maharajah and went along to see what he was doing. There he was in his beautiful blue pyjamas, chortling with joy as he methodically knocked out every German loophole within range with a 500 Express Elephant rifle, firing soft-nosed bullets. This was strictly against the Geneva Convention and the Germans registered their disapproval by putting over a heavy mortar concentration. I hated having to stop him but in any case we had to go to ground quickly, so that was the end of what I am sure was the most exciting big game shoot the Maharajah was ever likely to experience.

On 12 November 1914 my boyhood hero, Field-Marshal Lord Roberts, arrived out from England to visit the Indian Corps. It was well over sixty years since this very wonderful old soldier had first arrived in India. To the Indian soldier his name was a legend and they were thrilled by his visit. It was a bitterly cold day when he came to inspect us: he caught a fatal chill and was dead in three days.

My first leave home to England was certainly a milestone in my life which I shall never forget. In the early days of the war, when the people of England were still very worked up and every soldier back from the front was a hero, crowds used to meet the hospital trains and the leave trains at Victoria Station. People would leap forward to carry one's bag or offer a car. How terribly quickly the hours sped by! The good-byes at the departure platform were very moving, particularly as it was quite possible to be killed in action within twenty-four hours of leaving home, and indeed one of my friends suffered this fate.

In the early part of 1915 I went for a short time to Brigade H.Q. as A.D.C. to General Strickland, who had been given command of the Jullundur Brigade after doing splendidly as colonel of the 1st Manchesters. 'Strick' was a tremendous martinet and a real tiger to look at and to be with. His thin, lined face, beneath fierce, aggressive eyebrows, his spare figure and general air of active belligerence, struck terror into the hearts of a great many people. He was a born leader, but in those conditions of continuous lines of trenches protected by acres of barbed wire and dominated by that deadly queen of the battlefield, the Vickers machine-gun, there was little scope for generalship and at that stage of the war we were involved in a grim close-quarters struggle with a very tough and unyielding adversary. It has become fashionable for modern armchair critics to belittle the generals of the First World War. But I wonder what the critics would have done had they been in their place.

I personally had the greatest admiration for Douglas Haig, who, first as a Corps and Army Commander and then as Commander-in-Chief, saw the whole war through in France. He had of course many critics and was severely blamed for the blood bath of the Somme and Passchendaele, though the former was undertaken against his own wishes and advice, solely to bolster up the very low morale of the French. But what a colossal burden he bore, commanding for three years by far the largest army Britain has ever put into the field. How tremendously staunch and determined he was in the dark days of 1917, when the French Army's morale had been shattered by the costly struggle at Verdun and by General Nivelle's disastrous offensive. And in the even darker days of March and April 1918, when the Germans threw in all their reserves against the British Army in a last desperate effort to win the war by a knock-out, it was Haig's buoyant spirit and confidence which did so much to restore the situation.

Douglas Haig was a firm believer in the importance of the spiritual side to war, besides being a devout churchman himself. He gave many people the impression of being cold and reserved, but beneath the surface was a great depth of feeling and kindness of heart. He was dedicated to his profession and utterly concentrated on his job. It was he who founded the British Legion after the war and gave so much of the remaining years of his life to the care of war pensioners and the war disabled.

As soon as I heard that the Battle of Neuve Chapelle was on the tapis and that I had a chance of being adjutant of the Regiment (as our adjutant had become a casualty), I formed up to 'Strick' and asked to go back. He gave me a terrific dressing down.

But when I said : 'Well, what would you have done, Sir, if you had been a subaltern in my position?' a smile lit up his rugged countenance.

'I should have done just what you are doing,' he said. 'So go, and good luck to you. But try not to get killed.'

Later on, when he had got command of a division, 'Strick' wrote me an amusing letter from a hospital in England. At the Battle of Loos, much against the advice of his staff, he insisted on having his advanced battle H.Q. somewhere where he could actually view the attack, instead of in some underground dugout. Accordingly, a good, big, leafy tree was selected, in which a comfortable but hidden nest was prepared after the fashion of a *machan*, in which one sits up for tiger in India. There, he and his G.S.O.1 would be connected by a special cable line to Division H.Q. A rope ladder was fixed up, which they climbed under cover of darkness, and they were all ready for the 'off' at crack of dawn.

So far so good. But as soon as the barrage started every Boche machine-gun opened up and overs and ricochets began to buzz through and around the tree. When the artillery opened up shells started to crash around and the smoke prevented any visibility. 'Strick' said in his letter, 'I did not acknowledge I was wrong until one strand of the rope ladder was cut. I then told the G.1 to get down. But, being a heavy-weight, he broke the remaining strand of the ladder and I had to jump for it.' Strick was now repenting at leisure whilst fuming sulphurously to be allowed back to the front.

The 15th Sikhs were on the march up to Neuve Chapelle when I arrived to take over the adjutancy. The Brigade car decanted me at the rear of the battalion, where I reported to Major 'Rutter' Carden, the second-in-command. He was a rugged character of the old school, but with the heart of a lion. He hadn't much longer to live. His face lit up when he saw me.

'Hallo boy, nice to have you back. Do you know the plan and the orders?'

'No Sir.'

'Do you know where we are going?'

'No Sir.'

'Do you know the order of march?'

'No Sir, but I'll soon find out.'

'Good for you; you'll do,' he said, with a broad smile as I sped up to the head of the column to report to the C.O.

The Battle of Neuve Chapelle, which started on 10 March 1915, was the first large-scale attempt at a breakthrough which the British had made on the Western Front since the stalemate of trench warfare began. It went extremely well in the opening stages but then, as so often happened on subsequent occasions, it ran out of steam because of the difficulty of getting reserve formations forward quickly enough. In the end, the massive German counter attack won back almost all the ground we had won. A few days later the Adjutant Bill Barstow returned from hospital and my short but exciting period as adjutant came to an end.

On 22 April the Germans first used poison gas in the Ypres Salient against a French division. The gas was chlorine, discharged from cylinders previously established in the German front line trenches. It came as a complete surprise and its effect against entirely unprotected troops was devastating.

The situation at Ypres was very serious. A big gap in the allied defence system had been created and there were no troops in reserve except the new Kitchener's Army divisions which were being nursed gradually into the battle. I could quite appreciate that the last thing the British high command wanted to do was to throw one of these new divisions into this gaseous hell on earth.

At this time the Lahore Division was holding a line of trenches at Festubert, on the extreme right of the British Army – the very opposite end to the Ypres Salient. The 15th Sikhs had been in the front line trenches for over a week in the worst conditions I had ever experienced. The trenches were over a foot deep in mud and water and the condition of the men's feet can be imagined. Suddenly the Lahore Division received orders that we were to be relieved that night and were to proceed by forced marches to Ypres. The distance was thirty miles, behind the whole of the front held by the British. It had suddenly turned very hot, our wet boots dried up like boards and the men's feet became badly blistered. I have always felt that the Indian soldier was never given sufficient credit for this sacrificial affair; and indeed it was in the interests of the 'powers that be' to play it down.

As we passed through villages crowded with the new K's Army battalions they turned out en masse to cheer us on our way, and to have a look at Indian troops, whom they had never seen before. The new battalions were the pick of our British youth – 'the First Hundred Thousand' – and I was much impressed by their physique. It was certainly not by their choice that we had to do this dirty job for them. People were sometimes apt to criticize the Indian Corps and say that they should not have been employed in a Western theatre of war. They certainly had difficulties in the way of rationing and reinforcements with which British troops were never faced and, naturally, being Eastern people, were more suited to a warmer climate; but in those early days of the war in France, while the old British Expeditionary Force was dwindling rapidly and before the new armies were ready to take their place, their presence in France was invaluable and they were given some very unpleasant jobs, such as this one at Ypres.

As we passed through Corps Headquarters the Division formed single file and every man dipped his handkerchief in one of the rows of buckets by the roadside, which was supposed to contain some anti-gas preparation. The hot sun dried the handkerchiefs long before we reached Ypres – not that the lotion would have had the slightest effect. Meanwhile the Germans had contented themselves with consolidating the ground they had gained. They had reversed the captured trenches and wired them strongly. Immediately on arrival, after this very exhausting forced march and with very inadequate artillery preparation which left the wire completely uncut, the Lahore Division was put into the attack.

No one of the top brass had bothered about the way the wind was blowing, or indeed whether there was any wind at all, and yet where a gas discharged from cylinders was expected this was a matter of vital importance. As a matter of fact quite a strong breeze was blowing from the German trenches and this really made the attack futile before it had started. Even without the gas, to commit infantry to attack a strongly prepared position, protected by uncut wire, was murder and the inevitable cause of crippling casualties and lowered morale; yet at this stage of the war we kept on doing it. However, although at the time I was a toad under the harrow, I saw the difficulties involved. But the battle for ground was overdone : every bit of ground which was lost had to be regained, regardless whether it was of real tactical value. In this case it was of course imperative to plug the gap and prevent further exploitation. We didn't however have to possess that particular line of German trenches to do that; in fact we failed to take them and had to make do with a line of our own digging. In the interim we had suffered a large number of casualties from an unimaginative and ill-prepared counter-attack.

Our Brigade was in divisional reserve and I watched the attack from the roof of a small house. The two attacking brigades went forward steadily to face a hail of machine-gun fire. When the leading companies were only about 100 yards from the German trenches a cloud of heavy greenish-yellow vapour issued from them and rolled slowly over the attacking troops. It left behind a scene of complete confusion. Men were running blindly, some sideways, some forwards, some backwards, with their hands over their mouths or eyes, trying to escape from this dreadful choking death. The attack failed, with very heavy casualties.

I was so intent on the scene in front of me that I had not noticed that little swirls of gas were drifting round me. Being heavier than air the chlorine kept low but I got some in one eye and this affected my sight for some years.

Such was the obsession of the brass hats with the recapture of lost ground that just before dark we received orders that the 15th Sikhs and the 4th Gurkhas, under command of our own C.O., Johnny Hill, were to assault the Germas trenches by a surprise night attack. Where a division had failed, and without any attempt to deal with the uncut wire, or to introduce any new factor into the situation, these two battalions were to be offered up as a sacrifice to satisfy the higher command. It was one of those senseless operations, to 'keep up the offensive spirit', which created such bad feeling between the troops and the brass hats in France.

There was no time for careful reconnaissance or planning. Under cover of darkness the two battalions, tall bearded Sikhs and sturdy little Gurkhas, deployed silently and advanced with fixed bayonets. Johnny Hill however was determined not to allow the attack to go in unless there was some reasonable chance of success and he had ordered that it should not go beyond a certain point without a second confirmatory order.

When the scouts of both battalions reported thick, uncut wire all along the front and German patrols and sentries very much on the alert, Johnny Hill went straight to Brigade Headquarters and refused to carry out the attack. It was a very brave thing to do and earned him a severe reprimand, but it undoubtedly saved two good battalions from complete annihilation. The higher command very grudgingly cancelled the attack and we were ordered to dig in where we were.

Meanwhile the women of England had been working night and day on making rough-and-ready gas masks which were issued to us within a week. These consisted of some sort of impregnated cotton wool sewn into a gauze cover which came over the mouth but left the eyes unprotected. We spent a very unpleasant week on top of the German gas cylinders before their arrival, but fortunately the wind blew steadily from our direction all the time. In the end the Germans came to regret their introduction of cylinder gas as the prevailing wind was unfavourable to them for the greater part of the year. But it could well have won them the war in that April of 1915 if they had only realized how devastatingly effective it would be.

By the end of the week our trenches, in the very apex of the Ypres Salient, were strong and well wired. But someone in some château at the back decided that the British defence line would look tidier if the kink in it where we were was straightened out. Hence the staging of another abortive little attack, without any element of surprise or intelligent preparation, which was doomed to failure before it began. This was to take the form of a daylight attack, carried out by our Brigade, with the French Moroccan Brigade on our left. After a very short and entirely inadequate artillery bombardment we were to advance and do a complete right wheel, pivoting on the Moroccans, who had to do a much shorter and simpler one. But the success of their operation was vital to ours as its failure would result in our Brigade being completely enfiladed. In any case, complicated manoeuvres of this sort against such stern opposition generally invited failure. As the Moroccans didn't really get started at all it was murder for us.

By this time the 15th Sikhs were sadly reduced in numbers and, despite several drafts, only numbered about 450 men and eight British officers, of whom two were on leave. I was officiating as company commander for one of them. We were to attack with two companies forward, Major Muir's on the right and Major Vivian's on the left. I was to support Major Muir and Major Carden was to support Major Vivian. After the short and obviously ineffective artillery bombardment the awful moment came, familiar to so many who took part in the First World War. I shoved my watch in my pocket and, trying to disguise my state of blue funk with a nonchalant air, I swarmed up the parapet and led my company forward.

The men advanced coolly and steadily, but as we started our wheel to the right two machine-guns caught us in enfilade and the battalion suffered a hundred casualties within ten minutes, including all the other three company commanders. This was a crushing blow and the attack came to a full stop. Majors Vivian and Carden were both mortally wounded, the former dying within a few minutes. I went forward to 'Smiler' Muir and found him badly wounded and unconscious with a bullet clean through his stomach. I lay down beside him, produced a first field-dressing and a knife and started to cut away his clothes. The German machine-guns on the flank were rat-tat-tatting away, which made my job extremely difficult. The men were taking what cover they could.

Suddenly 'Smiler', who had the reputation of being the smartest and best-dressed man in the Army, recovered consciousness and said that on no account was I to cut the yellow waistcoat he was wearing under his tunic. Whereupon, as one is apt to do when one is frightened, I let fly such a volley of oaths at him that he relapsed into unconsciousness once more. However, Smiler lived to tell the tale. He became Controller of the Viceroy's Household in India, and still kept his neatly patched yellow waistcoat.

I was now left in command of the whole attack. On my right I could see no one. On my left the last of the Moroccans were withdrawing back to their own trenches. The attack had obviously failed completely and we were left alone out in no-man's-land. A runner arrived from the C.O. confirming this and telling me to withdraw the battalion. I replied that a withdrawal by daylight would result in heavy casualties but I would withdraw under cover of darkness, which I did successfully. So ended a very unpleasant day. Little did I think that twenty-four years later, in nearly the same place, I should be in an almost equally difficult position whilst getting my Brigade back to Dunkirk.

We were three weeks in the Ypres Salient, an eerie place to be when the Verey lights went up at night, as it always appeared that we were completely surrounded. We then returned to our old haunts round Neuve Chapelle and Festubert. It was during some heavy shelling here that Anthony Wilding, the famous New Zealand tennis player, was killed in one of our dugouts. He came along in one of his armoured cars, got out when heavy shelling started, and then took cover in a dugout which received a direct hit from a shell almost as soon as he entered it. His car remained on the road untouched.

May 1915 saw some terrible expensive trench raids by the Indian Corps, in many cases against uncut barbed wire.

And so to my own V.C. incident, regarding which I have always felt that the Sikhs with me did not get sufficient credit. This occurred in that little cockpit of the Western Front near Richebourg L'Avoue, which the troops afterwards called 'the Glory Hole'. At that particular time it was littered with the unburied dead of many battalions, stinking to high heaven, and typical of these grim battles for ground. We were suddenly hurried forward to take over some trenches from a British brigade which had just taken part in an unsuccessful attack to obtain some rising ground from which it was intended that a further attack should be launched. Only in one place had the attackers succeeded in gaining about 200 yards of German front-line trench. The two front-line battalions of our Brigade, the 15th Sikhs and the Highland Light Infantry, were each ordered to put one company into this bit of captured German trench. The company we sent was commanded by Captain Kenneth Hyde Cates, who had only just come to join us with a draft of the 45th Rattray's Sikhs. Their position was 300 yards forward of, and unconnected with, our own front line. They were really out on a limb.

Early on the morning of this, for me, momentous 18 May, the Germans started attacking the forward position and a few hours later we had a signal to say that our people were running short of ammunition, particularly bombs, which were the principal weapons in a close trench battle. The H.L.I. sent up a carrying party of twenty men under an officer, but all were shot down before they had reached half way. Then their forward company tried to send a party back, but with the same result. I had been watching these doings through my glasses with a by no means impartial eye. As I was the battalion bombing officer I felt certain that I should be next for the high jump; and sure enough, the C.O. came on the field telephone from Battalion H.Q. The conversation went something like this.

C.O.   'Hullo boy. You know what the set-up is?'

J.G.S. 'Yes, Sir.'

C.O.   'The Brigadier wants you to have a shot at it. Do you think you can do it?'

J.G.S. 'Quite frankly, no Sir. I've just seen two attempts fail. But of course I will have a go if I'm ordered.'

C.O.   'Look – stay where you are. I'll have a talk to the Brigadier and get it cancelled.'

But I knew very well what the answer would be. The Brigadier was just a pawn in the game of the struggle for ground. This order had come from a much higher source than he. Sure enough, when the C.O. came on the line again he was in tears.

'Sorry boy. The brigadier says you must have a shot at it. He has great confidence in you.'

'O.K. Sir. I'll get started.'

My company commander, Major 'Spooky' Hughes, who was a great martinet and a stickler for discipline, was very worked up indeed and begged me to refuse to obey such a suicidal order. However, I managed a rather sickly smile and told him not to be silly. The sooner I got started the better. It was already mid-afternoon and we had had no news from our forward company.

The men of my company had been insisting that on occasions like this I should wear a pagri to make me less conspicuous. I disliked doing this very much as I hadn't got, like them, long hair which would have kept it on my head and I looked, and felt, rather foolish. They had to tie it for me. Now, however, there was no time for this and I wore my khaki service cap. As I was the only one not killed or badly wounded I never wore a pagri again.

I must confess there was nothing heroic about my feelings. I was in an absolutely blue funk. But this disappeared when I asked for ten volunteers to go with me – and the whole company stepped forward. This was really incredible as they had been in the front row of the stalls watching the two fatal dress rehearsals. They really put courage into me.

I wanted to take as small a party as possible, which would give us a better chance of getting through, and yet we had to take sufficient

49

men to manhandle two boxes of bombs and have some spare for casualties. I chose ten stalwart Sikhs: four from the 15th proper and the other six from the 45th Sikhs and 19th Punjabis, who had recently joined us in drafts. There was an anxious hush as we made our preparations. I felt as though every German machine-gunner was waiting with his finger on the button – and how right I was! In mid-afternoon I led my little party over the top.

In order to make still more certain of defeating any further attempt at relief, the Germans had laid on an artillery concentration in addition to the machine-gun and rifle fire which had accounted for the other two parties, and it was that which really gave us an outside chance. The smoke and the earth and dead bodies thrown up from the bursting shells hid us from view for a time; and although it caused one or two casualties we had covered about a third of the distance before the machine-guns and rifles got on to us. Then it was a matter of crawling forward, taking what cover we could from the corpses with which the ground was strewn and from a small stream up which we managed to wade undiscovered for a short time.

Eventually I arrived with one man, Lal Singh, and one of the two boxes of bombs, in a shell-hole just behind our forward company. They, intent on their battle, had not been able to make out what all the shelling and machine-gunning was about. When Hyde-Cates looked round and saw me he thought he was seeing a ghost. I yelled to him to cover me with everything he had and Lal Singh and I went all out for the trench. The Germans at once started bombing up the trench but our people were now able to reply with interest and held on until nightfall, when more bombs and reinforcements from both battalions were sent up.

Unfortunately, in the last fracas, Lal Singh was hit through the head and killed instantly. I returned alone in the dark to report to the C.O. who had long given us all up as dead.

My devoted Sikh batman, Ishar Singh, was the only person who was quite convinced that I would return and, refusing food and drink, he had sat glued to the parapet, holding my British warm, which he helped me into, chanting the Sikh war cry: 'Wah guru ji ka Khalsa, Siri wah guru ji ki fateh. Sat Sri akal.'

I had indeed been lucky. I had several bullets through my tunic, one through the top of my service cap and my small cane had been hit no less than four times. I was utterly drained of energy and my inside felt as though it was trailing on the ground. The C.O. gave me a tot of rum, wrapped me in a blanket and I slept under the orderly room table until mid-day the following day. But although badly shocked I was young and fit and soon recovered.

Meanwhile, the stretcher-bearers had been out searching for my dead and wounded Sikhs. There were few survivors and those who still lived were desperately wounded. All ten of them were awarded the I.D.S.M. But at the time life went on much as usual and I had no idea that I, or any of my men, had been recommended for anything.

I had two rather amusing encounters with Sir Douglas Haig in the ensuing weeks. On the first occasion, during a short spell in rest billets, my friend Jim Willcocks, son and A.D.C. of the Indian Corps Commander, offered me one of their staff cars to take me into Bethune, which was our nearest town. It had been raining almost incessantly for days. I told the young British driver to go carefully and then curled myself up in the back of the car and went to sleep. On that day Sir Douglas Haig was visiting some Australian troops who had recently arrived, in their billets. As he and his staff were walking up the pavement of a narrow village street my idiot of a driver drove past them much too fast and a stream of muddy water flew up all over Sir Douglas's lovely polished brown field boots.

I was awakened by a roar of rage to find the alarming face of Sir Douglas asking me what the devil I thought I was doing and what my name was. I explained that I was Lieutenant Smyth of the 15th Sikhs and that I had been asleep and that the driver was young and inexperienced. I was allowed to go on my way.

I had tea and a haircut in Bethune, did some shopping, treated myself to a pint of champagne, which was both cheap and good, and feeling at peace with the world, wrapped myself in my greatcoat and prepared to sleep all the way back. I had taken particular trouble to work out with the driver a circuitous route which would avoid going anywhere near the vicinity of my unfortunate encounter with Sir Douglas Haig. However, once again I awoke to find the car halted by a military policeman and the awesome figure of a general officer approaching. To my horror it was Sir Douglas Haig again. He had motored to another village and was taking the salute of a brigade which was marching past in fours. My young driver in a hurry to get back to his supper, saw a big gap between Sir Douglas and the Brigade, which he thought was just right for him to make a dash for it.

'Good God, it's you again,' said Sir Douglas.

I could think of nothing to reply except: 'Yes Sir, very sorry Sir.'

As Sir Douglas seemed unable to say anything either, I departed, hoping that I would never encounter Sir Douglas again. But I was wrong.

Shortly after this regrettable episode I received my second precious seven days' leave. Again Jim Willcocks lent me a car to take me to Boulogne and insisted that I should lunch at Corps H.Q. first. I particularly didn't want to do the lunch as I was afraid it might make me late and the idea of losing one of those precious days made my flesh creep. However, I managed to start in reasonable time, though not as early as I would have liked. Alas, two punctures put me right in the red and I arrived on the quay just as the leave boat cast off her ropes. There was already a nasty gap of water between the boat and the quay; but as the quay was higher than the deck and I was rather a good long jumper, I was determined to have a go.

So, tucking my kit-bag under my arm and jamming my cap well down on my head, I took a good run and went at it. Suddenly the red-hatted and much bemedalled figure of Sir Douglas Haig rose up from the deck and shouted: 'Stop, you bloody fool.'

My legs shot from under me and I came to rest on my backside on the very edge of the water. By the time I had picked myself up the leave boat was chug-chugging its way across the Channel.

I spent a most miserable night in a pub near the port, indulging in a lot of alcoholic remorse. As I came on board the leave boat at Dover for the return journey Sir Douglas Haig happened to see me and sent his A.D.C. with the following message: 'Sir Douglas Haig presents his compliments to Lieutenant Smyth and is sorry to have done him out of a day's leave but is sure he would have landed in the water.'

I was still feeling very sore about my lost day's leave and replied thanking Sir Douglas for his kind message but saying that I was quite confident that I would have landed on the boat.

A few weeks later, on 29 June 1915, my V.C. was gazetted and Sir Douglas Haig chose me from a number of other V.C.s to receive the first Russian Order of St George, which the Tsar had presented to the 1st Army. It came with a personal letter to me from the Tsar telling me, amongst other things, that the Order entitled me to become an inspector of girl's schools in Russia and to have free travel on public transport anywhere in Russia. I have never had the opportunity of availing myself of either of these priviliges. Alas, I lost the letter, which would indeed have been a wonderful souvenir.

In the second week in July I was given special leave to return to England to have my V.C. presented by King George V at Buckingham Palace. It was the biggest investiture of the war up to that time and several other V.C.s were also being presented. I was one of the few who could walk. There were great crowds at the Palace and we were given a wonderful welcome. I was exceedingly nervous but the King could not have been more charming and quickly put me at ease. Having pinned on my Cross he handed me the box, a very plain cardboard affair, which I have always treasured. He explained that the reason the V.C. was enclosed in such a plain box was in order that the actual value of the Cross, made from the metal of one of the Russian guns captured at Sebastopol in 1855, should not amount to more than one penny. Some years later, in India, I had all my medals stolen, including of course my precious V.C., for which I had to claim a replica from the War Office. I remembered the King's words when they charged me £1 11s 6d for it! It was my first experience of dealing with a Government department! In 1975 a V.C. was sold by auction in London for £7,500.

I had only been back in France about three months and we were just preparing for the Battle of Loos when the 15th Sikhs suddenly received orders to proceed to Marseilles immediately. As our transport sailed with secret orders, which were not to be opened until we were well out at sea, I sat on the top deck to watch the sunset and brooded on the momentous year we had spent in France. I felt curiously sad to go. Bad times are soon forgotten and one remembers only the good. I pondered on the unique relationship which existed between the Indian soldiers and their British officers. The soldiers followed them, not because they were British, nor because they were white, but because they trusted them. How tragic that, when Hindus and Mohammedans had been such brothers in arms, there could ever have been such bloody communal massacres as have occurred in the transfer of power in 1947 and later wars between the troops of the new India and Pakistan.

The lovely Indian War Memorial near Neuve Chapelle remains today a fitting tribute to those soldiers of what are now India and Pakistan, who gave their lives in the cause of freedom, and to their British officers who died with them. Fifty-five years later, I was present when the Indian Army Memorial windows were unveiled at Sandhurst by Field-Marshal Sir Claude Auchinleck, then aged eighty-seven, and at the unveiling by Queen Elizabeth II of the Indian Army Memorial plaque in St Paul's Cathedral, both memorials to the soldiers of the old Indian Army.

CHAPTER FOUR

Egypt, India and the North-West Frontier

WE were bound for Egypt and we spent a very pleasant month on the Suez Canal at Ismailia resting and refitting. We were disappointed not to get a fresh draft however, as our total strength was now not much more than 300. The Indian Corps was being gradually withdrawn from France to go to fight the Turks in Mesopotamia. But the 15th had been withdrawn in a hurry as the number of fighting units in Egypt had been reduced below the safety limit, although the number of depots, hospitals and base organizations for the Gallipoli campaign were legion.

As it turned out our arrival was opportune as, towards the end of 1915, the Sennussi, a powerful Mohammedan tribe in the western desert, influenced by German propaganda and encouraged and reinforced by German troops and German money, started to advance along the North African coast with the object of attacking Alexandria. A force had to be hastily scraped together to deal with the situation. Part of it was sent along the desert road whilst the 15th Sikhs were embarked in three large North Sea fishing trawlers, with a small gun in the bows of each, with orders to steam westwards along the coast and then land and hold up the advancing Sennussi. Each trawler carried rations for ten days and the men were packed on board like sardines. It was frightfully rough and the small craft behaved like bucking broncos. The men were very seasick, and so were some of the officers.

On arrival at Mersa Matruh, then a small and peaceful village, we heard that the Sennussi had already captured Sollum, so we ran our ships ashore and leapt out on to the beach. We had no landing craft and there was no port or quay. We just let down planks from the ship's sides and slid the men down, plus all their equipment. There

54

were a number of splintered bottoms (not merely of the ships!) and one broken leg, but we were ashore and in action within a few hours. One had to act quickly in those days : a ponderous approach like the Suez operation of 1956 would not have been any good. We were soon joined by the Duke of Westminster's armoured car unit and a Horse Artillery battery and with their assistance we held off the Sennussi until the main force from Alexandria started to arrive.

The ensuing campaign was no picnic, but the movement, the bright sunshine and sparkling air, were a pleasant change from the muddy trench warfare of Flanders. The Sennussi had a variety of weapons and observed no civilized conventions. I had two orderlies shot by a left and right from a 500 Express elephant gun – a frightful mess. I was lucky not to be in the middle. The desert mirages were most eerie and the camel-borne Sennussi were difficult to catch. In spite of the bright sun the nights and early mornings were bitterly cold. Our Force Commander, who had a wooden leg, was so cold on some of the early morning operations that he insisted on dismounting and walking. This played hell with the march tables!

The 15th experienced plenty of hard fighting and suffered a further 200 casualties, which reduced the battalion to a mere skeleton. Eventually the Force became so big that they could do without us and the battalion departed with many congratulatory messages from all and sundry for a very fine job well done. Meanwhile the rest of our Brigade had arrived from France and had been despatched to 'Mespot', our place being filled by another battalion. So we were then sent back to India for duty on the Frontier. But first a period of complete replenishment was urgently required.

On arrival in Bombay we were sent to Peshawar in the North-West Frontier Province. I doubt whether there was any better military station in the world. The hot weather was of course very trying, but the winter was gloriously invigorating. Peshawar was a wonderful training ground; it also had facilities for every form of sport, including hunting with the famous Peshawar Vale Fox-hounds. And in the spring the country was pink with almond blossom.

Just as the hot weather was starting the Mohmand frontier tribes flared into violent revolt and we spent a very unpleasant summer in appalling heat on what was known as 'the Mohmand Blockade'. This was a fantastic operation in which about twenty miles of country were sealed off with a live wire fence. All sort of wild animals, and occasionally some humans too, got electrocuted.

By the autumn, however, we were back in Peshawar and during the winter of 1916–17 we were busy training and sending drafts to other battalions. I had some excellent hunting with the Peshawar Vale

Hounds over the most sporting country in India. I was also given a well-known racing pony called Lady Honor by a British cavalry regiment which had been ordered abroad on service, and this started me on a brief flat-racing career. At that time I could ride at nine stone and, as Lady Honor was almost always given top weight, I got quite a lot of rides. Later I had her trained for polo and, to everyone's amazement, although she had been raced for years, she took to it like a duck to water and I could have sold her for a big price as a first-class tournament pony.

In 1917 I had the wonderful experience of being invited by Jack Manners-Smith, V.C., the Resident in Kashmir, to spend a holiday with him and his delightful family in Srinagar and Gulmarg. He had been Resident in Nepal when I had spent two months there just before the war. What a heavenly place Kashmir was – a paradise on earth; and what a tragedy that it was subsequently to become a battleground between the forces of the new India and Pakistan after the transfer of power in 1947. I thought it was the worst mistake of the Government of that time that they didn't settle the future of that lovely country before leaving India.

However, I was abruptly recalled from my idyll in Kashmir to go with the 15th on yet another Mohmand campaign. The heat in the Peshawar Valley was truly terrific. This campaign was more mobile than the last one and was chiefly remarkable for the gallant but disastrous charge of the 21st British Lancers at Shabkadr. At the end of a long and exhausting day they contacted a large body of Mohmands who had positioned themselves in some high crops. The C.O. at once ordered the regiment to charge. In between the regiment and the Mohmands was a deep ditch known as the Shabkadar drain; it would have been a fair jump at any point-to-point and the officers, better mounted and less heavily laden, all cleared it, but the tired and heavily laden troop horses fell in heaps. By the time the men had scrambled over and remounted most of their officers had been killed, among them Captain Thompson, who had been my company colour-sergeant at Sandhurst. He was still alive when they found him, with nearly the whole of the top of his head cut off by a sword and with a ring of fourteen dead Mohmands around him. He was sitting up and smiling and his last words were : 'What a wonderful scrap that was!'

Private C. Hull (Shoeing Smith of the 21st Lancers) won the Victoria Cross rescuing his adjutant, Captain G. E. D. Learoyd, whose horse had been shot, by taking him up behind him and galloping to safety. The 21st also lost their commanding officer, Lieut.-Colonel Scriven, and Captains Percy Hume and P. N. A. Anderson, all killed in this action. This was a great tragedy for that fine regiment which, having been posted to India in 1912, missed the whole of the First World War and yet suffered such a disastrous loss in these unfortunate circumstances.

There was an interesting sequel to this action. Thompson's sword was the Sandhurst drill prize of 1911, which he had shared with C. J. R. Turner of the 15th Sikhs. The latter, who became an air commodore in the Second World War, still has his drill prize sword, which hangs over his writing desk today. Thompson's sword, with which he had wrought such havoc on the Mohmands, was captured by them and sold to the Afghans. In 1967 it was bought from them by a Pathan business man, who presented it back to the 21st Lancers.

As the end of the war appeared to be coming (though in actual fact it was far from over) I had to face another milestone in my life. I was giving promise of becoming a really good polo player, even though I had played so little, and not on good ponies. Most of the good polo players at that time were either fine riders without a very good eye for a ball or vice versa. The top players of course had both assets. I had a splendid eye for a ball at any game and was also a good rider; but I was already getting better than my ponies and could no longer afford to play first-class polo unless I exchanged into an Indian cavalry regiment. Several of the best polo-playing regiments would have been glad to have me, particularly the 17th Cavalry where my friend Joey Atkinson was serving, who became a British polo international. I admit I was very tempted and I would have loved it – for a time. But with my war experience I was rather committed to the serious side of soldiering and decided to stick to it; and I was loath to leave my beloved 15th Sikhs. How different the rest of my life would have been if I had taken the other turning! But having made the decision I hardly ever played polo seriously again, although I watched good polo whenever I could.

In January 1918 I was sent to the Staff School at Saugor and having passed out top was appointed brigade-major to the Bombay-Deolali Brigade, a very big job in those days for an officer of only twenty-four, and I had four staff captains. However, it was largely an administrative area and I hankered to be with troops; so I managed to get myself transferred as brigade-major to the 43rd Infantry Brigade at Lahore. This was a war brigade in the 16th Division, which was commanded by Major-General Beynon, an ex-Gurkha officer.

Lahore Cantonment, or Mian Mir as it was formerly called, was at that time one of the hottest and most unhealthy stations in India; but it was a splendid job for a young officer and I enjoyed every minute of it. We were responsible for the training and administration of all sorts of units in addition to the infantry battalions of the 43rd Brigade.

All through the hot weather my brigade commander, Brigadier-General J. L. J. Clarke, and I rode round to look at units training from daylight until 9 a.m. Then I bathed, changed, had breakfast and worked in the office until 3 p.m., went back to my bungalow in blinding heat, had a sandwich and an iced drink and slept for a couple of hours. Most evenings I went into Lahore Civil Station, seven miles away, played hard tennis, then had a swim in the splendid Government House pool, followed by a couple of long drinks at the Punjab Club, and so back home to dinner at the end of a pleasant if somewhat exhausting day.

Suddenly the news broke that the Armistice had been declared and this was celebrated with tremendous festivities in Lahore. But I felt very sad that I was not in France or England, and longed to get home. However, I still had quite a lot of battle fighting to do before that came about.

The so-called Punjab disturbances will be remembered always for General Dyer and the massacre at the Jallianwala Bagh at Amritsar. These events aroused then, and still do now, immense and heated controversy, and they have become distorted by passion and prejudice as the years have passed. As I was a close observer of the scene and of all the chief characters concerned, and was in fact ordered to give evidence at the trial, I will describe it as I saw it.

The two outstanding characters in these momentous events were Sir Michael O'Dwyer, the Lieutenant-Governor of the Punjab, who had done some marvellous work during the war and had recruited nearly 400,000 men to the Indian Army, and Brigadier-General R. H. Dyer, who was commanding the Jullundur Brigade next door to us. General Dyer was a short, thick-set man of more than average ability as a soldier and with great knowledge of, and sympathy for, the Indian. He was far from being the brutal murderer history has made him out to be. Micky O'Dwyer was a fine and lovable character and one of the greatest administrators we have had in India. He had personality and charm, a great sense of humour and with these human qualities he combined courage, wisdom, judgement, a cool temperament and a very firm hand. In these difficult and dangerous times he showed himself to be a fine leader; no one, soldier or civilian, who served under him, ever doubted that Micky would take full responsibility for anything that befell, and all knew that no subordinate would be cast overboard by him to placate a superior; and that knowledge gave great confidence.

In consequence of the disturbed conditions which became rife in various parts of India the Government had introduced the Rowlatt Bill, which gave the Executive certain additional powers in dealing with crimes of anarchy and revolution. This Bill was much resented by that portion of the population to whom it was particularly intended to apply; and at their instigation unrest grew into a widespread conspiracy. Great efforts were made to tamper with the loyalty of Indian troops and the one bright spot in the disturbance was the complete loyalty of the Indian soldiers to the British Raj.

Early in April 1919 a general hartal (closing of shops) was ordered by the agitators in Lahore and outbreaks of violence were expected beyond the power of the police to deal with. No one realized, however, how organized and widespread these outbreaks were to be. The 43rd Brigade was ordered to send troops to various points in the Civil Station, to be in position by 7 p.m. that evening. My General and I set off by car about 6 p.m. to tour round these positions and see that everything was in order. Suddenly we heard shots and the angry roar of a large crowd. We found that a violent mob of about 10,000 men, armed with staves, sticks, clubs and a certain number of firearms, had issued from the city and invaded the Civil Station. They had been held up by a small party of armed Indian Police only a few hundred yards from the Lawrence Gardens, where a number of white women, nurses and children were congregated. The mob was in angry and determined mood and it was clear that the police would not be able to deal with them.

We turned our car and hastened back to the Punjab Club and I telephoned for the 17th (Indian) Cavalry to gallop down the Mall and for the remainder of the troops to hurry to their positions. The 17th arrived just in time and the mob withdrew, most of them to the city, which became entirely subject to mob law, and the remainder to various parts of the Civil Station, from which they were gradually evicted.

All over the Punjab violent disturbances were taking place; railway stations were burnt down, railway lines torn up and telegraph and telephone lines cut. Mob rule continued in Lahore City for the best part of a week, until we finally forced our way in with a large body of troops. Martial law was proclaimed and Colonel Frank Johnson, commanding the 2/6th Royal Sussex Regiment, was appointed to administer it in the Civil Station. This set us free to cope with the situation in the Lahore area generally.

Meanwhile, in Amritsar, which was in General Dyer's brigade area, serious disturbances had been taking place. On 9 April a large mob from the city invaded the Civil Lines and the troops, very few in number, had to open fire. The mob raided the railway station and beat to death a British guard and an electrician. European women and children in the Civil Lines were collected in the Fort; but nothing could be done to help those in the city.

59

On 10 April the mob set fire to the Town Hall and the Post Office. They looted and burnt the banks and beat to death the European managers and staff. A search was made by the rioters for the lady doctor of the Zenana Hospital, but she was hidden by an Indian servant and escaped. Miss Sherwood, who was superintendent and manager of the City Mission Schools, was pulled off her bicycle, mercilessly beaten and left for dead. She was taken in and cared for by Indian friends and eventually recovered. General Dyer sent us an urgent request for reinforcements and we sent him 176 men of the 1/24th Baluchis and 125 men of the 2/6th Royal Sussex, though we badly needed every man in Lahore.

On 11 April General Dyer and his brigade major, Captain Briggs, who was a great friend of mine, motored over to Amritsar. Proclamations were posted everywhere and announcements made that gatherings and processions were illegal and would be fired on. It was evident that the Punjab was rapidly approaching a state of anarchy. On 13 April General Dyer marched through Amritsar City with a column of troops proclaiming with beat of drums that any large gathering would be dispersed by force. On his return to the Civil Lines he was informed that in defiance of his proclamation a meeting was to be held that afternoon in a large enclosed square called the Jallianwala Bagh. He decided that this deliberate challenge to law and order must be met. He selected a small, entirely Indian, force to take to the Bagh. It consisted of twenty-five men of the 1/9th Gurkhas, twenty-five men from the Frontier Force Rifles, forty Gurkhas armed only with Kukris, and two armoured cars. The remainder of the small body of troops which he had in Amritsar were employed on guards and pickets.

Although his force was such a small one General Dyer had no intention of saddling a subordinate with what he knew might be a very difficult and critical assignment. So he commanded the force himself and took Captain Briggs, his brigade major, with him. It was through the latter that I had an eye witness account of what took place immediately after the event. Reports had already reached General Dyer that the crowd assembled in the Bagh numbered from ten to twenty thousand; that several revolutionary leaders had already addressed them and they were in an ugly mood.

General Dyer's intention was to go in first with the armoured cars, from the top of one of which he would address the crowd and order them to disperse, keeping the troops in the background. The cars however could not get through the narrow entrance and had to be left outside. Having entered the Bagh with his fifty rifles the attitude of the vast crowd appeared to the General to be so immediately menacing that he decided that he must open fire at once to prevent his small

60

force from being rushed and overwhelmed. He therefore deployed his men and gave the order to open fire. Not a man hesitated. They fired 1,650 rounds, or an average of thirty-five rounds per man. The crowd fled at once, trying to clamber over the walls of the Bagh. The rifle fire in this enclosed space was ear-splitting and no order to cease fire could be heard above the clamour and the shrieks of the crowd.

The casualties have never been estimated accurately but it is possible that about 300 were killed and 1,300 wounded. It was estimated that the firing lasted about ten minutes. The effect of this incident was quite electric. In Amritsar itself, law and order were at once re-established and the police resumed their duties. News travelled miraculously fast in India and the rebellion in Lahore petered out like a pricked balloon. All over the Punjab there was a return to law and order and civil control. The Government had allowed the subversive elements such a lot of rope that they found themselves powerless to take any action against them. But General Dyer's action at Jallianwala Bagh gave rise to worldwide discussion and criticism, the chief points of criticism being that no preliminary warning was given that fire was about to be opened, that the firing continued too long and too many rounds were fired, and that no attempt was made to attend to the casualties.

With regard to the first point, General Dyer had to make up his mind in a matter of seconds. He would certainly have been gravely at fault if he had allowed his little force to be overwhelmed. As regards the number of rounds fired, I think the General was to blame. I have always been of the opinion that, if firing has to be resorted to in this most hateful of all duties of the soldier – aid to the civil power – a few rounds fired early by picked shots are always more efficacious and save the heavy casualties which inevitably result from confused and uncontrolled shooting. And I proved my methods to work when confronted by an even more menacing situation in Peshawar City in 1930. General Dyer was well aware of the sort of situation he might expect when he entered the Bagh. He should have been all the more careful, knowing that his men were not only rather raw troops but also religiously antagonistic to the populace of Amritsar. As regards the wounded, the casualties were so large, General Dyer's force so small, and the general situation in Amritsar so menacing that he was probably wise to get his force back and let the civil medical services deal with the casualties.

The Dyer incident would probably have faded into obscurity had it been allowed to do so. His action was enquired into and approved by his superiors, both military and civil, and he was given another responsible command. In November 1919, however, seven months after the disturbances had taken place, a Committee of Enquiry was sent out from England under the presidency of Lord Hunter, a Scottish judge. The effect of this enquiry could not have been worse. All the dying embers of forgotten controversy were fanned into flame. The very fact of the Committee coming out at all was a slap in the eye for the Viceroy and the Commander-in-Chief, both of whom had enquired into the matter themselves. Their findings were over-ruled, and General Dyer was summarily retired. The Hunter Committee, conducted in open court amid a barrage of abuse in language which the judge couldn't understand, engendered more racial hatred than was ever created by the Punjab disturbances themselves. I had been ordered to give evidence before the Committee, but by then I was engaged in an important frontier operation and the force commander, General Sir Andrew Skeen, flatly refused to let me go.

From Indians and Englishmen, both in India and from other parts of the world, letters of sympathy and support for General Dyer poured in, the *Morning Post* newspaper opened an appeal on his behalf. Contributions came in from all quarters, all classes and all races and the list was closed when it reached £28,000. Sir Michael O'Dwyer, as one would have expected of him, did everything he could, regardless of his own career, to support Dyer. Dyer himself however was sent into retirement, together with many other officers and officials who were concerned in suppressing the riots. Sir Michael's assassination later in London was a great tragedy.

Early in May 1919 the Third Afghan War had started and the 43rd Brigade was ordered up to Bannu – without the 2/6th Royal Sussex, who were still on civil defence duties in Lahore. The Afghan has never been much of a fighter, particularly in a regular role, and the 'war' was soon ended with the minimum of casualties. But far more menacing was the rising of the formidable frontier tribesmen, the Wazirs and Mahsuds, which followed. This was to result in the biggest and most difficult frontier campaign we had ever experienced, so much so that at one point it looked as though we might be defeated and forced to withdraw. In fact, had it not been for the inspired and determined leadership of one man, General Sir Andrew Skeen, that could well have happened.

Skeen had been an instructor at the Quetta Staff College and Chief Staff Officer to General Birdwood in Gallipoli. Of all the generals I have ever met I would put Skeen in the highest class. He lacked only one thing, important in a general, and that was robust health. He was a great and lovable man; and his superior commander in Waziristan General Sir Skipton Climo, was also a grand fighting soldier – tall, gaunt, hook-nosed, hard as nails and of indomitable spirit and vast experience. He and Skeen had been in the same Indian battalion: they were great friends and were two of the best leaders of troops the

Indian Army has ever produced – and they needed to be in this campaign. If only I could have had Climo and Skeen as my superior commanders in Burma in 1942 instead of Wavell and Hutton how very differently the battle for Rangoon would have turned out.

The Mahsuds, particularly fighting in their own tangled mass of mountains, were on a par with the Germans and the Japanese as being the most formidable fighting men I have ever encountered. They were ruthless, cunning, good marksmen, adept at concealment and masters of the use of ground. They were watchful and patient, and they never missed an opportunity of bringing off a surprise attack if they saw a chance. They were particularly formidable in following up a withdrawal, and if things were going well for them they would come to close quarters without hesitation. They have been called the best umpires in the world because they never failed to take advantage of a tactical error, or failure on our part to take adequate precautions. Now, armed with modern rifles firing smokeless powder, they were all the more difficult to spot in their mud-coloured clothing which merged into the background of their native rocks.

The Mahsuds alone had some 3,500 modern rifles, in addition to 10,000 of the older pattern. Moreover, they had a number of ex-soldiers from the Indian Army who knew our methods. Added to these were the many well-trained and well-armed Indian officers and 2,000 men of the Frontier Militia who had deserted at the beginning of the campaign. Our troops were stale and jaded from their great struggles against the Germans and the Turks; many of the units, and nearly all the junior British officers, were new to mountain warfare. The British troops in India were in the process of demobilization and repatriation and all my invaluable British signallers and clerks had to be weeded out. The forces deployed on our side therefore, in these toughest of all mountain operations, had to be almost entirely Indian.

On our arrival in Bannu in the Tochi valley on the last day of May we found the situation chaotic. The South Waziristan Militia had deserted and burnt their posts and Brigadier-General F. G. Lucas, commanding the 67th Brigade at Dardoni, was cut off. Our task was to proceed up the Tochi valley, reoccupy the militia posts and connect up with General Lucas. A lot of extra troops, whom we had to sort out and organize, were flung at us. Then, at dawn next morning, 1 June 1919, we started off.

It was the hottest day I have ever experienced. We had many cases of heatstroke and several deaths. We negotiated the difficult Shinki Pass successfully and did not have any excitements until we approached Idak Fort, which had been invested by Wazir tribesmen for over a week. The country opened out here and we let loose our cavalry squadron of the 31st Lancers. The tribesmen were quickly on the move, but they weren't quick enough and the Lancers got into the tail of them with deadly effect. First blood to us.

Brigade H.Q. remained at Idak for the rest of the summer – the most unpleasant one of my life: no fans, no ice, no comforts, burning hot tents, all in one of the hottest regions on earth. The troops were constantly employed on picketing and road protection duty and, to add to our troubles, we had an outbreak of cholera. It was much too much for my General Clarke, who went sick quite early on. He was succeeded by Brigadier-General Gwyn-Thomas of the 2nd Lancers, who had been commanding a British brigade in France. He had had no previous experience of frontier warfare but he was sturdy and of tough physique, though carrying too much weight. Considering he never appeared without his spurs during the whole of the campaign he got along fairly well, but he knew his limitations and never ventured up on the steep hillside. He was somewhat irreverently known to the Brigade as 'Tosh' or 'Where's Jackie'; but he was exceedingly kind to me and I think we formed a good partnership. He was a man of firm decision, absolute integrity and enormous personal courage. By the end of the hot weather we had had many casualties and changes and I was the only officer left who had been with the Brigade in Lahore.

The ending of the Afghan War in such tame fashion merely stimulated the Waziristan tribes, the Wazirs and the Mahsuds, to become more offensive. It was decided that two columns should be formed to deal with them – first the Tochi Column, to operate against the Wazirs, and then the Derajat Column, to take on the much more formidable Mahsuds. The infantry for the Tochi Column was to consist of the 67th and 43rd Brigades and the force commander was to be General Sir Andrew Skeen.

While the preparations for the first campaign were in progress a serious attack was made on one of our convoys in the Shinki Pass. The animal convoy, seven miles long, was moving up the line from Bannu, protected by road pickets on the hills and a certain number of infantry marching with the column. A raiding party of about a hundred Mahsuds, knowing that the convoy was arriving, had come over into the Tochi valley the previous evening and hidden themselves in the rocks on one side of the road, close to Khajuri post where the road debouched from the Shinki Pass. With amazing forbearance they had allowed Brigadier-General Gwyn-Thomas through when he motored past right under their noses on his way back to Brigade Headquarters. They waited until next day when the head of the convoy had reached Khajuri post. Then they opened fire, creating absolute havoc: the road became a shambles of dead and wounded men and animals. Keeping

Douglas Haig, 1st Earl, British
Commander-in-Chief in France in the
First World War, who gave me
my V.C.

One of the many artist's
impressions of myself
winning the V.C.
in France in 1915

After receiving the Victoria Cross on 18 May 1915, aged twenty-two

Leading a company of the 15th Ludhiana Sikhs on our return to billets from the trenches in France, 1914

the road covered they had only to wait a few hours until darkness set in before they could loot the whole convoy at their leisure. But the officer commanding Khajuri post managed to get through on the telephone to Brigade Headquarters at Idak and the Brigade Commander sent me off at once with 300 men of the 9th Jats, under Major McCalmont, in Ford vans, supported by two antiquated armoured cars.

We arrived on the scene within two hours and a very hectic scrap ensued. I sent McCalmont round at the back to get on top of the Mahsuds and then rammed the armoured cars straight down the road to take them on at point blank range. Unfortunately only parts of the old cars were bullet proof, but the crews stuck gallantly to their job and gradually gained the upper hand.

Regardless of his own safety Captain Henry Andrews of the Indian Medical Service, an elderly man and formerly a devoted Salvation Army official, came out from Khajuri post in the middle of the action, with a party of stretcher bearers, to tend the wounded, dress their wounds and get them evacuated in some of the 9th Jats' vans. A number of his men were killed in the process but Andrews seemed to bear a charmed life. He was killed just as he was getting the last man away. The Mahsuds had now had enough and were thoroughly alarmed when McCalmont's men started shooting them up from the back. In their flight the Mahsuds lost a number of men. We managed to get the convoy away and evacuated the wounded before dark.

Captain Andrews had set a magnificent example and was awarded a posthumous V.C.* McCalmont and I were given the M.C. I heard afterwards that General Gwyn-Thomas had originally recommended me for a bar to my V.C. – the only time he had done anything without consulting me! General Climo came up the line and pinned on my M.C.

* Some fifty years later, when I was Chairman of the V.C. and G.C. Association, I was invited by the Director-General of Medical Services to attend the unveiling of a painting depicting the exploit for which Captain Andrews won his posthumous V.C. It was to be unveiled in the anteroom of the R.A.M.C. Mess at Millbank, where they had several exhibits of other R.A.M.C. V.C.s. I said nothing about my having been concerned in the incident.

It was a private party with the V.C.s relatives, some R.A.M.C. and Salvation Army officers and a few special guests such as myself. I was interested to see how the artists had managed to recapture the scene from accounts he had read, in country which was strange to him.

One of the family said: 'I wonder what that camel was doing there?' And without thinking I said: 'It wasn't.' Everyone stared at me and I had to admit that I had been there too. They were eager to know more about the incident and about Captain Andrews. I said I had only known him for the last hour of his life, and that was an hour of which they could be very proud.

The Salvation Army and I became great friends, particularly in my parliamentary constituency where they were very active.

ribbon himself. The M.C. was presented to me later at Buckingham Palace by the Duke of York (later King George VI), who was taking his first investiture as King George V was sick. My brother, Bill, who was also getting the M.C., was marched up with me and we were decorated together. I don't know who was the more nervous, the Duke or Bill and me.

In October 1919, as part of the Tochi Column, the 43rd Brigade advanced up to Datta Kel with very little opposition and forced the Wazirs to accept our terms. It was then decided that the same two infantry brigades, 67th and 43rd, should form the infantry of the Derajat Column against the Mahsuds, although that meant moving us a considerable distance, from Datta Kel to Jandola. By this time however we had had a certain amount of experience of mountain warfare, and there were very few other troops in India who had; and in mountain warfare, as in jungle warfare, experience and training are everything. Needless to say Andrew Skeen was again selected to be the force commander.

CHAPTER FIVE

The Waziristan Campaign
1919-1920

ON the morning of 27 November 1919 the Derajat Column began its march from Dardoni to the Derajat via Bannu and thence by road via Pezu to Tank. This was a distance of 140 miles and it was not until 13 December that the column was concentrated on the Tank–Jandola line. The object of a frontier campaign of this nature was to inflict a decisive defeat on the tribesmen in the field by threatening their capital or some other place of importance or value to them, in defence of which they would be certain to stand and fight – or perhaps run and fight. There was no attempt at strategic surprise, which might well defeat the object. In this case the spearhead of the Derajat Column, based on Jandola, was pointed at Kaniguram, the Mahsud capital, and the tribesmen would obviously concentrate on defending it to the death, which they certainly did.

The advance of a column in this form of warfare was always along a river valley. Only thus could the column obtain water and only thus could it take along its guns, its transport, its supply columns, its hospitals and all the other impedimenta with which the tribesmen managed to dispense, but which were essential to the operation and maintenance of a regular force. To progress in this type of operation we had to picket the heights to enable troops and transport to be protected in their movement along the valley. Usually a column established its road pickets each morning and withdrew them to camp each evening, but in this campaign the Mahsuds put up such fierce resistance that the establishment of each picket became a battle in itself.

It was the fertile brain of Andrew Skeen, the column commander, which provided the only possible answer, in the shape of permanent pickets, just as at a later stage he dared to undertake night operations against the tribesmen which had always previously been considered to be courting disaster. Permanent pickets were established on commanding heights, on either side of the axis of advance to protect important camps and the lines of communication. The pickets were strongly built for all-round defence and protected by thick barbed wire entanglements. Their establishment and construction led to most of the actions which took place during the operations and, on many occasions, the full strength of the Derajat Column had to be used, first to capture the site, and then to cover the construction of the picket. The sites of all the main permanent pickets were chosen personally by Sir Andrew Skeen, who had a wonderful eye for ground.

As the hours of daylight were all too limited we aimed at getting started each day at crack of dawn and being securely established in camp well before dusk. There were innumerable administrative tasks to be undertaken in the morning and evening – such as watering and feeding the hundreds of animals (2,330 mules and camels), the provision and watering of the pickets and, most important of all, the construction and defences of the perimeter camp in which the Force was to pass the night. The Mahsuds, being master tacticians, imposed the maximum delay on our morning advance by skilfully posted riflemen hidden in the rocks. They kept up long range sniping fire on the picket builders, which hampered the work considerably and often caused a number of casualties. But their tour-de-force was always reserved for the afternoon withdrawal; they then moved like lightning to exploit any mistake, and did not hesitate to come to close quarters if opportunity offered.

As brigade major I used to move around the picket lines with a couple of orderlies, an Afridi and a Garhwali; they were very carefully picked, wonderful shots, splendid climbers and as staunch and brave as lions. I was pretty good on the hillside myself; but they were mountain goats and they guarded me as if I was their only child. They could sense danger when they couldn't see it. One day we were moving between two pickets when the Garhwali suddenly froze in his tracks and motioned us to take cover. I swept the horizon with my field glasses – and then I saw him as the sunlight glinted on his rifle barrel; just one ragged Mahsud crouched behind a rock. It seemed ridiculous to be held up by one man who looked to be nearly 900 yards away. I decided to push on despite the protests of my stalwarts. There was a dull report and I felt a pain in my left hand. He had got me in one, but the bullet had hardly penetrated and the wound didn't put me into hospital. Then my two stalwarts went into action and the Mahsud didn't live long to tell the tale.

What really complicated all our operations on the frontier was the absolute necessity never to leave a wounded man behind, and we didn't like leaving a dead one either. Whenever this had to be done (and it wasn't often) the sickening results when we covered the ground next morning were unforgettable and bad for the morale of any troops.

Our 43rd Brigade consisted, to start with, of the 4/39th Garhwal Rifles, the 57th Wilde's Rifles, the 82nd Punjabis and the 3/152nd Punjabis. We also had a squadron of the 21st P.A.V.O. Cavalry, but did not take it beyond Kotkai. There were three Indian mountain batteries in the Derajat Column and a mountain battery of the Royal Garrison Artillery.

The operations had begun with a programme of intensive air attack against the Mahsuds. As they had never been subjected to air bombardment before it was expected that it might well bring them to terms. However it only seemed to make them more aggressive.

On 11 December 1919 therefore, preparations for the advance of the Derajat Column from Jandola began. But the Mahsuds struck first on 17th December with a determined attack on the Jandola camp pickets and, despite the close covering fire of mountain guns and machine-guns, one picket was completely overwhelmed. The Mahsud swordsmen closed in with reckless fanaticism to finish the job. It was only with the greatest difficulty and after three days' fighting that the column established itself in a perimeter camp on the Palosina plain, three miles beyond Jandola. From Palosina further operations were conducted to establish a series of permanent pickets; but each operation was strongly challenged.

On 19 December a force consisting of two battalions of the 67th Brigade, the 1/103rd Mahratta Light Infantry and the 1/55th Coke's Rifles, crossed the Tank Zam river from Palosina camp with the object of establishing a permanent picket on a feature known as 'Mandanna Hill' to cover the further advance of the column up the Tank Zam. This action ended disastrously with both battalions being flung back across the river without completing the building of the picket.

It now became essential to restore confidence and the same operation was carried out next day by four battalions, under the command of General Lucas, with the strongest support from aircraft and mountain guns. The wily Mahsuds just disappeared into the mountains and waited their opportunity. The permanent picket was built and occupied by a British officer and 100 rifles of the 2/19th Punjabis without a casualty. The covering troops withdrew, leaving the picket garrison to complete the sangar defence at their leisure. But the lynx-eyed Mahsuds, who had been watching the whole operation, had spotted one possible weakness; from a jagged cliff a few hundred yards from the picket they could bring fire to bear on the inside of it if they acted quickly before the picket had been completed. They acted immediately and I watched the drama as it unfolded with awed fascination through my field-glasses. Whilst keeping the garrison of the picket closely engaged with heavy sniping a strong body of tribesmen swarmed up the other side of the hill, scaling a near precipice which appeared unclimbable. The British officer, Captain Cuthbert, gallantly led a charge against this main party but was killed instantly. The Mahsuds leapt over the wire and into the picket. Had I not seen it with my own eyes I would never have believed it possible.

The morale of the Mahsuds was now sky-high and the next day they threw two whole battalions back into the valley. Unfortunately we had some missing among our sixty-six fatal casualties and 256 wounded on this day, and that was very bad for the morale of the Force. However, in their completely reckless close-quarter attacks the Mahsuds themselves lost some 250 killed and 300 seriously wounded. These were fantastic casualties amongst their best fighting men, which they were bound to feel severely.

From the point of view of our Higher Command the situation didn't look at all good. In two days we had only advanced three miles and had suffered three resounding defeats; three battalions had been so badly mauled that they were in need of a rest and perhaps worst of all, the confidence of the troops had been badly shaken. We had realized that our troops were untrained in mountain warfare and that they would have to buy their experience, but we had hoped that the price would not be so high. Only a few people, myself included, realized how close we had come to a real débâcle. General Skeen had been quite frank with me about this.

General Skeen now flew to A.H.Q. Delhi to emphasize the seriousness of the situation. As a result four battalions of Gurkhas, the tough little hillmen from Nepal, were sent to join the column. These consisted of the 2/5th, 2/9th, 4/3rd and 3/11th. The arrival of these redoubtable battalions raised the morale of the whole Force and depressed that of the Mahsuds, who well knew their reputation and their fighting value.

On 29 December Column Headquarters, and my 43rd Brigade, made a further advance of four miles to Kotkai, where we remained until 7 January. During this period we built a series of permanent pickets north of Kotkai in preparation for the next advance. At first we had little opposition but on 2 January the 4/39th Garhwalis became involved in a real scrap during the construction of a picket about 2,500 yards from the camp. The 4/39th were as good a battalion as I have ever seen but they were obviously going to have a very sticky time getting away in this very steep and difficult country. And the building and occupation of a picket like this for anything from fifty to a hundred men under constant long range sniping was a long and hazardous business. It had to be really strong, well wired and supplied with food, ammunition and water and the garrison would then be out on a limb, subject to attack every hour of the day and night.

In the course of preparing the fire-plan for the withdrawal, to see what support we could give from guns and other units, I had been up with the C.O. of the Garhwalis and then went forward to Lieutenant Kenny's company, who were holding the key covering position. It was an absolute brute of a place, perched on a knife-edge, which they had done wonders to capture and hold, but from which it would be equally difficult to withdraw. Kenny was as good a young subaltern as any battalion could wish to have. He was tall, strong, red-haired, always smiling, and his men would have followed him anywhere. Kenny's broad smile was the last I ever saw of him.

As soon as the general withdrawal started the Mahsuds pressed him from all sides, but his company fought back fiercely and did not give an inch. When the rest of the battalion was well away, and at last he got the order to withdraw his own company, he trickled three platoons away cleverly, remaining behind himself with the fourth to give them cover; but when he had started to withdraw he saw that one of the other platoons was having difficulty in getting several wounded men away. Obeying the frontier code of never leaving a wounded man to the tender mercies of the tribesmen, he at once ordered the platoon he was with to about turn, fix bayonets and charge the pursuing enemy. It was of course certain death and Kenny and all his party were killed : but the wounded men were carried to safety. Kenny was awarded a very well-deserved posthumous V.C. The 4/39th had displayed the greatest gallantry and the Mahsuds ever afterwards treated them with considerable respect.

On 6 January the 67th Brigade came up from Palosina to join us. We were now confronted with the biggest task of the whole campaign, the capture of the Ahnai Tangi – the most formidable, craggy mountain gorge I ever want to see, flanked by precipitous cliffs rising to a height of 1,200 feet above the bed of the Tank Zam river. On 7 and 9 January General Skeen put in both brigades to try to get a footing on the Ahnai Tangi but found it so naturally strong and so heavily defended that he had to think again. On the 9th my Brigade had such a sticky time that we were glad to have the assistance of the 2/9th Gurkhas, who had just arrived to join the column, in getting us back to camp.

General Skeen then decided on a very bold move : a night operation by both brigades. This was indeed a headache for the two brigade-majors, myself and my friend, Ronnie Duncan. The moon was in its last quarter, which helped a lot, but I thought that the neighing of the animals, dislodged stones and the curses of the men who fell and rolled down the hillside, would awaken the dead. Some of the older frontier soldiers were convinced that General Skeen was about to involve the whole force in a disastrous massacre in the dark. The General told me afterwards that he lay in his camp bed with his hands over his ears waiting to hear the crackle of Mahsud rifles. But the noise of the swiftly flowing river and the unexpectedness of such a move completely surprised the Mahsuds and by daybreak both brigades had reached their objectives and we had got a grip on the Tangi. My Brigade then withdrew to Kotkai, leaving 67th Brigade in a new camp at Ahnai.

The R.A.F. gave us wonderful low-flying support as soon as it got light. As the campaign continued we resorted more and more frequently to night operations. The tribesmen never knew when we were coming and they hadn't the discipline to lie out on the hillside every night, nor indeed had they sufficient warm clothes and the bitter cold drove them into their caves and nullahs.

The advance through the Ahnai Tangi was an epic in the history of frontier warfare. The operation was directed personally by General Skeen and conducted by 67th Brigade, and it proved the most stubborn of the whole campaign. Our casualties were nine British officers killed, including two C.O.s; six British officers and two Indian officers wounded and 365 Indian other ranks killed or wounded. The enemy's casualties were reported later as being 400 killed and very seriously wounded. Though the Mahsuds were still ready to come to close quarters whenever an opportunity offered they never again fought with such reckless abandon.

This period, from 29 December to 20 January, had seen the turning of the tide. During those thirty days there had been twenty actions, in nearly all of which more than one brigade had been employed. We had demonstrated our ability to move over appalling country in the dark and the troops were now standing up to the Mahsuds and giving as good as they got. About one and a half miles north of Sorarogha Camp lay the Barari Tangi, a gorge some three hundred yards long and sixty yards wide, with sides rising precipitously from the river bed. It was almost as tough a nut to crack as the Ahnai. We had been able to establish an advanced aerodrome at Sararogha which ensured close support for the picket-building troops.

After some stiff fighting a hold on both flanks of the Tangi was secured and three camel tracks were made in preparation for the next advance. The Mahsud leaders had collected a 'Lashkar' of some 1,200 rifles to dispute our passage through the Tangi. General Skeen decided to seize the key position of Barari Centre by a night operation and then push our 43rd Brigade through the Tangi. The operation was a brilliant success and we captured this formidable position for the loss of only seven killed and sixty-two wounded.

North of Barari Tangi the area was thickly covered with scrub and bush and intersected by ravines. The largest 'Lashkar' of the whole campaign, amounting to some 4,500, was collected to defend this very difficult position. But on 1 February the 43rd Brigade completely surprised the enemy by another night advance and eventually we established ourselves in a strong and dominating camp at Piazha Raghza.

It now became bitterly cold and heavy sleet and snow made life very uncomfortable indeed. The winding Tank Zam river, thickly encrusted with ice along its edges, had to be crossed many times during the course of a day's operation and the men's boots and puttees became completely frozen. I can see now the portly form of General Gwyn-Thomas, still with those spurs on, being constantly carried across the river on the back of his orderly. But he kept going and was never sick or sorry whatever might befall. He gave me his complete trust and I had a great affection and admiration for him. All through this campaign he had carried along in his kit a large bottle of the best champagne which he intended to drink on the day the operations ended. Being a great stickler for the regulations he had cast out one much needed blanket from his bedding so that his kit should not thereby be overweight.

Towards the end of the operations there had been a difference of opinion between two of our C.O.s about the covering fire arrangements for their withdrawal from two particularly high ridges. I had been out on the mountainside all day in filthy weather when they asked me to go up and settle the matter, which involved another long climb. They got away successfully but I arrived back in camp absolutely whacked. I sent a message to the general to say that I was so tired I had gone straight to bed. Shortly afterwards, the general's servant entered my tent with a large tray, on which was a small plate of egg sandwiches and a huge tankard into which had been poured the contents of the general's precious bottle of Bollinger, which had come all the way from India via Bannu, Pezu, Tank and the Derajat.

On 7 May 1920 the operations came to an end and the Derajat Column was dispersed. Thus ended a frontier campaign of disastrous beginnings and unparalleled severity. And victory had been won over the finest mountain fighters in the world by a Force composed almost entirely of young Indian soldiers. With the exception of the R.A.F. and one British mountain Battery, all the troops employed were Indian Army. Of course all the units were led by British officers, few of whom had had any experience of mountain warfare and many of them little experience of Indian troops, but the guts and leadership of those British officers is something of which I shall always feel proud.

I would put General Sir Andrew Skeen very high among the commanders under whom I have served. I have never seen a general impress his personality and will-to-win on his officers and men as he did. And he was a joy to work with. He later became Chief of the General Staff in India and then his health let him down. He was forced to retire and died soon afterwards.

I have fought against Germans, Japanese, Wazirs, Afghans, Mohmands, Arabs and Sennussi and I have fought alongside many other races, but I think that the Mahsuds, armed with modern smokeless powder rifles, and fighting in their own stark and mountainous country, were about the most formidable fighting men of them all.

It is perhaps not generally realized how the tribesmen's possession of modern rifles with smokeless powder revolutionized warfare on the Indian Frontier. Lord Roberts's famous Kabul to Kandahar march would have been a very different kettle of fish if the Afghans had been so armed in those days.

CHAPTER SIX

Peacetime Soldiering

A S soon as the campaign was over I applied for leave to England
– my first long leave home since my arrival in India eight
years earlier. I was due to be married at the Brompton Oratory
on 22 July to Miss Margaret Dundas, to whom I had become engaged
in India towards the end of the war. Her father was in the Indian
Civil Service. Her mother – quite one of the most beautiful women I
have ever seen – was a strict Roman Catholic and Margaret had been
brought up as a very strict Roman Catholic also, which did of course
involve marital difficulties in those days.

Margaret was a very beautiful woman with a saint-like character.
She gave me four wonderful children, who were the joy of her life,
and of mine in later years. The fact that our marriage only lasted
twenty years was certainly not her fault. But the life of a successful
young soldier in the Indian Army demanded inevitable separations,
and marriage was made for togetherness, both sexual and mental. We
corresponded regularly after our divorce and from 1956 onwards I
was able to do her a real and much appreciated service by getting
over from Australia (in relays with my V.C.s) our children and grandchildren, the family of my second son, Julian, who had become a
naturalized Australian, as I was allowed to bring over two relatives
for each biennial Reunion.

On 26 June 1920 I attended the first Victoria Cross Reunion, a very
momentous and moving occasion, which was attended by great crowds.
The Garden Party at Buckingham Palace was preceded by a luncheon
at Wellington Barracks where the band of the Welsh Guards played
throughout the meal and later led us on our march along Birdcage
Walk, across the Horse Guards Parade and through the Mall to the
Palace. Our oldest colleague was Sir Dighton Probyn, then over eighty-
seven, who had won his V.C. in the Indian Mutiny of 1857. There

75

were 324 V.C.s present; these included twenty-four naval V.C.s and three from the R.A.F. The R.A.F. of course was a young Service, but it had thirteen living V.C.s, most of whom were too seriously injured to attend.

Each V.C. was allowed to bring three relatives so there was a big gathering in the Palace grounds. On the steps of the Palace terrace stood the King and Queen, behind them the Royal Princes, the Duke of Connaught and Princess Mary. Their Majesties received every V.C. separately. I think my most abiding memory of the occasion was the grace and beauty of Her Majesty Queen Mary. She was so obviously thrilled and delighted and communicated her pleasure to everyone around her. Some thirty years later, as Comptroller of the Royal Alexandra and Albert School for orphan and necessitous children, I had the honour of being presented to her again. And year after year, as a member of the All England Club at Wimbledon, I watched her intense interest in every stroke that was played on the famous Centre Court. No day was ever too long for her. When Queen Mary arrived in the Royal Box a sigh of content went round the Centre Court; and when she died each one of us at Wimbledon felt a sense of deep personal loss.

However, I had only been in England a few weeks when the Arab insurrection started in Mesopotamia and Brigadier-General A. le G. Jacob (brother of Field-Marshal Sir Claude Jacob) at once applied for me as brigade-major of his 74th Brigade which was being formed in India. I must say I did think that there was some other officer on the spot – who wasn't just getting married in England – who could have been appointed. I suppose I should have been flattered to be so much in demand: but I didn't see it that way. However, they graciously allowed me another ten days' leave and Margaret and I were married at the Brompton Oratory as arranged. The bride was given away by her great-uncle, the Marquess of Zetland.

Ten days later I was on the high seas bound for Basra. The campaign in Mesopotamia started with one or two unpleasant setbacks which encouraged the temperamental Arabs tremendously. The heat in July and August was terrific. During this period my old friends, the 1st Manchester Regiment, who had formed part of the Jullundur Brigade with my 15th Sikhs in France, were severely mauled in an ambush, in which, to my great sorrow, Captain George Henderson was killed, winning a posthumous Victoria Cross. He led three bayonet charges and was twice wounded, the second time mortally. His last words to his men were: 'I'm done now, don't let them beat you.' George Henderson was a very splendid young man.

My 74th Brigade was sent up to Nasiriyah on the Euphrates and we had a certain amount of fighting and a lot of heat, dust and discomfort before order was gradually restored. I was mentioned in despatches.

In 1923, after nearly two years' hard study, which was difficult to get down to after so much fighting, I qualified for the Staff College and was specially nominated to Camberley by Lord Rawlinson, the Commander-in-Chief in India. In peacetime the Staff College was the Mecca of all soldiers under thirty-five years of age who took their profession seriously. Promotion was slow and prospects of special advancement very small. The magic letters p.s.c. (passed staff college) after one's name were a great help and nearly all the top commanders and staff officers of the Second World War, both of the British and Indian Armies, had been Staff College graduates either at Camberley or Quetta.

About sixty officers were admitted to Camberley each year for the two-year course, making a total at the College of 120 students. The sixty officers in each term included two naval officers, two R.A.F., two Canadian, two Australian and six Indian Army.

When I joined the College in 1923 the Commandant was General 'Tiny' Ironside, who afterwards became Chief of the Imperial General Staff when the Second World War started. A colossal figure of a man, 'Tiny' Ironside was the youngest major-general in the British Army. Amongst our instructors (Dill had just left) were Gort, Alan Brooke, 'Bulgy' Thorne, Ronald Adams, Philip Neame, V.C., Haining and 'Boney' Fuller, all destined to become generals of high degree. In my own division were Arthur Percival, afterwards the ill-fated commander of our troops in Malaya; Teddy Schreiber, who became Governor of Malta at the end of a distinguished career; and Stephen King-Hall R.N., who later became a Member of Parliament and was given a life peerage just before his death. Our two Canadians were both to become famous, Georges Vanier as Governor-General of Canada and Harry Crerar as commander of the Canadian Army in France. There were also Robertson and Pain from Australia; Pargiter, Loch, Macready, Firebrace, Franklin, Halstead, Monty Stopford and Michael Gambier-Parry, all of whom were to become generals in the Second World War.

In our Junior Division in my second year were Willoughby-Norrie, later a corps commander in North Africa and a life peer; 'Tirpitz' Durnford, who became Quartermaster-General in India; Bill Barstow, who commanded my own regiment of the 15th Sikhs and was killed in action on 20 January 1942 in Malaya when commanding the 9th Indian Division. There was also another officer of the 15th, Jack Turner, who finished up as an Air Commodore. The 15th also had an officer at the same time at the Quetta Staff College. So, with an establish-

77

ment of only twelve officers, we had four at the Staff College at once – a unique record for any battalion.

The Camberley Staff College was a fine building in spacious and well-kept grounds, which included a cricket and hockey ground, grass and hard tennis courts and excellent squash courts. The College had its own drag hounds, and horses and grooms were provided for every officer by the Remount Department. The two years spent at Camberley were probably the best in one's military life. For the Indian Army officers it held the added advantage of a two-year break from India. The highlights of the course were the Foreign Tour, for which we formed our own syndicates and chose the particular country we wanted to visit; the Mountain Warfare Exercise in Wales; and the Combined Operations Exercise with our sister Staff Colleges of Greenwich (R.N.) and Andover (R.A.F.)

I played a lot of games, hunted and rode in point-to-points, much enjoyed the Staff College Drag and played a lot of good cricket, tennis, hockey and squash. Jack Turner and I, having been well grounded by our splendid Sikhs, were at once in line for English caps at hockey as well as being automatic choices for the Army and the Combined Services teams. I captained the Combined Navy, Army and Air Force XI in our first English International trial and Turner and I played in several more trials; Turner played centre half for England in all their international matches the year after I had left the College.

I also played lawn tennis and squash rackets for the College and for Devon County and the Army and was accepted for the Amateur Squash Championships. The Staff College cricket was great fun and of quite a high standard, and I also played a little Free Forester cricket.

Towards the end of the Staff College course there was naturally considerable anxiety as to what sort of report one would get. General Ironside started a scheme of picking out the top eight students, who were then put on a special list for accelerated promotion. I was included in this which was very flattering considering how high-class all the other seven were. I did however get such a good report that I was summoned back to India immediately to fill an important staff appointment.

Camberley was a happy interlude for the families – particularly for those in the Indian Army, and Margaret and I were fortunate to be accommodated in one of the College bungalows which had the advantage of being cheap and close to the College. Our first child, John, had been born in November 1921 and our second, Julian, was born at the Staff College on 16 October 1923. The family went back to India with me after the course and we lived in Delhi and Simla during my four-year tour on the staff at Army Headquarters.

The Director of Military Training in India was Brigadier Jack Collins, a British Infantry soldier, who had had a particularly distinguished career in the First World War and had been an instructor at the Camberley Staff College just before I went there. He was therefore able to pick the officer he wanted as his G.S.O.2, and I was glad he picked me, although he was a very hard taskmaster. He was very quick, a tremendous worker, a fine athlete and kept himself in first-rate physical condition.

In addition to the mass of work I had to tackle, Collins asked me to take on something to which he attached great importance. There was no doubt that officers stationed in India, both British Service and Indian Army, who wanted to study for the Staff College, were at a great disadvantage compared to their counterparts in England, many of whom could take courses from the various 'crammers' who existed for the purpose. Jack Collins therefore asked me to arrange, and to run myself, courses for officers studying for the Staff College to be held in Simla during the hot weather. These courses, which became known as the 'Backward Boys', lasted a month and took sixty officers each year. They entailed a great deal of work for me and my helpers but they became very popular: quite a number of officers attributed subsequent admission to the Staff College to them and were duly grateful. What with these courses and the five years I had spent at the Camberley Staff College as student, and later as instructor, I got to know a great number of the 'brains' of the Army, both British and Indian.

After our two years together Jack Collins was summoned home to take command of the so-called 'Experimental Brigade' at Tidworth. This was regarded as a key job and Collins was just the man for it. As soon as he got home he asked for me as his brigade-major. The War Office were quite agreeable, and so was I. But the everlasting problem of finance reared its ugly head and the Indian Financial Authorities refused to sanction it. This appointment would have been a milestone in my career and it was very frustrating that through no fault of my own I was unable to take it up.

The Commander-in-Chief in India after the death of that splendid battle commander, Lord Rawlinson, was Field-Marshal Lord Birdwood of Anzac. He was the fittest Commander-in-Chief India had ever had. In Simla his day used to start with an arduous climb straight down the Khud and up again, followed by strenuous physical exercises. Even at his age no one could keep up with him on the hillside. All the wise-acres used to say that over-exercise would kill him, but he long outlived all the other Great War commanders. If he had not been knocked down by a car in his late eighties he might well have reached his century. I was to become a close friend of 'Birdie' and his family and when he died the B.B.C., at the family's request, asked me to make an obituary broadcast to Australia, which I was proud to undertake. His own family – and many Australian soldiers – paid tribute to the broadcast in words I shall never forget.

General Sir Andrew Skeen, the brilliant Chief of the General Staff at Army Headquarters, whom I had come to know so well in the Waziristan Campaign, was soon unfortunately to suffer a breakdown in health which necessitated his retirement from the Service – a great tragedy for himself and for the Army in India. He was succeeded by that fine cavalry leader, Sir Philip Chetwode, who afterwards became Commander-in-Chief in India.

When I first went to A.H.Q. the Viceroy was Rufus Isaacs, the first Lord Reading. He was a charming and extremely handsome man and I used to enjoy just looking at him. When the first Lady Reading died he married his secretary, Stella Charnaud (in 1931), who became a close friend of myself and my wife Margaret. A few years before Lord Reading's death we stayed with them at Deal Castle. It was a unique event to play golf with Rufus. He played the ball hard and straight along the ground and it ricocheted towards the hole, outdriving by yards those whose ball described a perfect parabola. I asked him once how he first made his reputation at the bar and he replied : 'I set myself to know just a little bit more about every case than anyone else concerned with it. It was just sheer hard work. For several years I worked until 3 a.m. and rose at 8 a.m., allowing myself only five hours' sleep. And at the end of three years of that – I had arrived.'

Rufus Isaacs was one of the most brilliant and attractive men I have ever met. Despite their difference in age his marriage to Stella Charnaud was a love match and they were both delightful people. In 1958 Stella became Baroness Swanborough, being one of the first life peeresses to sit in the House of Lords.

Lord Reading's successor as Viceroy was Lord Irwin, later Lord Halifax, also a brilliant and charming man. I had of course met him before when his daughter, Anne, was bridesmaid at my wedding. His great relaxation was fox-hunting; he had been a Master of Hounds at home and when he was appointed Viceroy he cabled out to say that if someone was willing to hunt them he would bring out a pack of foxhounds. There had been foxhounds in Delhi previously but they had been abandoned for the simple reason that there wasn't any scent. However, all that had been forgotten and the foxhunting enthusiasts, myself included, rallied round and cabled back an optimistic 'Yes'.

Meanwhile I was becoming increasingly interested in lawn tennis and if I had had the opportunity of playing earlier in my life I might have become rather good. As it was I played for my county at home and for the Army and the Combined Services, both in England and in India, and would probably have played at Wimbledon if I hadn't always been stationed abroad.

Now however I became closely associated with the Delhi foxhounds. Lord Irwin was as good as his word and arrived complete with a fine pack of English foxhounds. An old ammunition magazine on the banks of the River Jumna made excellent kennels, the thick walls making for coolness and the many trees on the river bank giving plenty of shade. I whipped-in to the first two Masters and was then invited to become Master myself. I very much doubted whether I could possibly find time for this but my boss, Brigadier Jackson, who had a passion for hunting himself, insisted that I should accept. So I duly became Master (and huntsman) of the Delhi Hunt.

The main hunts in India were Ootacamund, the Peshawar Vale, Lahore, Poona, Kirkee, Bangalore, Bombay, Belgaum and Quetta; but there were comparatively few places where the scent, the climate and the jackals (or foxes) were suitable enough to provide enjoyable sport without some form of artificial aid. The Peshawar Vale, with whom I had hunted quite a lot, was a very sporting country with some formidable obstacles and quite good hunting conditions, but there was a great shortage of jackals and a number had to be imported. In hunts like Lahore a bagman always had to be provided and in many other places also where scent was poor or non-existent. In Quetta they had a good system of artificial earths from which a jackal, on emerging, got his pads in some sort of smell.

In Delhi the problems were briefly as follows : the field were nearly all soldiers or civil servants who had to get back to their offices at a reasonable time. So there had to be an early start from that point of view alone. Also the early morning was the only time there was any scent, before the sun gained power. Another factor which made an early start imperative was that English foxhounds very soon went sick if they were kept out too long in the heat of the day. So, as Master, I used to aim at moving off from the meet as soon as it was light enough for the horses to see where they were putting their feet; and that probably meant a 4.30 a.m. start for myself and the hunt staff for a meet at 6 a.m. But all the field had to be up betimes too because the hunting country was about ten miles from Old Delhi, plus another five miles for the Viceroy and many others who had to come out from Old Delhi. All the horses had to go out to the meet the night before or very early in the morning and hounds came out in a van.

During the year when I had been first whip to Scottie (Lieut.-Colonel R. S. Scott of Army Remounts), who was a first-class huntsman, I was able to study the form. To start with the hounds had been an enormous success, largely because it was a new venture which had the enthusiastic support of the Viceroy and his family, and of the Commander-in-Chief, Sir Philip Chetwode. Lord Irwin and his sons and daughter not only came out hunting but paid frequent visits to the kennels, which was a great encouragement to the hunt staff. The size of the fields and the number of cars were almost embarrassing. Then there was the beauty of the early cold-weather mornings; and every now and then we got a good run. But Scottie and I knew very well that it couldn't last and we began to realize why foxhounds in Delhi had never been a success. You can't hunt with scent dogs if there isn't any scent.

From the point of view of transport and the necessity for moving off soon after sunrise the meets had to be on one of the main roads leading out of Old Delhi. The dry, scrubby country on either side of the road was always teeming with jack (there were not many foxes and they never ran well) but hounds always found at once. However, scent was so weak that any line they picked up faded quickly and they at once changed on to another jack. The result was lots of hounds music, quite a lot of fun for the hunt staff, but very little for the field, who either followed us around in the scrub or stayed patiently in one place, waiting for us to go away.

What were we to do about it? Earth-stopping or artificial earths were quite impossible. We tried putting down an impregnated bag-man, which Scottie and I both hated doing. It certainly took us through the scrub but a bagman never ran well and was always obvious to any acute observer. During that hunting season, which extended from November 1927 to March 1928, hounds were out thirty-seven times and we accounted for eight and a half brace of jack. Scottie's 'Master's Report' finished as follows: 'On the whole it is considered that the season has been reasonably good and it is doubtful whether better average sport can be expected considering the difficulty of the conditions under which we hunt in Delhi.' But it was poor praise.

At the Hunt point-to-point I won the light-weight race on my grand little country-bred mare, the Queen, and the heavy-weight race on my chestnut Australian mare, Mary Rose. In the latter race I had to carry 13 stone 7 lb, which meant a terrible amount of lead as I could ride 9 stone with a racing saddle.

With interest in the hunt undoubtedly on the wane it was not a very favourable moment for me, or anyone else, to take over the Master-ship. However, I had a splendid hunt staff and some fine hounds and we could only do our best to provide reasonable sport and a good gallop now and then. English foxhounds could not be kept down in the plains of India during the hot weather and we had to make some arrange-ment for them at a hill station for the summer months. This time we sent our eighteen couple to the Imperial Institute of Veterinary Research at Muktesar in the Kumaon Hills. Unfortunately, despite the care taken of them, we lost three and a half couple, one and a half couple of these being the result of an encounter with a wild boar.

We started hunting again on the 29 October; and on 18 November I got a new draft of eight and a half couple from England, which were very kindly presented by the Masters of the Sinnington, Middleton, Holderness, Tiverton and Bramham Moor Hunts. The conditions which faced us that season were the worst we had encountered. There had been an exceptionally dry summer and there was very little rain during the hunting season itself. This made for very bad scenting conditions at all our usual meets. Nevertheless we had far and away our best season and we had much bigger fields. Hounds were out forty-three times and accounted for twenty-one brace of jack and one fox.

Now, how did we manage to have such a successful season? The critics of course said: 'Bagmen', and then, when we had so many long straight runs, they wondered mightily, because the bagman seldom runs straight. And when we killed several times in a morning, after long runs, they began to realize that bagmen were out. One or two jealous spirits posted themselves under cover out in the country I was proposing to draw, and remained more mystified than ever.

I kept the secret entirely to myself. You can't hunt with smell dogs if there isn't any smell, nor can you show good sport in a country full of earths which you can't possibly stop. I could have resorted to bagmen, as so many other hunts in India did, but I never did. What I had discovered however was that wherever there was water there was scent, even in Delhi. If only we could get away from the belt of dry, scrubby terrain which bordered the roads, and out into the damper grassy country beside the rivers, we had every chance of finding a strong wild jack which would not immediately run to earth.

The problem was to get hounds through the wide belt of scrub teeming with jack that at once went to ground and into these green pastures. It was here that my experience with the Staff College drag at Camberley came in useful. I laid a short drag line from my first draw through the scrub and out into the open country – and having got there, I relied on picking up a wild jack, either in the open or in the reeds bordering the river banks. This provided a solution to the problem which had seemed insoluble ever since hunting with foxhounds had been first attempted in Delhi.

During this time I was very lucky to get away with an outbreak of rabies. We destroyed one or two hounds immediately and segregated others. Then every hound was inoculated fourteen times and every precaution was taken to prevent the spread of this terrible disease, which of course can also be passed on to humans. Had my good Honorary Veterinary Officer, Major S. W. Marriott, not tackled the matter immediately in such a thorough fashion we might have lost the whole pack.

At the end of a very successful season I gave up the Mastership as I was going on home leave. I had enormously enjoyed being a Master of Foxhounds and had never missed hunting hounds myself. Had I been staying on in Delhi I would have agreed to remain as Master for another year, although it was a very great strain on top of my busy job on the General Staff at Army Headquarters. Lord Irwin almost always brought his daughter, Anne Wood (later Lady Faversham) out, and his two small sons, Charles and Peter. Richard, later the Rt Hon M.P. for Bridlington, was too young. One day Peter's horse kicked one of my hounds and Lord Irwin sent him over to me to apologize. On arrival Peter was so overcome by the enormity of his offence that he burst into tears. I hadn't the heart to scold him and said something to the effect that it didn't matter. Peter went back to his father beaming. 'The Master said it didn't matter,' he said. For this I was strongly reproved by Lord Irwin who had hoped that I would row Peter severely.

In the point-to-point that year I won the Hunt Pony Race on the Queen for the third year running, but failed to repeat my success on Mary Rose in the Hunt Horse Race. However, I had a splendid ride in the Open Race on a gallant little mare called Evergreen Eve, belonging to Mr S. H. Wise, being only beaten on the post by a big striding racehorse called the Soarer.

Although rabies was of course always a background menace in India it did not prevent any pack of hounds or long dogs, as far as I was aware, from hunting the jackal, or, in some places, the fox – both of which are likely carriers of this horrible disease. In all my thirty years' service in the Indian Army I never came across a case of anyone, British or Indian, who contracted this complaint. I did of course know of several people who, under suspicion of infection, had been compelled to undergo the painful injections which alone could prevent its fatal progress. There was never any question of eradicating rabies from India. What was all-important was that any person who had been bitten or licked by a rabid animal should seek immediate advice from a veterinary surgeon. The injections had to be administered within a comparatively short period of time to be effective.

I lost four dogs from rabies during my thirty years in India. In each case the dog was put down as soon as the first symptoms appeared and of course was followed by a thorough investigation into any person who might have been in contact with the dog beforehand.

My last experience of this caused me the most anxious dilemma of my life. It was described in the book, *Plain Tales from the Raj,* by Charles Allen. It occurred in Delhi in the late 1920s, when my much beloved dog Kim suddenly contracted rabies and had to be destroyed immediately. As Charles Allen writes in *Plain Tales*: 'The vital need for treatment (of possibly infected persons) at an early date and the impossibility of knowing for certain whether rabies had been transmitted could turn a brush with the disease into a frightful gamble with death.' And this is what happened in this case.

Shortly after the time limit for treatment had passed I was having drinks at the Adjutant-General's house, when one of his daughters said to me: 'Oh Jackie, I forgot to tell you that when I was passing your bungalow a short time ago I saw Kim in the garden and took him out for a run. He was so pleased to see me and licked me all over my face.'

My heart stood still. I rushed off to the vet who was a great authority on rabies and he said: 'Injections at this point of time would be absolutely useless.'

I then had to make up my mind whether to tell her parents. Her mother, who was in frail health, would hardly have stood the anxiety, which I decided would have to be mine alone. I started calling at their house almost every day, until they began to think I had designs on their daughter, for whom I always asked if I did not see her in the flesh. At last the danger period passed and I breathed again. I never told them.

There was a great deal of social life in Simla but not so much in Delhi. The British, exiled temporarily from their own country and their own kind, worked willingly with the people of the country, but for recreation and amusement tended, in those days, to foregather in their own clubs and associations. In many ways this was a great weakness because the various races never got to know each other properly; on the other hand it avoided many difficulties. The Viceregal and Government functions were of course completely mixed as regards race and colour, but there were still comparatively few mixed social clubs of any sort. However, I made a point of playing a lot of tennis with Indians; for one reason, I liked them, and for another, they played better tennis!

Simla was apt to be a very depressing place in the rains, and dances and theatricals relieved the gloom. Margaret and I used to go fairly often to stay the weekend at a lovely rambling old house in the Simla Hills, called Dukhani. This was owned by an elderly gentleman by the name of Buck (always known as Bucky), who was Reuter's correspondent in Delhi. Bucky was a great character, a wicked but very

85

charming old man who had a host of friends, male and female, but chiefly female. The house next door to Dukhani was known as 'The Bower' and it was supposed to be haunted by the ghost of the Indian mistress of a British officer who had left her for another. Certainly no one would ever rent The Bower, although it was going absurdly cheap. On one or two occasions I had brought myself to enter the garden, which must have been beautiful once but was now a wilderness. Each time I had begun to feel so very queer that I had taken to my heels in a panic. Nevertheless the place fascinated me.

On one occasion Bucky was having a very special weekend party at Dukhani — I think it was to celebrate his seventieth birthday. Margaret had gone out there on the Saturday morning and I had decided to walk out as soon as I could get away from my office in Simla. It was quite a long ride on horseback and a very tiring walk indeed, up and down khuds and through the pine woods. I arrived in Dukhani, hot and exhausted, to find that owing to difficulties of accommodation the sexes had been segregated and I was to sleep in a camp-bed in Bucky's own room, which was down in the old part of the house at garden level. Since Bucky was a notorious snorer I didn't relish the thought of sharing a room with him, even though it was a big one. However, there was nothing to be done about it; so I wallowed luxuriously in the tin tub of very hot water brought in by the Indian servant and dressed leisurely for dinner.

Bucky was in his most impish form and told us some quite unrepeatable after-dinner stories. But I was tired and very early I slipped away from the music, the singing and the bridge, to seek my camp-bed, and was fast asleep almost as soon as my head touched the pillow.

I woke quite suddenly. The light of a half moon was filtering into the room through a french window which led into the garden. What had woken me was the curtain blowing into the room and making a flapping noise in the wind. Should I get up and shut the window, or shouldn't I? I had just decided to do nothing and go to sleep again when, in the middle of the room, I saw the figure of an elderly, grey-haired gentleman in a dressing gown.

Naturally I thought it was Bucky. 'Oh, do shut the window,' I said to him.

But at that very instant, from Bucky's bed in the far corner of the room came a loud snore. I suddenly had the same eerie feeling that I had had in The Bower and my hair felt as if it was standing on end. What to do now? Pull the clothes over my head and pretend nothing was there, or pluck up my courage and investigate?

Rather reluctantly I decided on the second course, swung my legs out of bed, felt for my slippers, stood up and started to advance in a trembling fashion towards the middle of the room. The old gentleman looked sad and lonely; he was perfectly clear in the moonlight. As I advanced he retreated towards the window. Then he just quietly melted away into the garden. I dashed to the window. I could see all the way up the garden. The path, the lawns were empty; there was no one there. The garden lay bathed in moonlight and a gentle breeze soughed in the trees. But of my old man there was not a sign or a sound. I fastened the window securely and went over to my bed and lit my candle: there was no electric light in Dukhani. I felt very shaken.

After breakfast someone searched out an old history of Simla and found that, exactly forty years previously, an old man in a dressing gown had shot himself in that very room. Naturally the story got around and, in due course, both Lord Birdwood, the Commander-in-Chief, and Lord Irwin, the Viceroy, wanted to hear from me personally the story of the Dukhani ghost. But what impressed them most was that I had never believed in ghosts, and most obviously didn't *want* to believe in them now.

Lord Irwin was the first Viceroy of India to take leave in England during his tour of duty. Margaret and I were staying with his wonderful old father, Lord Halifax, in Yorkshire when he arrived. There had been references in the newspapers over the previous week or so to troubles with Gandhi and riots in India which had worried him a lot. 'My poor Edward,' he said; 'he will be in a terrible state when he arrives.'

However, when the day came Edward was in tremendous form, had put on about a stone in weight and bounded up the steps.

'But Edward.' Lord Halifax said; 'the papers all said you were having a terrible time.'

'Father,' replied Lord Irwin; 'never read the papers.'

While I was in Delhi I was initiated into the art of pig-sticking and I only regret that I did not have time to go in more for this thrillng and marvellous sport and perhaps have competed in the Kadir Cup. I shall always remember my first encounter with the mighty boar. Glen Macartney, on Lord Rawlinson's staff, an expert and experienced hoghunter, took me out, together with 'Mossy' Owen of the Governor's bodyguard. Neither of us had ever been pig-sticking before. I rode my own little mare, the Queen, and Mossy was riding an enormous body-guard horse. We had made no arrangements for beaters and planned to ride around on the chance of picking up a pig. Glen explained to us that if we did put up a pig he would probably make for the thick cover on the river bank, so therefore we must try to spear him quickly before he got there.

For a long time we saw nothing. Suddenly there was a shout from Glen and a lean and tough-looking old boar shot out between Mossy and me and made for the river. The Queen, naturally well-balanced and on her toes, was off after him like a flash. I had never felt so excited in my life. The going was appalling, potholes and thick roots over which in the ordinary way one would have ridden at a walk and with extreme circumspection. Now they might not have existed. The only thing that mattered was the pig, well out in the open, but going straight as a die for the river and safety. There was no need to encourage the Queen with whip or spur; her blood was up.

With only a hundred yards of open going left we got on terms with this formidable animal. I tried to remember all I had been told about how to spear, but only succeeded in making a very inexpert jab much too far back. However, it temporarily paralysed the pig and he squatted in a bush, winded and furiously angry.

Mossy was the first to arrive just behind me. He eyed the pig some-what gingerly and then, looking as though he was starting on a quiet morning's tent pegging, he cantered in with his spear levelled. What happened then almost took my breath away. The pig came out of the bush like a shot from a gun and the next thing we saw was Mossy and his enormous horse rolling on the ground. Glen came to the rescue immediately, or it might have gone hard with Mossy, and hustled the pig off. Just as he was going to spear the pig it jinked and slashed at the same time, inflicting a nasty cut on Glen's horse, which he was planning to ride in the Kadir Cup. The pig once more squatted in his bush, ready to repeat the tactics which had proved so successful. I was left on my own with the pigsticker's most difficult problem – an angry and wounded boar at bay.

However, I had profited to some extent from Mossy's discomfiture and did not need Glen's shout of 'Go fast, Jackie, go fast!' to realize that speed was vital; so that when the pig charged I was going faster than he was. That pig was very very angry and I had been initiated rather too quickly into the gentle art of pig-sticking. What would have hap-pened if our two charging bodies had met I do not know. I might have disabled the pig but I doubt if I could have kept him off my beloved Queen and she would probably have been badly damaged. As it was, the Queen deemed discretion the better part of valour and threw the most enormous leap into the air, the pig just cutting her very slightly on the fetlock as he struck upwards with his tusks. Then, with a wicked and triumphant leer, he disappeared into the jungle.

Mossy's horse was in a bad way; and so was Mossy, for he had not asked anyone's permission to bring it out. It died in the night, but the Viceroy was quite nice about it.

After this my blood was up and I went pig-sticking whenever possible. Much as I loved hunting I must confess that if I had to choose between the two sports in India I should choose pig-sticking every time. But there were not many places where one had this difficult choice.

Half way through my term of duty at A.H.Q. I had been given a brevet-majority and was selected by the Chief of the General Staff as 'pre-eminently the first choice of the Indian Army for selection as Instructor at the Staff College Camberley.' This of course was the plum job the Indian Army had to offer. But in the end it was decided that I was too young and should wait until 1931. How frustrating these foolish ideas about age were to the keen young soldier. I suffered from it on more than one occasion and it really almost ruined my soldiering, as it did for many others – some of them resigned in disgust.

When my time at A.H.Q. came to an end I handed over my job there and my secretaryship and editorship of the United Services Institution to G. B. Henderson of the old 15th Sikhs, and the hounds to Victor Wakeley, than whom there was no better nor more enthusiastic Master of Hounds in India. I and my wife and family, now consisting of John aged eight, Julian aged six, and Robin, aged three, went back to England on leave. Jill was born a year or two later. We were soon to be faced with the problem which beset so many British families in the Indian Service : should the children be left at home in somebody else's care while the wife stayed with her husband in India, or should the wife make a home in England and leave someone else to look after her husband? It was fortunate that we decided on the latter as in two years I was to come back for another term of duty at the Staff College, after which the family remained at home, with the children at school.

CHAPTER SEVEN

England and India
1929-1933

THE great event of 1929, the summer of which I spent in England, was the dinner given to recipients of the Victoria Cross in the Royal Gallery of the House of Lords by H.R.H. the Prince of Wales (Patron), Admiral of the Fleet, Earl Jellicoe (President) and the National Executive of the British Legion. The dinner took place on Saturday 19 November and it was followed next day by a special performance of the most popular of all war plays, R. C. Sheriff's *Journey's End*, at the Prince of Wales Theatre. Then, on Monday 11 November, there was the Remembrance Service at the Cenotaph in the morning and the Festival of Remembrance at the Albert Hall in the evening.

The British Legion were wonderful hosts and those three days will remain imprinted on the memories of all who experienced them. But the big event was the dinner itself, in which H.R.H. had taken the closest possible interest; in fact he had been the originator and the inspiration of the whole affair. By his special wish it was to be marked by a complete absence of formality, so we all wore lounge suits and medals.

The police arrangements were of course wonderful or we should never have got through the crowds which thronged Old Palace Yard. Over the entrance to the House of Lords was a huge emblem of the Victoria Cross in Flanders poppies. There were 321 V.C.s at the dinner as compared with the 324 who attended the Buckingham Palace Garden Party in 1920. They had come from all parts of the Empire. There were veterans from Rorke's Drift, the Afghan and Burma campaigns and the Boer War. But the great majority consisted of the younger men of my generation who had been through the 1914–18 war. Subadar Ishar Singh, 2/8th Punjab Regiment, had been flown over from India for the ceremonies and had been put in my special charge; and I took him back with me to India on *The Viceroy of India* afterwards.

Seats at the dinner were arranged by ballot. The Prince of Wales had Sergeant W. F. Burman of the Rifle Brigade on his right and on his left was Colonel Lord Gort. The Prince's speech, which was excellent by any standards, was received with rapturous applause. He described the V.C. as : 'The most democratic and at the same time the most exclusive of all the orders of chivalry – the most enviable order of the Victoria Cross.'

What with the emotion and the champagne some of our members required a helping hand from the police in order to get safely home.

When the order to fall in for the parade at the Cenotaph was given I inserted myself and Ishar Singh at the very end of the line, not wishing to face the massed crowds in Whitehall in the forefront of the parade. However, in manoeuvring us out of the barracks the officer in charge about-turned us and Ishar Singh and I thus marched on to this very historic ceremony in the front row of fours. In the pictures of the parade Ishar Singh's white pagri makes him quite unmistakeable and my wife and mother, perched on the balcony of my friends and bankers, Messrs Grindlay and Co, who then lived at 54 Parliament Street, could pick me out quite easily, knowing that I should be next to him.

All the other troops were formed up before we appeared and the crowd started to cheer, which was really 'not done' at a memorial service of such solemnity. Nevertheless, they did it, and cheered us again as we marched off. This may have been the reason why the V.C.s never paraded at the Cenotaph again.

Just before 11 o'clock the Prince of Wales took his place, wearing the uniform of the Welsh Guards. He was accompanied by the Duke of Gloucester and Prince Arthur of Connaught. The impressive service which then took place followed much the same lines as all those subsequent ones with which we have become so familiar over the years. The anthem, the laying of wreaths, first by the Prince of Wales on behalf of the King, who was not well enough to attend, and then by the Duke of York, the Prime Minister Ramsay Macdonald and representatives of the Dominions, India and the Services. At last Big Ben struck the first note of the Armistice hour; a gun boomed and the two-minute silence started. The silence was so intense that one could almost feel it, and it was heightened by the steady drip of the rain which had started to fall as soon as we arrived on the parade.

After these excitements I returned to India to do a year's regimental soldiering in Peshawar with my old battalion the 15th Sikhs, now officially called the 2/11th Sikh Regiment, before taking up my appointment at the Staff College. The battalion was being temporarily commanded at the time by Johnny Marshall of the 45th Sikhs (the 3/11th). A few months after my arrival he left to command his own battalion and Bill Barstow got command of the 15th. Bill was killed in 1942 commanding a division against the Japanese in Malaya.

The Regiment was very keen to have a try for the regimental race in the Hunt point-to-point, which had never been won by an infantry battalion. The unit team was three; we had two good riders, reasonably well mounted, in Captain Tom Ker and Captain Windsor Aubrey, and they roped me in to make a third. Unfortunately the Queen sprained a tendon three weeks before the race; but I had Mary Rose to fall back on. Two days before the race Mary Rose split a pastern and eventually had to be destroyed – a terrible bit of bad luck which appeared to put a stopper on our entering as there was no other horse in the battalion which had any hope of getting round the course, always a very stiff one.

I went to see the Queen in hospital. She was quite recovered and was looking full of herself, but of course had only been in light work. I decided to take a chance and run her. I told the other two members of the team that I would not push her but that, barring accidents, I might come in about half way up; so if they could be in the first ten we might have a chance, as there were always a great many falls.

There was a terrific field from fifteen units, making forty-five starters at the post. We somehow managed to survive the jam at the first few jumps and then started to get a bit more elbow room. I kept the Queen well back, expecting that she might 'blow up' before the end, as the course was both long and stiff. Half way round however she was going so easily that I let her stride out a bit. The leaders gradually came back to us and we finished third with the Queen none the worse – a really wonderful performance on the part of the gallant little mare. The other two clung on to me well and finished 4th and 6th, which gave us the cup easily. I was surprised at the delight of the men in the 15th who might have been expected not to take a great deal of interest in such horsey goings on; but they were as pleased and proud as we were.

I was happy at getting back to troops again; but, as always seemed to happen whenever I did so, we were not left long in peace and, in fact, as soon as I arrived the Mess said: 'Now there will be trouble.' And there was.

Gandhi had been on the warpath again and, judging by his former appearances in the 1919 disturbances, I expected rioting and bloodshed to follow. It did. There was a riot in Peshawar City in which the Deputy Commissioner was injured, troops were ordered out, the crowd attacked them with bricks and bottles, several officers and men were badly hurt, confused firing started and there were a lot of casualties.

The 15th were ordered down into the city and spent a few very sticky days on that most unpleasant of all jobs for the soldier – duties in aid of the civil power. Meanwhile the Afridis took advantage of our internal troubles to raid the Peshawar Vale and got right down as far as Peshawar itself. The first we knew of this was one morning, in the middle of a P.T. parade, when bullets started to kick up the parade ground. The men were hastily got under cover, the alarm blown and the quarter guard turned out.

One solitary Afridi, greatly daring, had come across the golf course, crept through the crops and started to shoot us up. Having fired five shots he thought it was time to beat it. But a Sikh sepoy, who was washing under a pump, had spotted him. Clad only in a pair of drawers he snatched up a rifle from the guardroom and gave chase. The Afridi in his own hills is very hard to catch, but on the flat and in strange country the Sikh soon got on terms with him. The Afridi swung round, the Sikh dropped on one knee. The two shots rang out almost simultaneously and the Afridi pitched forward. The bullet had taken him in the centre of the forehead.

Peshawar Cantonment was then completely wired and the wire lit by arc lamps and patrolled day and night. Columns were sent out from Peshawar and the Afridis were eventually driven back to their own wild hills.

Meanwhile the situation in Peshawar City was anything but satisfactory and in the middle of May I was appointed to the very unpleasant position of City Commandant. Peshawar City was very different from a down-country town as it contained a large number of real frontier toughs who required extremely firm handling if they once set out to make trouble. I had the equivalent of two and a half battalions in complete companies from several different units, billeted in and around the city, and a squadron of the Poona Horse, at the race course on call. My city magistrate was the Deputy Commissioner Peshawar, one Olaf Caroe, later India's Foreign Secretary. We worked together throughout the disturbances with complete harmony and understanding, and have remained close friends ever since.

Peshawar City in May was a very unpleasant place. The heat was terrific and the smells indescribable. Towards the end of the month we got a case of cholera in the city, which was hardly surprising but which caused the greatest anxiety in medical circles. On 31 May I was taking round a party of doctors and, at about 9 a.m., we arrived at our last port of call, the guardroom at the Kabuli Gate, where there was one platoon of the K.O.Y.L.I. The British guard turned out; I looked at them quickly, dismissed them and went into the guardroom, which opened right on to the pavement of the main street. The lance-corporal of the guard, who had been cleaning his rifle when I arrived, had somehow got the magazine jammed and was still in the guardroom wrestling with it. As I came in he slammed the magazine home, closed the bolt, and forgetting he had now got a round in the chamber, pressed the trigger and let off the round within an inch of my head. It passed through the chick (blind) which separated the guardroom from the street. For one moment I was uncertain if I was alive or dead – a rifle shot fired in a small room makes a deafening sound.

Then there was a blood-curdling scream from the street outside. If that soldier had tried for a hundred years he could not have fired a more unlucky shot. The bullet had killed an Indian woman and two children who were driving past in a tonga, or Indian trap. She was sitting in the back seat with her arms round the two children, who were on either side of her. Her husband was in the front seat with the driver. The bullet hit one child through the head, went clean through the woman and had then set up into a lump of lead which almost blew the head off the second child. The whole terrible, bloody mess was thrown into the middle of the road.

The city once more flared into riot and, within ten minutes from the Kabuli Gate and the whole way along the Kissa Khawhani Bazaar Road, an enormous and violent crowd was gathering. I walked across the road to the small police station and telephoned for the Deputy Commissioner and the troops to come to me at the Kabuli Gate. Until they arrived I had only twenty rather young British soldiers and about ten Indian policemen and the situation was uncomfortable to say the least of it as the vast crowd gathered in an ugly mood.

The first troops to arrive were a company of the 15th Sikhs and a company of the 36th Sikhs and I drew them up outside the gate where they would be handy but out of sight of the crowd. Throughout these disturbances, and indeed in all my experience of civil disturbances in India, the Indian soldier was always absolutely loyal and staunch and obeyed unhesitatingly every order given in support of law and order, regardless of class or creed.

Meanwhile the Deputy Commissioner had arrived with more police, but they soon got so roughly handled by the crowd that, having warned the rioters of his intentions by loud speaker, he asked me to take over. All the way down the street the rooftops were black with rioters armed with stones, bottles and bricks. The stage was set exactly as it had been for the previous riot in the same place, when eventually about sixty-five rounds had to be fired and many casualties were inflicted on both sides. The D.C. and I had been able to discuss such an eventuality together with the lessons of the former riot to help us.

I had maintained, and still do most strongly, that it is not fair to any troops to call them in during a civil disturbance – which is never done unless it is a serious one beyond the powers of the police to deal with – and then allow them to be pelted with bricks and bottles. It encourages the rioters, leads to loss of morale on the part of the troops and nearly always ends in the situation getting out of hand. This results in uncontrolled firing and heavy casualties to the crowd. Neither is it fair to the vast majority of the populace, who are not concerned with the riot and only ask that law and order shall be restored and that their lives and property shall be protected. My contention therefore was that, in this most unpleasant task of duty in aid of the civil power, the soldier must put up with *gali* (Indian abuse), flag waving and hysterical screaming, but bricks and bottles NO!

I called in the leading company commander, Captain Eustace of the 15th Sikhs, who had with him, as instructed by me, four picked shots with their rifles loaded with one round in the chamber, who would only fire on my order. I then ordered him to clear the street. As he saluted and turned to go, a man on the roof of the nearest house leant over and threw a brick which hit the British officer full on the side of the face, cutting his cheek open and knocking him unconscious. I immediately ordered one of the escort to fire one round at that man. It hit the brickwork just beside him, sending up a big spurt of red dust.

The effect was electric. All the way down the street you could see people on the rooftops putting down their bricks and bottles and going inside. The crowd melted away and the street was cleared and picketed in exactly seven minutes with only that one shot fired. Truly it was a case of a stitch in time. The troops were able to be withdrawn very soon after and the populace settled down to business as usual.

It was only to be expected that Congress would try to make much of this incident of the shooting of the woman and her children and an inquiry was demanded, with a murder charge against the British soldier. I was called down to Delhi and interviewed first by one of the Secretaries to the Government and then by Lord Irwin himself. The Viceroy adopted an absolutely firm attitude from the start and refused to have any inquiry beyond the quite informal one he had with me personally to clear one or two points about which he was doubtful. He completely accepted my statement that the incident had been an accident. Later I was mentioned in despatches for my part in these disturbances.

In October 1930 I said goodbye to the 15th Sikhs – for the last time as it turned out although I did not know it then – and sailed once more for home and the Camberley Staff College, being now deemed old enough to take up the appointment of Indian Army Instructor.

It was certainly a great honour to be appointed an instructor at the Staff College. The Directing Staff of the College consisted firstly of the Commandant, Major-General John Dill (afterwards Field-Marshal Sir John Dill), and two first grade general staff officers with the rank of full colonel. These were Colonel H. M. Wilson, always known as 'Jumbo', who became Field-Marshal Lord Wilson of Libya, and Colonel E. K. Squires, who died later in Australia as a Major-General. Then there were thirteen second grade general staff officers ranked as (local) lieut.-colonels and an R.A.F. teacher who was an old friend of my boyhood days in Oxford, Squadron Leader Jack Slessor. He afterward rose to dizzy heights in the R.A.F., becoming Chief of the Air Staff and a Marshal of the Royal Air Force.

When I took up my three-year appointment General Dill had just been appointed Commandant. Although he had great ambitions to become a commander and was disappointed when, on the outbreak of the Second World War, Gort was appointed Commander-in-Chief of the B.E.F. over his head, he was perhaps an even better staff officer – and he made a great reputation as such during the war. Field-Marshal Alanbrooke had the very highests opinion of him, both as a commander and a staff officer.

Dill was a terrific worker and had few interests in life outside soldiering. He was however a very keen rider to hounds and in fact his keenness was somewhat in advance of his ability as a horseman. He had been issued with a wonderful remount called Dalgetty which the Director of Remounts had told me (I'm sure rightly) was a horse which might well have won the Grand National. Dalgetty had already won the Staff College Past and Present race in 1927, 1928 and 1930, against high-class opposition; but he was now considered to be too old for racing. General Dill however wanted something he could win the race on and offered to pass Dalgetty on to me, on condition that I would school the young horse he had just bought. I jumped at the offer of Dalgetty but didn't fancy the look of the General's young horse. The first drag line on which I took him he went straight through the middle of every fence and we arrived at the end, somehow still together, but looking very dishevelled indeed. I strongly advised the General to get rid of him at once.

But Dill was nothing if not courageous and he insisted on having a go himself. The result was a bad fall, with two broken ribs, which put him out of action for quite a long time. Fortunately for me he didn't

A point-to-point in 1924 at the Staff College, Camberley. Major Franklin (foreground) is on Hortense and I am on Skylark

British and Indian officers of the 2/11th Sikh Regiment, Peshawar, 1930. I am in the front row, second from left

My second wife Frances, around whom my life has revolved for the last forty years

want Dalgetty back, and for three years I had a lovely hunter who never put a foot wrong.

The 360 students who were pupils at the Staff College while I was a teacher included: Captain M. C. Dempsey of the Royal Berkshire Regiment, who became one of Monty's most famous Army Commanders; Captain 'Strafer' Gott, K.R.R.C., a really grand fighting soldier, who was selected to command 8th Army in North Africa and was then shot down and killed in the air before he could take up his command. His death gave General Montgomery his great chance, which he took with both hands. Captain N. C. D. Brownjohn, R.E., later General Sir Nevil Brownjohn, who had been Quartermaster General and held other high appointments in the Army; Captain Brian Horrocks, the Middlesex Regiment, who became one of Monty's finest Corps Commanders and later a considerable TV personality; Captain Ian Jacob, R.E., who became one of Winston Churchill's war staff officers and then head of the B.B.C.; Captain Pete Rees, Indian Army, who took over the 19th 'Dagger' Division, which I had raised in Secunderabad in 1941, and who commanded it most successfully in Burma; Major A. G. Salisbury-Jones, Coldstream Guards, who attained high rank in the Diplomatic Corps; Frankie Festing, Rifle Brigade, who became Chief of the Imperial General Staff and was the only one of my Camberley pupils to become a Field-Marshal.

Lastly, there was my brother, Bill Smyth, Oxford and Buckinghamshire Light Infantry, whom I mention particularly because I was told that this was the only occasion in the history of the Staff College when brother taught brother. (In September 1975, however, when I was asked to review *Goughie – The Life of General Sir Hubert Gough*, I discovered that in 1904 Hubert was a teacher at Camberley and his younger brother Johnnie Gough, V.C., was a student.) Bill was unlucky to be wounded whilst commanding a brigade early in the war and he never really recovered from that initial setback so far as higher command was concerned.

My biggest job at the Staff College was in running the Mountain Warfare exercise at Harlech in Wales. This was our most popular course, but for me the most strenuous, both physically and mentally. To start with I had to take the directing staff through the scheme, and some of them had no experience of mountain warfare at all. But in May, given good weather, it could be very pleasant indeed, even though it did entail a lot of scrambling over high country. Some of the students considered it rather a nightmare, but the majority enjoyed it enormously.

I much enjoyed the Combined Operations exercise with our sister staff colleges. During each of my three years my syndicate did its preliminary work at Andover with the R.A.F. Staff College and I made many friends there, including Air Marshal Joubert de la Ferté, the Commandant, who was afterwards in charge of Coastal Command and later made a considerable reputation as a broadcaster and writer.

General Dill was tremendously keen on the Staff College grounds and gardens, and also on the games, although he was not a games player himself. In 1932 he made me 'President of Games and Gardens'. I had under me the various captains and secretaries of cricket, hockey, lawn tennis, squash rackets, golf and gardens, and I was directly responsible to the Commandant for the way they were run – and particularly for the care and upkeep of the grounds.

I had by this time cut out cricket and hockey from my games, and refused to allow myself to be persuaded to take them up again seriously, but I had become very keen on lawn tennis, played golf passably well, and rode as hard as ever. I also played a certain amount of first-class squash rackets and was always first string for the Staff College at tennis or squash when I wasn't wanted for the Army or my county (Devon).

But of all my memories of that happy and strenuous time some of the pleasantest are those connected with the Staff College Drag, when I rode my lovely Dalgetty in friendly rivalry with Otto Lund on his grand horse, Twinkle, and with Jack Slessor who, despite his gammy leg, was always thrusting his way to the top of the hunt. I think they were all agreed however that my Dalgetty was the best horse of them all.

During my last holiday in England after I had finished at the Staff College I played tennis several times for the Army and was selected to represent them at Wimbledon in the Inter-Services Championship. All three Services were strongly represented by several well-known Wimbledon players. The Army team, headed by Lieut. C. R. D. Tuckey, who won the Wimbledon doubles title in 1936 with G. P. Hughes, and the highly ranked Australian player, Lieut. Clynton Read, an Australian Davis Cup player, was one of the strongest teams the Army has ever put out. I played second pair with Lieut. E. P. Percival. The Army were successful in all their doubles matches for the loss of only one set, and we lost one singles match, which gave us an overwhelming victory. I had hoped during my last year at home to play at Wimbledon with Clynton Read; but I had an unlucky accident at the St George's Hill tournament at Weybridge just before the Wimbledon fortnight and broke my wrist.

Before leaving the Staff College I had a most interesting trip to Germany with Jack and Hermione Slessor. We paddled canoes down the Saar into the Moselle, and down the Moselle into the Rhine. All the way down the Saar and the Moselle there were special camp stations where we and the canoes could be housed for the night for some incredibly small sum.

Canoeing is a fascinating pastime and very good exercise. Clad only in bathing slips, with the small despatch case which was our only luggage, stowed away in the bow, we soon got extremely fit and a beautiful mahogany in colour. I was much struck by the very fine physique of the Germans we met on the river. Germany had become enthused with physical culture and bodily fitness had become almost a religion. Clad in the minimum of clothes the youth of Germany took their holidays in the open air and canoeing was fast becoming a national sport. But Hitler disapproved of nudity and the bronzed bodies of Germany's young men were soon to be clothed in coloured shirts and semi-military holidays were to replace the carefree river life. Already it seemed to us that the youth of Germany were turning their thoughts to war.

On our way back through France we spent a night at Bethune and, with the aid of some locally purchased maps, went in search of 'the Glory Hole' in Richebourg L'Avoué, where I had won my V.C. in 1915. The countryside of course was tremendously changed and it was almost impossible to see through the present peace and prosperity to the scars and ruins of war. In many places however one could still trace the trenches and one would suddenly come upon a bit of trench which had been left just as it was. To my great delight we discovered 'the Glory Hole' trench in this condition with an old rusted unexploded shell and some bombs still lying beside it. And, still reviving past memories, we came to the Indian Army war memorial at Neuve Chapelle and various other war cemeteries, all most beautifully kept. I went back again some years after the Second World War and found them still immaculately tended and very moving. Many years afterwards my son Robin, then in charge of the *Daily Mail* office in Paris, took me on a similar tour and wrote an article in the *Mail*, 'Father and Son'.

My three years at Camberley as a teacher were now coming to an end. They had been memorable and happy years for me. I lived with my family in one of the Staff College bungalows which, though not much to look at, were very comfortable inside – and had the merit of being a great deal cheaper than any other available accommodation. And during those years one lived a strenuous but very pleasant life among congenial people.

In my last year at Camberley General Dill had asked me if I would recommend an Indian Army officer who might replace me as the Indian Army Instructor. I gave him a few names headed by Major Slim of the 6th Gurkha Rifles. A few days later Dill said to me: 'No one I have consulted about your Major Slim has ever heard of him.' I suggested he should ring the Chief of General Staff in Delhi. Anyway, Slim was appointed and duly appeared to take over my bungalow and my job.

Bill was always a loyal and generous friend. On 22 January 1934 he wrote :

Dear Jackie, it was awfully nice to get your note wishing me luck on my first day at the Staff College. Everybody is so kind and you have left me such complete notes etc, that if I do make a mess of it, it will be my own fault. Again thanks for all your help. I feel that apart from myself my only handicap is that I have to succeed you – yours Bill.

Some thirty years later when we were both Masters of our City Livery Companies he invited me to be Guest of Honour at his Court Dinner. In his speech he 'confessed' that for the whole of his first year at Camberley he had used all my lectures just as they were.

In the last years of Bill's life, when he was blind and knew he had not long to live, we had some unforgettable talks – the last one only just before his final fatal stroke. He was one of the greatest, if not *the* greatest, British general of the Second World War.

I had been made a Brevet-Lieut.-Colonel in 1933 and was then about the youngest one in the Army. In 1934 I sailed once more for India leaving the family at home. John's first school had been the Dragon School at Oxford and he was later transferred to that splendid Catholic School, Ampleforth, where he was followed by Julian and Robin. Our daughter, Jill, had been born on 23 April 1929.

CHAPTER EIGHT

The Years Before the Second World War

1934-1939

ON my arrival back in India I was terribly disappointed to be told that I was not to return to the 15th Sikhs but was to be posted as second-in-command to the 45th Rattray's Sikhs (the 3/11th) with a view to succeeding Lieut.-Colonel K. G. Hyde-Cates, who was then commanding. This cross-posting was done in order to give me an earlier command, but it only gave me a seniority advantage of about six months and, much as I admired the 45th, I was sad that I couldn't command the 15th, with whom I had won my V.C. in France. This was certainly another milestone in my life, and one over which I had no control.

The 45th was a fine battalion with great traditions and a high reputation and I soon became almost as fond of them as I was of my own 15th Sikhs. They had rendered particularly distinguished and loyal service during the Indian Mutiny of 1857. In the Great War of 1914–18 they had fought in Mesopotamia (Iraq), where they had greatly distinguished themselves. Like the 15th they were all Sikhs – an even mixture of Malwas and Manjhas from either side of the Sutlej River.

I motored up from Bombay and joined the battalion at Rawalpindi. I had not been with them very long when the Mohmand Operations of 1935 started and the Rawalpindi Brigade was ordered up to the frontier under command of Brigadier Cyril Noyes. As Lieut.-Colonel Hyde-Cates was sick I was given command of the 45th Sikhs. The Peshawar Brigade under Brigadier Auchinleck, and the Nowshera Brigade under Brigadier Alexander (both future field-marshals) had most of the fighting. It was in this campaign that 'the Auk' really started to become known as a leader and commander as well as a brilliant staff officer.

The march up into Mohmand country was hot and dusty and the 45th distinguished themselves greatly by arriving in the best of shape. Years afterwards I had a letter from a retired British officer who wrote:

> The most inspiring thing in the whole of my military service happened to me on the 13 September 1935 in the Mohmand country. I was standing on the top of a high pass to watch the arrival of the Rawalpindi Brigade. The heat was absolutely blistering, and the British battalion which was leading had completely disintegrated. Then suddenly round the corner you appeared at the head of the 45th Sikhs. Not a single man had fallen out; not a single man was even out of step. It was just magnificent.

On 20 August 1974, when I took Field Marshal Auchinleck to look at the Gurkha Museum at Church Crookham, he recalled this incident and expressed the same sentiments about it.

The 45th prided themselves on their marching and their discipline, and wherever we went on that campaign we were given the highest praise by our friends and our commanders – and a very wide berth by the Mohmands. I certainly felt very proud of them.

There was a good deal of sharp fighting and a tremendous lot of unspectacular but essential picketing and convoying before the tribal forces were defeated. The famous battalion of Guides were ambushed and suffered severe casualties in a night advance up a particularly difficult and precipitous hill. Night operations on the frontier, which had formerly been considered suicidal, had by now become quite common. But they required careful preparation and rigidly enforced secrecy if they were to be successful, and I think that in this disaster these essentials were lacking.

Coming out of the Mohmand country I commanded the rearguard for the whole force – generally the most arduous and ticklish job in frontier fighting. I had some light tanks among my troops. I had always believed that tanks would prove a big factor in frontier warfare, even when the ground was too bad for them to move off the road. The Mohmands however had had enough and the withdrawal was not followed up.

I received another mention in despatches for my part in this campaign and further strengthened my relations with Auchinleck and Alexander, both of whom remained my lifelong friends.

Towards the end of 1936 the 45th Sikhs were posted to Chitral.

In 1865 the territory of Imperial Russia and the North-western frontier of the Indian Empire were far apart. Thirty years later they almost touched and the British became concerned with the possibility of a Russian incursion from this direction. This borderland, protected and defined by the mighty mountain ranges of the eastern Hindu Kush, swept northward in a great arc: three hundred miles of tangled mountains and precipitous valleys thrusting into the very heart of Central Asia. It might have been thought that the very ruggedness and impassability of this part of the world, with its lack of communications, would have been considered protection enough; but the British considered that the advance of Russia was a threat which they could not disregard and Chitral provided the most obvious back door for a possible Russian incursion. And so this little country became an important frontier station at an apex with Russia to the north, Gilgit and Kashmir to the east and Afghanistan to the south. And it has remained so ever since. Although the Russian menace decreased with the passing of the years the presence of a small British–Indian force in this part of the world had a peace-keeping influence.

For its size Chitral is probably the most mountainous country in the world, containing forty peaks of over 20,000 feet, including that beautiful mountain Tirich Mir, which at that time had never been climbed. Although Tirich is only 26,000 feet it gives an impression of height and grandeur far greater than many mountains such as Everest, which are only *primus inter pares*. Tirich Mir seems to rise straight out of the Chitral valley, supreme, aloof and dominating.

The people of Chitral were as hard and wild-looking as the country in which they lived. They were desperately poor, but keen sportsmen who rode their hardy little Chitrali ponies prodigous distances to play them in a game of polo, which may be said to be the traditional game of Chitral. There was also good shooting to be had, and ski-ing and skating for the British officers.

However, Chitral was not everyone's cup of tea as a military station. It was cut off and lonely, no families were allowed and the men got no leave for the two years they were up there. (I did get the Government of India to modify this rule.) Both officers and men were apt to get depressed there, the former to take to drink and the latter to run amok. I know of no station where a battalion could go downhill so rapidly, and many did.

In former days I understand the force commander on arrival received presents from the Mehtar (the Ruler) consisting of two fat sheep and one slender Chitrali maiden. Whether the presents were accepted (or acceptable!) I know not. This time the two fat sheep arrived alone, looking a bit sheepish. But as I had to be shut up in a fort for two years with 1,500 sex-starved soldiers the addition of one Chitrali maiden would have been murder – and the first casualty would have been the force commander!

Of course so far as the troops were concerned the entire absence of women for a prolonged period was a problem; and as I was taking a Sikh battalion to a land of Mohammedans it was all the more important that there should be no 'regrettable incidents' between the troops and the local inhabitants. There had been such incidents from time to time with other battalions, and they had almost always led to murder or some form of violent retaliation.

Also of course one has to realize that in such conditions homosexuality is almost certain to rear its ugly head. This is apt to happen whenever males are herded together for any length of time, and it is extremely prevalent among frontier tribesmen in India, where women are in scarce supply. I know it has become fashionable to regard such people as 'queers', unlike other people and unable to help themselves. This may be so in some cases, but homosexuality, like lesbianism, is an unnatural state which is due either to abnormality in the personality or in the circumstances (mainly the latter), and in my belief it is far more preventable than is currently supposed. Certainly in any military unit it can be extremely destructive and must be stamped out quite ruthlessly. My Sikh officers were adamant about this and they knew the form. They inflicted their own punishments without asking me – and it didn't happen again.

I was determined to make our two years in Chitral a test of leadership; to take advantage of everything good the country had to offer, and to forget the bad times as quickly as possible; really to enjoy our time there and to see that the battalion left the country in even better form than when they arrived. The fact that I succeeded in this resolve beyond my wildest dreams was due to the help of a few British officers, who were with me in Chitral throughout, and to the most loyal and splendid team of Indian officers.

In 1969 I met General Sir Charles Richardson, Master-General of the Ordnance, at the Chaplain-General's Garden Party at Bagshot Park. He had been my sapper subaltern in Chitral and said it had been the happiest two years of his life.

One or two highly placed officers, who knew Chitral and knew the Sikh, were extremely nervous of a Sikh battalion being sent as garrison to a Mohammedan country. They were certain that I should have trouble with one or the other, or that they would have trouble with each other. But I bethought me of my visit to the Yugoslav Army during my Staff College days. When I asked the commander of a frontier division there how he kept his men amused in the evenings, he replied:

'When my men have finished their day's work they are only too glad to get their supper and go to sleep.'

The Chitral Reliefs, which took place in August, used to be quite an operation. The ingoing and outcoming battalions were escorted and protected during their long march by the Nowshera Brigade and the local levies of Swat and Dir States. In this year (1936), however, it was decided that we should go up under our own steam by air and M.T. – the first battalion to do so. This was a great compliment to me.

Owing to lack of aircraft less than a company went by air and were the first troops in India to be air transported. There was some doubt (not on my part) as to how the men would take to the idea. But as a matter of fact the competition to go by air was intense; and as the Granthi (Sikh priest) asked to go by air, taking the Granth Sahib (Sikh holy book) with him, air transport – anyway, so far as the Sikh was concerned – had a good start.

The air passage into Chitral was not easy as it meant flying over the Lowarai Pass of 10,000 feet, with hills of 14,000 on each side, and the ceiling of the old troop carriers when fully loaded was only about 15,000 feet. Unless the pass could be clearly seen (it was often covered by cloud) the flight was very dangerous. Had anything gone wrong with our flight it might have had wide repercussions among Indian troops and there was considerable anxiety in high quarters until the air reliefs had been safely accomplished. The Northern Army Commander asked me to convey to all ranks of the battalion who took part in the air lift his great appreciation of the way in which it had been carried out.

For the land journey I was given seven light tanks, ten armoured cars, and about a hundred lorries, and off we set on our own, protected only by the local levies of the States through which we passed. About ten shots were fired at us during the journey, but at long range and without effect.

Then began the four days' march over the Lowarai Pass into the Chitral valley. The top of the Lowarai Pass is bleak and windswept at most times of the year; in winter it is deep in snow, frozen hard into a sheet of ice, subject to sudden blizzards and a very dangerous pass for the uninitiated to negotiate. There were a number of deaths on it every year.

At 'Lowarai top' we were met by the two British officers of the Chitral Scouts, Bobbie Lawder and Hamer Stansfield, and by one of the brothers of His Highness the Mehtar of Chitral, who was sent by H.H. to welcome us to his country. The Scouts had affixed the traditional notice board at Lowarai top which showed on our side 'The First Time',

and on the reverse side, for the outgoing battalion, 'The Last Time!
Thank God!' From Lowarai it was three marches along the turbulent
Chitral river to Drosh Fort where the units of Chitral Force were accommodated, except for one company in Chitral Fort twenty-five miles
further up the valley.

As senior officer of the garrison I automatically became Chitral
Force Commander. Chitral Force consisted of my battalion, the Chitral
section of mountain gunners, the Chitral section R.E., and the various
transport and administrative units. A very pleasant little command. The
battalion and the gunners were housed in extremely good new barracks
in Drosh Fort; we had an excellent Mess; my own little 'Flagstaff
House' was quite comfortable, and we were promised electric light
within a few months, so things were not too bad.

The men were as happy as children just arrived at the seaside. They
were getting extra pay and good rations, and had better barracks than
they had ever imagined – and they were kept busy from morning to
night. But I knew that in due course they would start feeling rather
isolated and home-sick and I was anxious to get the existing ban on
leave altered. There were many difficulties in the way, such as the great
distances involved, no rest camps, no transport, the danger of crossing
the Lowarai Pass, the possibility of men overstaying their leave or
worse, and so on. However, these difficulties were gradually overcome
and I was eventually allowed to send small parties of men off in regular
batches to India on leave. They never abused the privilege and it made
all the difference to their life in Chitral to know that they could get
away in case of urgent necessity.

I was very keen that the British officers of Chitral Force should play
polo, the game of the country, which was cheap, kept us in touch with
the Chitralis and the Chitral Scouts, and took people's minds off the
inevitable boredom of life in a fort. Chitrali polo is played on a long,
narrow ground with a mud wall round it, or even in a village street.
There were no rules, except that it was rather bad form and indeed a
definite foul to hit your opponent with your stick unless he had caught
the ball in his hand. He could do this, at his peril, and gallop down
the ground with it, but he could expect to get his neck broken en
route.

The game starts with one of the side which had won the toss galloping down the centre of the ground, holding the reins in his left hand
and his stick and the ball in his right. Before reaching half way, the
ball must be thrown up in the air and struck before it touches the
ground. I have never seen a British player able to do this more than
three times out of five at the very best, but a good Chitrali player will
do it every time without fail and hit right up to the goal line. Behind

him come the rest of his side with flying sticks and waving legs; and they took a lot of stopping!

The British player, who may perhaps have played rather gentlemanly polo before, was rather out of his element at first and apt to be distinctly annoyed if he was deliberately crossed or his stick hooked from the wrong side, or expertly knocked out of his hand.

The ponies were nearly all stallions, small, lean, hardy little animals of about thirteen hands. They got little food, a tremendous amount of work, were very seldom sick or sorry and generally played polo until they were over twenty. The Chitralis maintained that British officers' ponies went lame because they were overfed and got too heavy for their legs. They thought nothing of riding a pony ten miles to polo, playing him two chukkers of twenty minutes each, and then riding him home.

In a tournament in Chitral there were two chukkers of twenty minutes each, both of which had to be played on the same pony, with a fifteen-minute break in between. Teams were five aside. A Chitrali band played the players and spectators on to the ground and continued playing throughout the game with varying intensity, rising to an absolute crescendo if someone got knocked over the wall, or something else exciting happened.

The Chitrali used a polo stick shaped like a straight-handled walking stick. He had an eye like a hawk and could hit the ball from any angle. His weaknesses were lack of direction and control in shooting at goal, and disregard of combination. We tried to exploit these weaknesses in our second year when we entered a British officers' team in the big Chitrali tournament.

I took the earliest opportunity of getting on friendly terms with the Mehtar of Chitral, and both he and his staff and his sons were more than cordial to me and my officers. He invariably addressed me in correspondence as 'My dear Friend'. The old Mehtar of Chitral, Sir Shuja-ul-Mulk, had been on the throne for nearly forty years – since the siege of Chitral, when he was under British protection in Chitral Fort as a boy of fifteen. He was an absolute autocrat and had his turbulent countrymen well under control. He had fifteen sons and the Government of India was rather apprehensive as to what would happen at his death as a revolution on the death of the ruler was almost traditional in Chitral.

Soon after our arrival Bishop Barne of Lahore, whom I had known from Oxford days, paid a visit to Chitral at my invitation to consecrate the two cemeteries at Drosh and Chitral, both of which had been in use for many years but had never been consecrated. The little Chitral cemetery was situated 400 yards south of Chitral Fort. It contained the graves of Captain J. Baird, 24th Punjab Infantry; Sergeant G. Williment, Commissariat Department; Major H. T. Marshall, 1st Brahmans, and Victor Fenin, a Russian. Captain Baird died on 4 March 1895 of wounds received in action on 3 March when making a reconnaissance prior to the siege of Chitral in that year. Sergeant Williment died on 11 August 1896. Major Marshall was murdered in Chitral Fort on 21 February 1915. Victor Fenin was the child of a Colonel and Madame Fenin who, with a party of about fifty Russian refugees, almost all officers, fled from the Bolsheviks in 1918 and made their way to Mastuj. As Madame Fenin was ill she could not go with the rest of the party to Bombay and then to Vladivostock, but remained in Chitral. Their son, Victor, died on 15 March 1919. They finally left Chitral with their small daughter in September 1919.

Ever since I went out East I have been interested in cemeteries. Such a lot of history that is now forgotten is written in them. I was glad that the British, in a very far outpost of Empire, had sheltered a Russian family in distress, and for some twenty years had carefully tended the grave of a little Russian boy, and that a British bishop had endured a long and arduous journey to consecrate the cemetery in which he slept.

But first we had to consecrate the cemetery at Drosh in which were buried a small number of British officers of Chitral Force who had died (or been killed) during their tour of duty in Chitral. I had no knowledge of the Consecration Service, and that I left to the Bishop. But as Force Commander I had formally to request him to perform the Consecration Ceremony. I still have the little piece he wrote for me to say, in his own handwriting on bishopric notepaper. It ran as follows:

Right reverend Father in God. On behalf of the Christian residents quartered in Drosh I request you to set apart and consecrate this plot of land that it may be used as a cemetery for the burial of persons belonging to the Christian religion.

I was absolutely word perfect. If only the bishop had taken me into his confidence as to what was to happen next we might have been spared one of the most exhausting and frustrating experiences either of us had ever undergone.

The Bishop arrived in full regalia with his crook. I was wearing my Sam Browne and sword. All the British officers of the garrison were present, dressed in their best uniforms. The Bishop then explained to me that he would read the Service in the course of circumnavigating the outside of the cemetery walls, with me, as Force Commander in attendance. With the fierce winds and the heavy snow and ice of winter it had been difficult enough keeping the inside of the cemetery neat and tidy : the outside was a complete jungle.

We started off with the Bishop in front and me behind. But soon I had to do advanced guard, hacking away with my very blunt sword, which was only meant for show, at the stubborn weeds and thick brambles which blocked our path. Finally the Bishop had to interrupt his prayers to assist me by holding back the branches with his crook.

I would venture to state that never has this Service been performed under more trying or spectacular conditions. We were exhausted and our clothing torn to shreds by the time it was all over. I am afraid the officers of Chitral Force rather enjoyed it. There was nothing in the Service which said they should join in, and I think they had a friendly dig at me in their thoughts. 'Well, what do you know? Mr Fix-it couldn't fix-it after all.'

The Mehtar then asked us both to go up to Chitral and stay in the Palace. On the evening of our arrival we had tea with him. He was a very fine-looking old man. He was most interested in the Bishop and all he stood for in the Church of England, and bombarded him with questions. That night there was a big banquet at which the Bishop and I sat on either side of H.H., and we were all three served from the same dishes throughout the meal, as is the custom on such occasions.

Next morning, after breakfast, the Mehtar had arranged to take us round Chitral. He looked so ill when we met that I suggested that some-one else should go with us instead. The Bishop and I were feeling like death ourselves and so, after a short drive round, we arrived at the house of the Political Agent (Ian Scott), where we were to stay that night. I couldn't face lunch and retired to bed, having been very sick. I was just getting into bed when Ian Scott ran in and said : 'The Mehtar is dead !' This made me feel even worse.

However, all sorts of precautions had to be taken : and I had to drag myself out of bed and into some uniform. Ian Scott went to the Palace and proclaimed that the Government of India nominated the eldest son, Nasir-ul-Nulk, as the new Mehtar, and I went to Chitral Fort. When I got back I found the Bishop prostrated and we were both very ill for the rest of the day. Thanks to my having been so sick early on I recovered quicker than the Bishop, who was extremely ill for several days. It was officially announced that the Mehtar had died of heart failure ! But the Chitral Scouts were in no doubt as to what had happened; it was just unfortunate that we had been poisoned too.

We dragged ourselves up next day for the Mehtar's funeral, at which my Sikhs provided a guard of honour. It was an unusual sight, and rather a triumph for British rule, to see Sikh soldiers escorting the body of a Mohammedan potentate with crowds of Mohammedan mourners lining the route. I should like to think that it could still happen nowadays – but know that it couldn't.

There was a state of considerable tension for some days. The Sikhs were seething with rage, thinking that these . . . Mohammedans had tried to bump off their Colonel, and the Mohammedans were suspicious that someone had bumped off their Mehtar – which was true enough. However, everything passed off peacefully. The new Mehtar asked me to ride with him in his coronation procession between Chitral and Drosh, which I did – and never shall I forget it. My horse didn't much like the showers of balloons and streamers, but whilst passing under the archway leading into Chitral City some lovely Chitrali maiden emptied over us from a high window a large bowl of boiled sweets. Doubtless it was very kindly meant. I am sure the Mehtar's horse must have been doped as it didn't bat an eyelid, but mine precipitated me right into the middle of the band. As we neared Drosh the levies on both sides of the road fired off their rifles in a sort of joyous salute – a most dangerous performance as they had no blank ammunition and had to fire ball.

Here the band of the 45th and all the officers of the garrison met us, and with the 45th band playing a march and the Chitral and Drosh bands playing Chitrali music, the levies shooting, and the Chitrali cannon firing a salute, we processed up to the Palace of the Governor of Drosh.

Nasir-ul-Nulk was kindness itself to me and to the officers of the garrison during the remainder of our stay in Chitral. He did everything he could to give us good sport, and to make our two years as pleasant as possible. Unfortunately he was stricken down with some form of paralysis soon after he became Mehtar and he did not survive very long after we left. He was far removed from the strong autocratic character of his father. He was convinced when he came to the throne that his life would not be of long duration and he had a rather pathetic reliance on me personally. I felt very sorry for him; he was a gentle man, out of place in those rugged surroundings.

We stuck to our daily morning battalion P.T. parade all through the bitter winter weather, and everyone, from myself downwards, turned out. And I am convinced that this firm discipline and hard exercise was one of the reasons for the tremendous fitness of all ranks during our two years in Chitral, for the absence of any serious trouble, and for the very high morale maintained by the battalion.

The District Commander asked me to carry out an experiment in Basic English during the winter months. I decided to experiment with the Indian officers and took the class myself three nights a week. Their progress in a short time was very favourably reported on by the District Education officer.

During our first summer in Chitral London Films sent out a party to make the film *The Drum*, and I was asked by the Government of India to give them every possible assistance. I took Chitral Force out into camp where most of the fighting scenes were shot. We found film work very trying in the middle of summer and we felt we had thoroughly earned the Rs 50,000 (£3,000) they paid us. In those few weeks I had a good insight into the making of a film, and was rather horrified at the tremendous extravagance of the procedure. We were all very disappointed that none of the principals – particularly the beautiful Valerie Hobson (later Mrs Profumo) – came out.

I renewed my acquaintance with my film friends when, at Sir Alexander Korda's invitation, I went later to Denham studios and saw the film in its final stages, and was then introduced to Valerie Hobson and the rest of the cast. Later of course I met her often when she was the wife of Jack Profumo, who was in the House of Commons with me.

In the summer the Chitral valley gets stiflingly hot and muggy, and I sent as many troops as could be spared up to Madaglasht, a very pleasant little valley perched up at 10,000 feet. The road up to Madaglasht, such as it was, had to be reconnoitred and repaired each April after the winter snows. Both officers and men loved this place, and the officers used to go up there to ski in the winter. My brother Bill, who had come out to India on a staff appointment, came up and spent his leave with me there.

In October 1937, to celebrate the first anniversary of his reign, the Mehtar gave a big 'Jhalsa', which included polo and football tournaments, tug-of-war, a khud race and Chitrali sports and dancing. There was also an Accession Anniversary Parade and a Durbar, at which we provided a guard of honour. The Political Agent Malakand (Major Evelyn Cobb) and Brigadier Alexander (later Field-Marshal Earl Alexander), who was commanding the Nowshera Brigade, came up to Chitral for it. I had previously invited Alex to come and stay with me and he was anxious to do so, so this seemed an excellent opportunity.

Evelyn Cobb was a firm friend and supporter of mine and a great lover of Chitral. He was a hard, tough sportsman and it was he who persuaded us to play moonlight polo, an old tradition in Chitral. I must say that despite the bright moonlit night we chose for our game, I did find it rather akin to blind man's bluff.

Chitral Force entered a British officers' team for the big polo tournament. This had never been done before. The Chitralis had a supreme contempt for British officers' polo but we had been practising hard and were determined to see whether marking, riding off and good combination could not offset the more brilliant individual play of the Chitralis. Our team consisted of Tony Maunsell, who had replaced Ian Scott as

A.P.A., one; myself, two; Richardson (later General Sir Charles), sapper subaltern, three; and Edge and Koko Cumberledge, two gunner subalterns, four and back. We were fairly well mounted. I played a little chestnut stallion which I had bought in Chitral for £10. He was handy and well trained but getting on in years and a little too slow.

Seventeen teams entered altogether and the enthusiasm was terrific. We astonished everybody by winning our first match by twelve goals to one. However, in the second round, we were drawn against the famous Chitral team which for years had been considered the best in the country. After a gruelling first twenty minutes the score was three goals all. The Chitral team were very worried indeed, and the spectators were almost stunned. The band had worked itself up into a veritable crescendo.

Soon after the resumption of play we took the lead. Chitral were now playing not only all out, but all they knew, which was a considerable amount! Koko hit a lovely shot up the ground within reach of goal; the Chitrali back and I raced each other for it. He was better mounted than I was, but about four stone heavier. I was gradually drawing away from him when he leant out of the saddle and grabbed me by the back of my breeches and all but pulled me off my pony. There was a roar of wrath from the men of the 45th who had turned out *en masse* to see the game. However, the umpire said nothing and I just had to take it. The play then got rather rough and one of their ponies was killed. I sent Richardson off the ground to equalize the sides. They scored again to draw level and then for five minutes there was no score. Our ponies, however, were finished and just before time was called Chitral scored two lovely goals to win the match by six goals to four.

But the Chitrali team had had a nasty shock and had it not been for the breeches episode we might have beaten them. We felt very pleased with ourselves. After the game we gave them one of our ponies, as a Chitrali is very lost without his mount.

The Jhalsa however nearly brought about just the sort of fracas between my Sikhs and the Chitralis which some people in high places had feared when it was decided to send a Sikh battalion to Chitral. Our relations with the local inhabitants had been so good and there had been such a complete absence of 'incidents' that I had perhaps been lulled into a sense of false security. International or inter-racial sport can generally be relied upon to arouse high feeling.

The tug-of-war is a form of sport about which the Chitralis were almost as fanatical as they were about polo and for their size and weight they were amazingly good. In the very first round we came up against one of the toughest tug-of-war teams I have ever seen. For fully ten

General Sir John Dill,
Commandant of the Staff College
in my time,
later Chief of the Imperial
General Staff

Field Marshal Sir William Slim,
in my opinion the greatest
British general of the Second
World War, and a great personal
friend

General Alexander, who led
the Nowshera Brigade in
1935 and afterwards became
a Field Marshal

Brigadier Alexander (left),
the Mehtar of Chitral, myself
and the Mehtar's personal
staff during celebrations to
mark the first anniversary of
the Mehtar's reign

The most beautiful mountain in the world, Tirich Mir, Chitral

As Commander of 127 Brigade at Dunkirk, 1940

Director of Intelligence
General Mason-Macfarlane,
Commander of MacForce at Dunkirk

General Sir Claude Auchinleck.
The Auk was a brilliant leader of men

minutes we failed to budge them an inch; then when we started to move them the fun began. They sat down, they lay down, they caught hold of bushes and eventually their end man on the rope swung to one side and wound himself and the rope round a tree! This was too much for the feelings of the Sikhs who were looking on. They flung themselves upon him and started to unwind him. Several Chitrali spectators then started to belabour the Sikhs with sticks. I saw a bayonet flash, then the A.P.A. and I and the Subadar Major rushed in between them and a very dangerous free for all was averted.

The Chitrali team was disqualified and we got through and eventually won the whole event, by which time anything might have happened. All the old Hindu–Mohammedan feelings had been aroused and the atmosphere was heavy with the thought of old forgotten wrongs and battles long ago.

I made the men of the 45th fall in immediately and marched them straight back to Chitral Fort, where they were confined to barracks until tempers on both sides had cooled down. Although we very soon resumed our cordial relations and everything was peaceful I never allowed our men to compete with the Chitralis in athletic contests again.

Alex enjoyed every moment of his stay and, being a natural athlete and superlatively fit, he revelled in the hard, outdoor existence of Chitral. He had been flown in and as it was now late October and the Lowarai Pass was icing up I suggested I should get a plane to take him back. But he was keen to tackle the pass and invited me to walk over with him and stay the night with him and his wife Margaret in Nowshera, which I much enjoyed.

At 4.30 p.m. on 14 November 1937 there occurred the most severe and unpleasant earthquake shock which any of us had ever experienced. It was even worse than the one which occurred in Quetta in 1935 and it was felt over the whole of northern India. But Chitral, Kashmir and Afghanistan felt the worst of it. It began gradually and continued more and more violently for over two minutes – and two minutes of a bad earthquake seems like a year. At the end of two minutes the ground was rocking so severely that it was impossible to stand up. I lay down on the ground and hoped it wouldn't swallow me up. The houses in Drosh were starting to crack and chimneys began to fall. Avalanches of rocks were roaring down the surrounding hills in the most terrifying manner as the tops of the mountains fell off. Years later I was describing this to Enoch Powell, the Greek scholar and Member of Parliament, and he brought me his own translation of Herodotus in which the description of the tops of the mountains falling off occurs in almost identical words. He said to me then: 'I would not have believed your description had I not read it for myself!'

113

Chitral is notorious for its earthquakes and the houses are low and strongly built, but another half minute of the 'quake would have seen appalling devastation. Drosh Fort stood up to it pretty well but the Lower Fort had to come down. Chitral Fort was so badly damaged that our company there had to evacuate it and go into tents borrowed from the Chitral Scouts – a very cold and miserable proceeding in the bitter weather. We had to withdraw one platoon back to Drosh and patch up the fort sufficiently to house the remainder of our detachment for the winter. Half of Chitral Bazaar fell flat and H.H.'s palace and mosque were badly damaged. There was also a good deal of damage in the northern parts of Chitral. It was fortunate that the earthquake occurred at a time of day when all the troops were out training or playing games and most Chitralis were outside too.

Now that I had got permission for the men to take leave out of Chitral I thought I might be permitted to get away for ten days myself to spend Christmas with my old friends, Colonel Rosie and Hilda Lloyd, in Jhelum, where Rosie was commanding the Carbiniers. It entailed crossing the dreaded Lowarai Pass in mid-winter, but I had done it so easily with Alex in October that I was lulled into a false sense of security. Lowarai Top was simply a large sheet of ice. The first step I took on the downward side my feet shot from under me and I fell about fifty feet, sustaining a badly bruised arm and any thoughts I had been nurturing of Wimbledon in the summer went by the board.

The battalion holding Chitral had never entered a team for the Peshawar District Athletic meeting before and I wanted the 45th to be the first to do so. There were all sorts of difficulties. The meeting was held in the winter when Chitral was under snow and training was difficult; also of course it was the worst time of year to cross the Lowarai Pass.

We cut a running track out of the snow on the aerodrome and got down to training in earnest. The battalion sports were run on a platoon basis so that we had the maximum number of men running and a wide choice of good level performers – rather than just a few gladiators. We chose the day for the selected teams to set out on their journey carefully; but, even so, the party ran into bad weather on the Lowarai and two men got frostbitten, one losing a toe and another a finger.

I had offered to eliminate with the Nowshera Brigade as it would obviously not have been fair for us to be let straight into the semi-final rounds. The team was not fully recovered from the effects of the journey down and they only just won the Nowshera Brigade Sports. But by the time the District Championships came on in Peshawar they were at the top of their form and won fairly comfortably, their crowning glory being to defeat both the 15th and the 36th Sikhs in the cross country race, which was regarded as a certainty for one or other of these two local Sikh battalions. I had many messages of congratulation – it really was a wonderful effort and raised the morale of the battalion sky high.

People have often tried to get the Indian soldier to play Rugby football but he seems temperamentally unsuited to the game. After the snow, when the aerodrome was soft and too rough for soccer. I tried to get rugger going and the men did get a lot of amusement and exercise out of it; but they never really liked it. Also of course the Sikh's hair and beards came down, which added to their difficulties, and created some very angry incidents. So I ruled rugger out.

In July 1938 the battalion was inspected by Brigadier R. N. O'Connor D.S.O., M.C., who was officiating Commander Peshawar District. He afterwards became General Sir Richard O'Connor and was a grand soldier and a delightful person. He stayed with us a week and went through every unit of Chitral Force with a fine tooth comb, and this is what he wrote about the 45th in his official report :

During its two years in Chitral the battalion has added greatly to its already high reputation. It has in every way shown itself an example of how a battalion should behave in a foreign country. Both officers and men have not only made the fullest use of all the existing amenities of the place but have greatly added to them. This is undoubtedly one of the chief reasons why the battalion is such a happy one, and has enjoyed so much of its stay in Chitral. All the officers play polo which has done much to establish a good liaison with the Chitralis. The relations with H.H. the Mehtar, the A.P.A., and the Scouts are excellent, and there will be regret on all sides at the departure of the battalion. [This very creditable record is very greatly due to the efficiency, tact and sound judgement of Lieut.-Colonel Smyth, the Commander.]

Our two years had passed unbelievably quickly and I think those officers and men who were with me in Chitral will always consider it about the best station they have ever been in.

The behaviour of the battalion had been exemplary and they had won golden opinions from everybody concerned. The Mehtar told me that he and his councillors had viewed the coming of a Sikh battalion to Chitral with dismay but in the event they had never known one that had given so little cause for complaint there or British officers with whom they had been so friendly. The men were fit and hard and their individual training and junior leadership were first-class. How I should have liked to have had them with me later on in Burma against the Japs.

I received the thanks of the North-West Frontier Government for the action I had taken to keep the situation in Chitral stable at the time of Sir Shuja-ul-Mulk's death and a fine cutting whip from the Political Agent Malakand in recognition of my services to Chitral polo. The whip hangs in my study today, together with one of the small knotted whips which every Chitrali horseman carries with him.

Chitral was certainly one of the toughest assignments I have ever had, and the job of Force Commander was necessarily a lonely one. But more than the official recognition of a job well done I valued the trust and confidence of the grand team of British and Indian officers who, by their loyalty and cheerfulness, made it all possible.

My time in Chitral was somewhat marred by a personal worry. I had been cited as co-respondent in a divorce case which was to be held in Lahore. Obviously it was considered that from such a faraway place on the roof of the world I would not be able to defend the case, but General Dashwood-Strettell gave me special leave to travel down to Lahore to do so and I won the case with costs. At that time the Army Council had issued an order that all officers involved in a divorce case must report the matter to them. In fact very few did so and the order was allowed to die a natural death, but as a very law-abiding man I duly reported my case, to which I never had an acknowledgement.

In August 1938 it was time for the 'Chitral Reliefs' again, this time with the 45th as the outgoing battalion and the 1/9th Jats the incomers. Our last crossing of the formidable Lowarai Pass held an element of nostalgia for me. Lowarai Top was reached quickly as we wanted to do the stiff climb in record time. Our good friends the Chitral Scouts were waiting for us at the top with very welcome refreshments. Our liaison and friendship with them had been one of our pleasantest memories of Chitral. Instead of the notice board 'The First Time', which had been displayed to us two years previously, we were now greeted with the other side, 'The Last Time, Thank God!' The Scouts had also put up a new notice board which read, 'Men Only', pointing towards Chitral, which was the greatest compliment these very tough chaps could pay us.

Before leaving Drosh we had been very pleased to receive the following personal message from Major-General C. B. Dashwood-Strettell, C.B., G.O.C., Peshawar District:

I very much regret that I was unable to visit you this year or to say goodbye to you personally. I congratulate you all, from the Commander to the youngest soldier, on the very high state of efficiency to which the battalion has attained. Despite the loneliness of Chitral nothing has occurred which could mar the excellent behaviour of all ranks and I am especially glad that your relations with the people of the country have been so good. I am very proud to have had you under my command and I am very sorry that I am losing you but I am confident that, wherever you go either in peace or war, you will surely live up to the magnificent reputation of Rattray's Sikhs.

God be with you all Sat Siri Akal.

Sir George Cunningham, Governor of the North-West Frontier Province wrote to General Sir John Coleridge, G.O.C. in Chief, Northern Command:

Dear General,

As the 3/11th Sikh Regiment have just left Chitral, I would like to take this opportunity of bringing to your notice the excellent impression they have left upon Chitral and its people. The tact and courtesy shown by Colonel Smyth and his officers, and the standard set by the whole battalion, have been of great moral assistance to His Highness the Mehtar at the difficult time, when His Highness ascended the 'gadi' on the death of his father. The local Political Officers have spoken to me in the highest terms of the very fine example set by the battalion.

If you consider it proper to do so I would be glad if you could convey a message of my appreciation to Colonel Smyth.

The G.O.C. added that he appreciated very much all that the battalion had done in Chitral. This was all very heart-warming for me and the 45th Sikhs.

We arrived at our new station in India at Allahabad on 9 October 1938. It was the beginning of a momentous period in my life. On the railway station at Allahabad I met Frances. It was love at first sight.

CHAPTER NINE

War Clouds Gather

ON my last leave home to England Lord Gort had told me that he had been ear-marked as Commander-in-Chief of the Expeditionary Force if the gathering tension with Germany should result in another world war, and in military circles this was considered inevitable. He also told me that it had been decided that the Indian Army would not take part in any European operations as they had done in 1914. This plunged me into the depths of gloom as it was for war in a Western theatre that I felt I had been specifically trained at Camberley, and it was there that all my good Staff College friends would be fighting.

My acute disappointment must have shown in my face for Gort said : 'But if you happened to be home on leave when the war started I would requisition you to command one of my brigades.'

This was a very flattering offer to an Indian Army Lieutenant-Colonel, of which I was determined to take advantage if it was humanly possible and, on my return to India, I had it constantly in mind. But the matter was fraught with difficulties. I would not be eligible for any more leave home, except possibly short leave on urgent private affairs, until my tenure of command of the 45th had ended. If I delayed my departure from India too long and the war had started, or even if a state of crisis had arisen, then all leave would be stopped and I would have had it. When Italy invaded Albania in May 1939 I was in an acute dilemma. Surely the war would begin now? I confided my anxiety to my Brigadier in Allahabad and he was completely co-operative and willing to let me have short leave on 'urgent private affairs' at any time I wanted. But if I took the leave and was back in India without the war having started then I would have missed the bus. I could hardly ask Gort when the war was going to start and he would be unlikely to tell me even if he knew. But wars with Germany generally did start in August or September. Anyhow, I decided to send him the following cable: 'Will fishing keep till August or shall I come now?' To my great relief a reply came back: 'Fishing should keep until August.'

During the next two months in Allahabad, as war clouds gathered in Europe, I was in a fever of anxiety. Looking back now I can only think how foolish I was to be so anxious to get myself killed. But war was my business, for which I had been trained and conditioned.

I left Allahabad by air on Saturday 15 July 1939, and by cunning use of the weekend I arrived in London the day after my leave had officially begun in India, six weeks before the war actually started.

The War Office wanted to get me into a job right away because if the war started and I was still on leave I would have to return to India. They asked me therefore if I would go temporarily, until a brigade command became vacant, to the Home Office to help them with their Civil Defence preparations. I gladly agreed to do this, particularly as Wing Commander John Hodsoll (later Sir John Hodsoll), who was the moving spirit in Civil Defence, was a close friend of mine. Had it not been for his efforts, and those of his little band of enthusiasts, Britain would have been totally unprepared to contend with the German blitzes.

The Home Office welcomed me with open arms as they were terribly overworked; so much so that when, on 30 August my mobilization papers arrived from the War Office, they absolutely refused to let me go. And as at that moment the chief anxiety of the Government was with regard to the possibility of massive air raids on Britain the Home Office request to keep me had precedence over that of the War Office.

This was ghastly. After all my trouble and scheming my promised brigade went to France under another commander. At last, under constant pressure from the War Office, who offered two other officers in my place, the Home Office agreed to release me. But, as there was no brigade command vacant just then I went as G.S.O.1 to the 2nd London Division, which was commanded by Major-General Harry Willans. The two London divisions were unique in that they were the only British divisions commanded by Territorial Army officers. General Claude Liardet commanded the 1st London.

All through that first winter of the war Harry Willans and I did our best, under every sort of difficulty, to train the 2nd London Division for war. One of our first priorities was to get our own divisional office going. We had a collection of clerks, typewriters, paper of all sorts, clips and files, but no one knew what was important and what was not, nor how to set about making order out of this chaos. Harry Willans, a business man himself, said: 'Jackie, what are we to do about all this?'

I replied: 'I know what we can do. I can get my friend, Colonel Lyn Urwick, the chairman of Urwick Orr, the well-known business management firm, and he will fix it.' And he certainly did. He arrived with a couple of assistants. They lived at Divisional H.Q. and in a matter of a couple of weeks we had an office of which any division might be proud.

I realized that the same problem would be facing every new division and Urwick Orr could do a real service to our rapidly expanding army if they would tackle the job in a big way. Urwick Orr were only too willing. It was just the sort of war work for which they were fully equipped. My proposal was well thought of until some stuffed shirt at the Treasury shot it down with the old cliché, 'We have never done this before'. But we had never had a world war quite like this before.

When I got command of a brigade shortly afterwards I called in Colonel Urwick again and he sent me off to France with a smoothly running Brigade office.

But the training of the 2nd London was terribly handicapped by all the anti-sabotage guards and duties which the division had to undertake. The divisional staff were also tested out in a series of T.E.W.T.s (tactical exercises without troops) arranged by the higher command. I very soon tumbled to the fact that these were really designed to test out the divisional commander himself. General Liarlet, a most talented and delightful man, was undoubtedly too old to command a division on active service. Harry Willans, however, was a good deal younger, extremely fit and active, and he was really keen to command a division in war. General Ronald Adam, who had been with me at the Staff College, had been instrumental in appointing me to be Willans's chief of staff and I was determined to do everything in my power to help him. But he just didn't quite know the patter. The bowling was fast and bumpy and there were a lot of people 'clustering round the bat' so to speak, waiting to catch him out. We cleared three big hurdles together, but he fell at the last one shortly after I left him, and was relieved of his command. He was bitterly disappointed, but I think he was probably of greater service to the Army in the important administrative assignment he was given, which was brought to an end by his tragic death in an air crash.

I began to feel that Gort had forgotten me, as well he might have done with all the responsibilities he was facing, but I had a great friend in Ronald Adam, who had been appointed Commander of 3 Corps in the B.E.F., and he had kept me very much in mind. On 1 February 1940 I was ordered to take command forthwith of 127 Infantry Brigade (The Manchester Brigade), of the 42nd East Lancashire Division. They were a first line Territorial division, due to leave for France almost at once. Bidding a fond farewell to Harry Willans and all my friends in the 2nd London Division, I set out for Rainscombe House just outside Marlborough, where my Brigade H.Q. was located.

The Divisional Commander was Major-General W. G. Holmes, aged forty-eight, who had been the youngest Major-General in the Army when he had been appointed to command the division three years earlier. He was a strikingly handsome man of fine physique. We had been brought up in the same military school and our association was of the happiest.

He came to see me at my Brigade H.Q. as soon as I had arrived, and made it clear that 127 Brigade was in a bit of a mess, both with regard to the standard of training of the battalions and, more immediately, the situation with regard to the Brigade Staff, of whom the brigadier, the brigadier major and the supply officer had all been removed. Only a few days before my arrival the Inspector of Infantry had reported the Brigade as 'unfit for service', and they were due to embark for France with the rest of the Division within a matter of weeks. Naturally there was an air of acute depression at Rainscombe House, and also at Divisional Headquarters.

The immediate problem was staff, particularly a Brigade Major. George Holmes had produced for my inspection three or four possibilities. Three of them were experienced staff officers but rather elderly.

'There is also,' said the General, 'a young Sapper subaltern called Jones, who has no staff experience at all but is quite bright and I would like you to have a look at him.'

Five minutes with 'Jonah' (who was afterwards known as 'Splosh') were enough to decide me that he was the man for us. And how right I was! He did the job for me in France superlatively well, got an M.C. at Dunkirk, and never looked back until, having been Master General of the Ordnance from 1963 to 1966, he retired and became Governor of the Royal Hospital, Chelsea in June 1969 as General Sir Charles Jones, G.C.B., O.B.E., M.C., and also President of the Royal British Legion.

I next engaged Jackie Stevens as my Supply Officer. Large, rotund and expansive, he turned out to be a Supply Officer of anyone's dreams – certainly of mine. With Phil Phillips as Staff Captain, Derek Kay as Transport Officer and Johnny Dodds as learner (and later on invaluable Staff Captain) and with the streamlining that Urwick Orr had given us, we had a first-class Brigade Headquarters by any standards.

The three battalions were the 4th East Lancashires, commanded by Robbie Robinson, the 5th Manchesters, under Ronald France and the 8th Manchesters, commanded by Lieut.-Colonel Kay. The men were excellent material, good, tough Lancashire stock, many of them miners. The officers too were splendid material and a number of them were athletes of county and international repute. The three C.O.s were capable men, fit, keen, trustworthy and stout-hearted. I found them loyal comrades and subordinates and, considering their lack of training, they put up a magnificent show against what was then the most highly trained and formidable army in the world. Certainly Britain would have been in a bad way without the Territorial Army at that time. But of course they were far from being fully trained by Regular standards, and that put a great strain on me and my Brigade Staff.

The units of my brigade group which, besides my infantry battalions, included a regiment of Field Artillery, a Field Ambulance, and a Field Company of Royal Engineers, were billeted in the back streets of Marlborough in acute discomfort, added to by the bitter winter weather. But these conditions were not allowed to interfere with my programme of intensive training, and every day that passed the Brigade became harder, fitter and more battleworthy. Realizing that time was short I cut out all the frills and concentrated on essentials. I made certain that the battalions could dig in quickly, move anywhere at the shortest notice, either on foot or in M.T., and above all that they knew how to conduct a withdrawal.

'Why the withdrawal?' a senior visiting officer asked me. 'There isn't going to be another retreat from Mons.'

'Maybe not,' I replied, 'but I'm not taking any chances.'

Suddenly all the Brigadiers and Commanding Officers of the Division were summoned to a conference at Marlborough town hall. The whole place was stiff with Military Police and it was clear that something very hush-hush was afoot. When we were all seated, in strode the huge figure of General 'Tiny' Ironside, Chief of the Imperial General Staff. He had on an enormous pair of black rubbery-looking boots, which seemed to reek of winter snows. Having sworn us all to secrecy he proceeded to tell us that we were to be sent to Finland to fight the Russians. He went on to speak of the snow and ice and the midnight sun. We were to be equipped with shorts and topees to make everyone think we were going East, and then, when the transports were at sea, we were to don our special Arctic dress and make for Finland. But how we were to get there through Norway and Sweden remained a mystery. The atmosphere was heavy with the silence of unspoken questions as Tiny rose and made for the door. Suddenly he caught sight of me and came over to wish me luck. I felt I should need it.

We then returned to our billets looking too furtive for words. Within three days the whole thing was in the national Press. But we remained part of 'Finn-Force' for another ten days. However, our role soon died of inanition, and our intensive training for operations on the Continent of Europe continued throughout February and March. Then, on 29 March an event occurred which was invariably the prelude to action or at least to embarkation, the inspection of the whole of 42 Division in Savernake Forest by His Majesty the King.

The weather had at last taken a turn for the better and the sun shone brightly; the forest was full of primroses. It was a great day for my Manchester men, hardly any of whom had ever seen the King except in pictures. The battalions were lined up in single file on either side of the road and the King walked with me up the centre, stopping every now and then to talk to some of the officers, N.C.O.s and men. He talked to me of the day twenty years earlier when, as Duke of York, he had presented the Military Cross to me and my brother Bill at Buckingham Palace. The men threw out their chests as they marched back to Marlborough and sang as they marched.

On 5 April our advance parties, which had been recalled because of Finland, returned to France. We were to complete our training somewhere south of Paris and the division started to move across the Channel by brigade groups, with my brigade the last to go. George Holmes was very keen on this breakdown of his division into brigade groups. It was certainly useful for training purposes, but he more or less made it a permanency for operations also. In a withdrawal such as Dunkirk turned out to be it had certain advantages. It greatly eased the task of the Divisional Commander and his staff, but put a very great burden on the brigade staffs.

On 9 April the Germans occupied Denmark and invaded Norway.

During the past years my marriage to Margaret had been drifting on to the rocks and I had fallen deeply in love with Frances Read, whom I had met in Allahabad after my two years in Chitral. We decided that we would marry when circumstances made it possible, which was not until 12 April 1940, when we were married from my mother's flat in Southsea. We both realized we would have little time together before I departed for France.

General Holmes and the rest of 42 Division had already sailed for France. On the night of Saturday 13 April I received a telephone message from the War Office to say that all further moves to France had been cancelled and that my Brigade was to stand fast. On Monday the 15th I was informed that my Brigade was to go to Norway, and that our advanced parties had been ordered back from France. I felt that poor Phil Phillips, the Staff Captain who was in charge of them, must be getting dizzy with all these 'ordres and contre-ordres'!

The next day I was summoned to the War Office. I was ushered into the operations staff room, next to General Ironside's office, and greeted by my old friend, Brigadier Otto Lund, now D.M.O. (Director of Military Operations) who had been a fellow teacher with me at the Staff College. He and his colleagues, all of whom I knew well, wore on their faces that frozen smile which I recognized at once meant that there was a bit of a flap on. And no wonder, the speed and unexpectedness of the German move had taken us completely by surprise. I was told that my Brigade was to land at Andalsnes. I had to admit that I had never heard of it and had never been to Norway. So we were going in the general direction of Finland after all, though now to fight a different enemy. Maps were produced and I sat in an armchair poring over them while staff officers buzzed about like bees.

I understood that General Ironside was holding an important conference in the next room with Lord Gort in France, the result of which I should await. I was left alone with my thoughts.

I could hear the rather acrimonious telephone conversation going on in the C.I.G.'s office. And then suddenly a staff officer came out. There had been another change of plan; the Andalsnes landing had been cancelled. I was to return to Marlborough and stand by at six hours' notice – to go where? I understood that Gort had objected strongly to 42 Division being broken up in this way and had insisted that my brigade should join him in France. I must say, when I remembered all the background of my somewhat extraordinary appointment to command a brigade in Gort's Expeditionary Force it would have seemed even more extraordinary if I had been whisked away to command a brigade under my friend, Claude Auchinleck, in another theatre of war. However, when I arrived back in Marlborough I found that my Field Artillery Regiment had been ordered off in my absence – presumably to Norway; I never knew, and I never saw them again. What a queer war this was going to be.

But, although we were not in the end destined for Norway, Andalsnes was to be kept in the family. My brother Bill was commanding a battalion of the K.O.Y.L.I. in the 5th Division in France. On relief by my own 42nd Division 5th Division was brought into reserve and my brother's brigade was hurried back to England and given exactly the same job of landing at Andalsnes which had been originally given to me and then cancelled a few weeks earlier. They were railed up to Glasgow while the Brigadier and his staff were summoned to London to receive their orders. They were then flown up to Glasgow, but crashed on landing and their unconscious bodies were transferred to hospital, and Bill found himself in command of the Brigade – but what to do about it? As the Brigade was embarking he received a somewhat confused telephone message from the War Office to say that he was to disembark at Andalsnes, where he would be met by an officer, whose name sounded just like Colonel Rumpelstiltskin, and then proceed inland to meet the German invaders. On landing, brother Bill enquired everywhere for the Colonel. At last they met and fell on one another's necks. At that moment a small German shell came meandering over and exploded almost on top of them. When Bill recovered consciousness he was being carried away on a stretcher and Colonel Rumpelstiltskin had disappeared. Bill was badly wounded in the leg and the brigade, attacked by a greatly superior German force, retired severely mauled, and re-embarked. It was an abortive operation which my Brigade was lucky to have missed.

On 20 April 127 Brigade Group were told to proceed to France on the 23rd; advanced parties were to leave immediately. But the strain had been too much for Phil; he went down with German measles and Johnny Dodds took his place.

My Brigade H.Q.'s last days at Rainscombe House were very beautiful. The sun shone and the air was filled with the bleating of young lambs. After the hard winter spring had burst forth in a blaze of primroses and daffodils; the trees burgeoned and blossoms dropped trails of petals on my Bren-gun carriers. Frances and I wandered around the countryside in my car and picnicked in Savernake Forest.

Goodbyes are always odious and this one was no exception. The windows of the little flat we had rented in Marlborough overlooked the main square of the town, which was full of the bustle of departure and the tramp of marching feet. Down below my Humber brake stood waiting, with its little blue 127 Brigade pennant fluttering in the breeze. Tranter, my sturdy Lancashire driver, was exchanging wisecracks with Wright, my excellent Cockney batman. Suddenly the first battalion came swinging through the square. The men were in tremendous spirits. The long winter of training and waiting was over at last and they were off to the war. They were singing 'We'll hang out the washing on the Siegfried Line' – but what years of death and tribulation, defeat and victory were to pass before we did so. Truly it is a dispensation of providence that the future comes to us one day at a time.

The next battalion came past singing 'Roll out the barrel'. Then there was a pause of several minutes and the last battalion approached to the nostalgic strains of 'It's a long way to Tipperary', to which I had marched to battle twenty-six years before.

And then it was time to say goodbye. Frances, smiling bravely, waved from the window, and I was off to yet another war.

CHAPTER TEN

The Miracle of Dunkirk

DUNKIRK was both a disaster for Great Britain, and a miracle. It was a disaster in that the French and British armies suffered complete and abysmal defeat at the hands of the new model German Army and their powerful supporting Air Force. The British Expeditionary Force only started their advance into Belgium on 10 May and were all back inside the Dunkirk Salient some twenty days later. It was a far graver defeat than that suffered by General Percival at the hands of the Japanese at Singapore, but it did not have the same unhappy outcome.

Prime Minister Winston Churchill said in the House of Commons on 4 June 1940: 'I feared it would be my hard lot to announce from this box the greatest military disaster in our long history.' Dunkirk was only saved from being so by the fact that over 336,000 troops, 234,000 of them British, and most of the remainder French, were evacuated by the British Navy and 'the little ships' under the air cover of British Fighter Command. Even so the B.E.F. lost everything in the way of weapons and equipment except for a proportion of their personal weapons.

This evacuation by sea of a defeated army under the noses of greatly superior German forces was certainly a military miracle; yet it happened, and that wonderful ditch, the English Channel, gave the defeated British Army time to re-arm and live to fight another day. And the British people gave their defeated Army a great welcome home. It has always been considered an honour to have been at Dunkirk and I count myself fortunate that I was the only Indian Army officer to command a fighting formation in that momentous operation. From the time I took over my brigade sector on the Belgian frontier at Halluin to the time we arrived back in England was a space of just over a month. Yet in that month was crowded one of the most hectic and exciting periods of my life.

It had been intended that 42 Division should undergo a period of six weeks' intensive training somewhere south of Paris but, on our arrival at Cherbourg, we found that this plan had been cancelled and that we were to go straight up to the Belgian frontier to take over a portion of the defences from 5 Division. The troops of course were delighted and so was I, although I fully realized that they could have done with those six weeks of training, and more besides. I was to take over the sector held by the brigade commanded by Monty Stopford (later Lieut.-General Sir Montagu Stopford who gained fame as one of Bill Slim's Corps Commanders in Burma) north of Lille and just south of Menin. I myself was to motor on ahead, leaving the Brigade to follow by road and rail.

As it was on my way, I decided to pay a call on Lord Gort at his G.H.Q. at Arras and then branch slightly west to Bethune where General Sir Ronald Adam, my Corps Commander, had his headquarters. In Arras I found Gort was out, but General Sir Henry Pownall, his Chief of Staff, was in his office. He and I had been at the Staff College together, served in India together and were old friends. He had a resourceful brain and great strength of character; he was to prove himself in various theatres of war as one of our most distinguished British staff officers.

Bethune brought back many memories of the 1914–18 war. The damaged clock tower in the centre of the square had been rebuilt and was permanently flood-lit at night as a memorial. When the lights went out in Europe for the second time in May 1940 this light went out too. I had tea with General Adam and his Chief of Staff, Brigadier Watson (later General Watson), and we had a good talk.

The road from Bethune to my journey's end at Halluin was signposted with memories of 'old, unhappy things and battles long ago'. But they had not all been unhappy and visiting places again brought the events with which they were connected vividly to mind. Festubert, Neuve Chapelle, Richebourg, La Bassée, were all familiar places where I had toiled and fought with the 15th Ludhiana Sikhs in that first bitter winter of 1914–15.

At 6 p.m. on Sunday 26 April I arrived at the palatial Château Larache at Roncq, which I was to take over from Monty Stopford as my Brigade H.Q. Next morning Monty and I set out to look round the defence line. But we had not got very far when an orderly suddenly appeared with a message to say that Monty and his brigade had to leave immediately. This was a bad blow for me as the defence system was very complicated. However, the late Duke of Gloucester arrived from

G.H.Q. to spend a day with me and he knew the position backwards and was immensely helpful.

The units of my Brigade group were billeted in and around Roncq and Halluin; the three infantry battalions of my Brigade proper, a whole regiment of Field Artillery, an anti-tank battery, and R.E. Company and a Field Ambulance. We had taken over the defence sector and every day was spent improving the defences and in studying the lines of fire for all weapons.

On 3 May the Brigade commanders of 42 Division were bidden to meet Lord Gort at Division H.Q. The heat was almost unbearable and there was hardly a breath of air. But the C.-in-C. was in terrific form and inspired the utmost confidence and enthusiasm. Thick-set, red faced, dynamic and tremendously tough, 'Fat Boy Gort', as he was affectionately known to his friends, had already had a remarkable career. In the Great War he had commanded the 4th and 1st Grenadier Guards and won the M.C., three D.S.O.s and the Victoria Cross. In reaching his present position he had passed over the heads of several other distinguished and ambitious general officers, who were not above giving his pedestal a gentle shake when opportunity offered. In every military disaster there must be a scapegoat, and Gort was made the scapegoat for Dunkirk. He was never offered another field command. But let us always remember that if he had not taken the vital decision to disengage the B.E.F. from the disorganized French Army and re-embark it at Dunkirk, the Second World War might well have been lost.

There were two particular matters about which Gort wanted to talk to the brigade commanders, and he interviewed each one of us separately, with only the divisional commander present. Being the senior brigadier I was interviewed first. Gort wished to replace one of my territorial battalions with a regular one. I very much welcomed this idea, though I hated losing any of the battalions I had got to know so well. I decided that the junior battalion, the 8th Manchesters, should go. A few days later I saw them off and heard that they were destined for Malta, where they did splendidly in the very critical days which lay ahead for that George Cross Island.

Gort then handed me a list of available battalions from which I could take my pick. To his obvious surprise I chose without hesitation the 1st Battalion Highland Light Infantry. This particular battalion had apparently been giving a bit of trouble, largely owing to their boredom with the 'phoney war' period. But I had been brigaded with them in World War I and they were closely associated with the incident in which I won my V.C.

'They will give you a hell of a lot of trouble, Jackie, before the show starts,' Gort said.

General Sir Archibald Wavell

Major-General H. L. Davies,
Chief General Staff Officer to
General Hutton and General Slim
in Burma, 1942, later Commander
of the 25th Indian Division

My eldest son, Captain
John Smyth, who was
killed in action at Kohima
leading his men of the 1st
Battalion Queen's Royal
Regiment on 7 May 1944,
aged twenty-two

James Gomer Berry,
1st Baron Kemsley. When I
knew him he controlled
perhaps the greatest chain of
newspapers in the world

'Maybe they will,' I replied, 'but they'll fight like hell when it does.'
And I was certainly right.

But Gort's next proposal I did not welcome at all, although I would
certainly have done so had it been made three months earlier. He wished
to replace my two Territorial C.O.s by regulars. The weakness of most
T.A. commanding officers was that they did not have the professional
knowledge to train their officers and men for war. But the training
period was over now. My two C.O.s, Robbie Robinson and Ronald
France, were both fine leaders and knew their men inside out. I was
convinced that to remove them now would do more harm than good.
Gort told me that my view was contrary to that of the other Territorial
brigade commanders; nevertheless, as he had personally selected me
to fight the battle, he respected my opinion and let me keep my
C.O.s.

I never regretted my decision, although command of a T.A. brigade
in battle, particularly in the type of operation we were soon to conduct,
was a far greater strain on the brigadier and brigade staff than in a
regular brigade, where the C.O.s and adjutants were much more highly
trained in all the niceties of staff duties within a brigade in battle conditions. And this strain was accentuated in 42 Division, where the
brigadier had to control the other arms of a complete brigade group
through the whole of the operations. This was actually the last time I
saw Gort, though we corresponded from time to time in the years to
come.

The end of the phoney war and the start of the real thing occurred
with startling suddenness. Thursday night, 9 May, was oppressively
hot. I have an instinctive sense of danger where war is concerned, and
I had felt for days as though we were sitting on the edge of a volcano.
I couldn't get to sleep. My bedroom window looked out across the
beautiful grounds of the château on to the ridge where the concrete pill
boxes of the defence line stood sharply etched against the night sky.
At 3 a.m. I was awakened from a fitful slumber by the hum of large
numbers of aircraft and the crash of falling bombs. This was it. I leapt
out of bed and switched on the wireless and heard a voice, speaking in
French on Radio Paris, announcing that the Germans had invaded
Belgium and the Low Countries.

The first job for 3 Corps was to picket an area to cover the advance
of 1 and 2 Corps for their advance on Brussels. This was a most exhausting job and we envied the other divisions rushing through in their buses.
On 11 May we were all heartened by the news that Winston Churchill
had become Prime Minister. On Monday the 13th we were informed
that 1 and 2 Corps were taking up a position on the River Dyle, north
of Brussels, and that 3 Corps were to hold a reserve position on the

River Escaut, with my 127 Brigade holding the sector from Tournai to Pecq.

Just before leaving we were issued with the long-awaited 25 mm anti-tank guns. These were excellent little weapons against light tanks, but of course it was a crushing handicap that we had been given them so late. As it was, only about half the gun teams had tried the guns, even once, before they had to use them in action against German tanks. Our lack of tank support and of anti-tank weapons necessitated our always taking up positions behind some form of natural tank obstacle.

The refugee problem had already become a major factor in all our operations and it increased every day as the situation worsened. It was cleverly and deliberately fostered and exploited by the Germans, both by rumours and direct action. The roads became choked with panic-stricken civilians, going they knew not where. The streams of refugees were used by the Germans to hamper our movements, but were merci-lessly shot off the roads they themselves wanted to use. The main road outside my Brigade Headquarters at Templeneuve was one solid block of slowly moving refugees, numbed with fear and fatigue and long past all reason.

I spent my daylight hours going round my battalions, deciding problems, adjusting and co-ordinating boundaries and lines of fire. The more I saw of 127 Brigade the more proud of them I became.

On 16 May, as I was returning from a morning with the 5th Man-chesters, I found Ronald Adam, the Corps Commander, waiting to see me. He gave me the disturbing news that the Germans had succeeded in crossing the Meuse on the front of the French 9th Army. This part of the front had been considered impregnable.

Next morning I was summoned urgently to Division H.Q. where the Corps Commander wanted to see me. George Holmes had no idea what it was about. Presently Ronald Adam arrived, bringing grave news of the German Panzer breakthrough on the Meuse. Not only had the 9th Army failed to close the gap but it had been considerably enlarged and through it had poured several Panzer divisions. This move danger-ously threatened the right flank of the B.E.F. and also Gort's Army H.Q. at Arras. To counter this threat Gort had ordered his own Director of Intelligence, Major-General Mason-Macfarlane, to form a scratch force to be known as Macforce, which was to move at once to the River Scarpe. It would operate under the direct command of Lord Gort. My infantry brigade was selected to be the basis of Macforce and General Mason-Macfarlane was already on his way to my Brigade H.Q.

I fully realized the need for speed, but my battalions were at that moment digging in on their River Escaut defence line. Before leaving

Division H.Q. I demanded from Ronald Adam and George Holmes the immediate supply of sufficient lorries to lift my three battalions, and some quick arrangements whereby they could be relieved in their present defensive positions. I then jumped into my car and made my way back to Templeneuve as quickly as the refugees would allow.

Mason-Mac, who had married Ronald Adam's younger sister, was a very old friend of mine. In India we had soldiered together and played cricket and polo together. Although he had no experience of command, as he had been in semi-political intelligence appointments for years before the war, there was no one in the British Army under whom I would have served with greater confidence. With his powerful physique, cool temperament, dynamic energy and, above all, a grand sense of humour, he had all the basic attributes of an ideal leader of men. Also he spoke French and German fluently, which was to prove of great use to us in the somewhat hair-raising adventures which followed.

What really delighted me was the way my Brigade Staff and my C.O.s and their units rose to an occasion which was to mean rapid movement, uncertain meals and very little sleep, to say nothing of considerable danger. Mason-Mac and I made a quick simple plan, the main ingredients of which had to be simplicity. I had somehow to get my brigade on to the Scarpe before the Panzers – if the latter weren't there already. Mason-Mac had been able to obtain no information from French G.H.Q. as to what was happening there, so we just had to chance our arm. Mason-Mac planned to set off at once with his staff to Orchies, which had been the headquarters of the French 3 Corps before the breakthrough, and I was to endeavour to join him there with my brigade before dawn next morning. The distance was some thirty miles over unknown roads and with the possibility of bumping into German or French formations.

By superhuman efforts on the part of brigade and battalion staffs we had our whole outfit withdrawn from their defensive positions, embussed and ready to move by the time darkness set in. The length of my whole column, at regulation intervals, was thirty-six miles, but in a move such as this it was no good observing the safety precautions laid down. Also if we had tried to proceed without lights our progress would have been painfully slow and many lorries would undoubtedly have been ditched. We should be no good to Macforce if we did not arrive quickly, so I divided my column into unit blocks, gave each unit commander the itinerary, turned on all the headlights and left them to find their way there with all possible speed. I saw them started and then told my good driver, Tranter, to tread on the gas in my Humber brake and Jonah and I sped ahead of the column to find Mason-Mac.

We arrived at Orchies in the small hours of the morning and found the whole place in pitch darkness. It had been fairly heavily bombed and was in consequence showing no lights. Jonah and I wandered along the main street by the light of a single torch. I knew Mason-Mac would leave me some clue as to his whereabouts and, sure enough, after a bit we came upon a large blackboard with the words 'Mason-Mac' printed on it in white chalk.

We found him with Major Gerald Templer (later Field-Marshal Sir Gerald), who had been his G.S.O.2 at G.H.Q., and the few other staff officers he had brought with him, busy establishing a Force Headquarters in an empty house. Mason-Mac suggested that we should share a headquarters, which seemed a very sensible arrangement. It would also simplify clerical, signals and messing arrangements. Thus was born 'Macforce', which was to play a not unimportant part in the operations to come.

As I anticipated Mason-Mac had made full use of his time; he had already contacted the French 3 Corps H.Q. in their new location. They were in a considerable mess. Some of their formations were north of the Scarpe and some south, but their supply and communication arrangements seemed to have broken down completely. Of the German forces in the vicinity there were only rumours, some of which were very alarming and others over-optimistic.

By 11.30 a.m. on Saturday, 18 May, my brigade had arrived and taken up its allotted position on the Scarpe, with a French Moroccan division on our left, and nothing whatever on our right. We were strung out on an extended front with everything in the shop window. I could not have been more pleased with my brigade. They were behaving like veterans and taking everything in their stride, and despite lack of sleep they were in the highest spirits. This was the twenty-fifth anniversary of my gaining the V.C. at Richebourg l'Avoue in 1915, and here we were, at it again with the same old enemy and in almost exactly the same locality.

We were a very cheery party at Macforce H.Q. Mason-Mac himself set a splendid example of terrific energy combined with complete coolness and an unfailing sense of humour. Whether we were hiding in some ditch from German low-flying bombers or conferring in the middle of the night with an excited French staff officer, he kept that crooked grin on his face and the inevitable cigarette in his mouth. Generally speaking, either Mason-Mac or I remained at Force Headquarters and he authorized me to take any urgent decisions for him on matters which might arise in his absence. But occasionally we paid visits together which I much enjoyed. Together we visited several French Corps and Divisional Headquarters. I gained the impression that most of the French higher commanders were far too old for their jobs and quite out of touch with the positions and morale of their troops. The majority appeared to be either over-confident or over-anxious.

Mason-Mac combined his activities as commander of Macforce with a sort of self-imposed role of liaison officer and morale raiser with our neighbouring French formations. They were obviously shattered by the suddenness of the German breakthrough. I believe that if Mason-Mac could have become French Army Commander at that critical stage he might well have pulled them together. Certainly all the head-quarters we visited appeared immensely heartened by his visits, by his command of their language, his cheerful and confident approach, and the fact that he had been around and knew more about the situation than they did themselves. Every day Macforce was being strengthened by the addition of some new formation.

Our few days in Macforce were packed with incident and excite-ment. My own battalions were digging in and pushing forward recon-naissance patrols, and the Germans were obviously concerned to find out what our strength and locations were by means of armoured car patrols and low-flying air reconnaissance.

Having heard from the French 3 Corps that their formations south of the Scarpe were retiring northwards in some confusion Mason-Mac and I decided to go and have a look at the situation for ourselves. We were enabled to do so by the addition of an armoured car reconnaissance unit under command of Lieut.-Colonel Hopkinson. 'Hoppy' had been one of my pupils at Camberley and was fast making a reputation as a bold and fearless leader of armoured formations. Having warned us that we might well be fired on by Germans, French or British, and that his armoured cars were old-fashioned and difficult to turn, he firmly placed Mason-Mac and me in separate cars – 'Mustn't put all our eggs in one basket, Sir,' – and with a beaming smile he led the way.

I think Mason-Mac and I were beginning to realize that we were being rather naughty, and we were somewhat lucky to get back alive from this adventure, in which we ran into all sorts of trouble and were shot up by low-flying aircraft. However, we did manage to make con-tact with the forward French divisions, and got valuable information from them which was of the greatest use to Lord Gort and which we could not have obtained in any other way. We arrived back at Orchies desperately weary to find a message from Gort demanding Mason-Mac's immediate presence at G.H.Q. Leaving me in charge of Mac-force he set off at once.

He was back next morning, bright as a button, and spent the whole day with me, touring my battalions. German air activity had greatly increased and they were clearly desperately anxious to find out more about our strength and positions. During this one day we shot down no less than eleven German aircraft, and every battalion had iron crosses and other souvenirs to show to the Force Commander, beside dead and wounded German airmen.

Next day General Damme, the very alert and capable commander of the French Moroccan division, demanded the presence of Mason-Mac and myself to discuss a vital problem with regard to the adjustment of our interdivisional boundary. The drive was hair-raising. The road was blocked solid with streams of refugees going in all directions. They fled from the bombing, from the Panzers, from the main German armies advancing from the east – and from rumours. When two streams met going in opposite directions each would suddenly realize the utter futility of it all.

It was late in the afternoon when we arrived at General Damme's H.Q. at St Amand. He was being strongly pressed on his left flank and wanted Macforce to take over a mile of his front. However, when he heard the length of the front we were already holding he fully realized that it couldn't be done. He therefore unhorsed his cavalry brigade and put them into the line. We never saw General Damme again. He was a fine commander and a splendid man. I heard he was killed shortly afterwards.

The journey back in the gathering dusk was a nightmare. Mason-Mac, a driver of racing standards, took the wheel and Tranter and I had to leap out of the car continually to urge a cart or other vehicle out of the way or to rouse a group of exhausted refugees who had flopped down in the middle of the road. We arrived back at Orchies very late, very weary and black with sweat.

After dealing with all the routine matters with Gerald and Jonah we had a quick meal and were just thinking of an early bed when the next bombshell arrived in the shape of an express message from Gort to Mason-Mac. The rearguard divisions of the B.E.F. had withdrawn across the River Escaut in the direction of Lille, leaving 44 Division and 42 Division holding rearguard positions on the Escaut. The advancing Germans had broken the 42 Division front; 127 Brigade was to return immediately to 42 Division. I don't know when I have hated an order more. We had an exciting and tremendously interesting job in Macforce, under a commander we all liked and admired. The order was also a tremendous blow to Mason-Mac.

This was one of the many occasions during these operations, and indeed during the Burma campaign of early 1942, when one just had to forget one was very tired and realize one would have a sleepless night. On such occasions it was always my practice to start by shaving, and then treat the coming night as if it was the beginning of another day. For a time one can kid the weary body that this is really so.

There was a great deal of planning to be done with Gerald Templer and Jonah to get the brigade relieved in their positions by other units and then embussed and ready for the move. Shortly before midnight we were ready to start, which was really almost a miracle of planning and action in the dark.

Mason-Mac insisted on being woken up to see me off. He was in his pyjamas, his hair tousled and his face grey and lined with fatigue, but the few words of thanks which he spoke to us touched me more than any 'Order of the Day'. None of us will ever forget those few exciting days under his command. Much was expected of us but, to those who served him well, he gave his complete confidence and trust. Himself however he never spared, but even his robust frame had to suffer eventually from the strain he imposed on it. In the foreword he wrote to my book, *Before the Dawn*, he said :

During the morning of the 17th Lord Gort sent for me and put me in command of a force with the initial task of taking up a defensive position on the River Scarpe to deal with any enemy action against our exposed flank. The first infantry brigade I was given was Brigadier Smyth's. Jackie Smyth was a very old friend of mine and a fighting commander of the very best type. His brigade – the 127th – were first-class fighting material and, confronted as I was by an obviously awkward job, it cheered me enormously to know that it was round this brigade that I was to start building my scratch force. For three very hectic days we worked together in the most intimate collaboration. I always look back on this brief period of co-operation with Jackie Smyth and his brigade as a very happy example of real comradeship.

I did not see Mason-Mac again for several years, and then he was an embittered and desperately sick man. He was embittered because he was never again given a fighting command after Dunkirk, and he had developed a spinal disorder which eventually crippled him completely. In his last years, which were of increasing pain, I visited him as often as I could and got him into Stoke Mandeville hospital, where, despite all attention, he failed to recover and died in 1953, shortly after my last visit to him.

Meanwhile 127 Brigade arrived back with 42 Division early next morning to find that the whole division was about to withdraw that night to a system of fieldworks known as the Lille defences. It was Wednesday, 22 May and the men of my brigade were almost asleep on their feet. During the late afternoon of the 23rd German patrols made contact all along our front. The rest of 3 Corps had gone back with Ronald Adam to organize the Dunkirk defences; 42 Division now formed part of 1 Corps, with General Alexander's 1 Division on our left and Monty's 3 Division beyond him again.

The 24th and 25th of May found us holding the Lille defences with my Brigade H.Q. in the old French fort of Sanguin, which I shared with Brigadier Miles commanding 126 Brigade. On the night of 26/27th both of us had to make adjustments to our defence lines owing to the sudden withdrawal of some French formations on the flank. This took us most of the night and we had hardly got back to Sanguin when orders came from Division H.Q. that we were to withdraw that night through Lille to the River Lys, round Armentières. It was quite impossible for Division H.Q. to work out a plan as the situation might have changed appreciably by nightfall. The Divisional Commander gave us our route, the hour at which we were to leave our rearmost defended localities, and told us that 1 Division (Alex's) would withdraw on our left and a French Corps on our right. The only thing I impressed on the staff officer who brought us the order was that Division H.Q. must keep our one road clear.

In such a situation it was obviously a great advantage for two brigadiers concerned to share a headquarters. 'Miles the soldier', as he was generally known, was a grand type of regular officer with whom I got on extremely well. I offered to do rearguard, as his position was more difficult to get away from than mine, and both brigades withdrew smoothly without the Germans being any the wiser. All went well until we arrived at Lille, which was blazing furiously from a heavy German air attack. There I found a very tired French cavalry brigade and parts of a disorganized French infantry division completely blocking our road. In fact many of them were lying asleep on the road, and the horses were asleep standing. Jonah and I abandoned the car and slogged along the road on our flat feet in a confused mass of French cavalry, French infantry, French refugees, Manchesters and every sort of oddment from the French and British armies.

I arrived at my predestined Brigade H.Q. at Le Bizet at 4 a.m., sorted out the battalions as they came along and by 11 a.m. the whole of my brigade group, the three battalions, the field regiment of lorry-drawn 25-pounders, the anti-tank company and the machine-gun company were digging in on their new defence line.

The general situation in our new area might now be described as 'fluid'. I was out of touch with Division H.Q. and with the formations on my flanks, and had received no further orders about any further moves, which was strange as the situation was obviously rapidly becoming precarious. I decided to take Chambres, my Intelligence Officer, with me in the Humber brake and see what I could find out. I discovered Division H.Q. on the outskirts of Neuve Eglise, which was being heavily shelled. But they were out of touch with Corps H.Q. and with 4 Division, with whose movements 42 Division was supposed to conform. The Divisional Commander decided that Tim Moorhead, the G.S.O.1, should try to contact Corps, whilst I went in search of 4 Division. I ran the latter to earth eventually and found the G.S.O.1, Basil Denning, who had been at Camberley with me, in his field office. They had received their orders from Corps an hour before. Our two divisions, the 4th and the 42nd, were to withdraw to the Yser River that night, a march of thirty miles. There wasn't a minute to lose; I jotted down the gist of the orders in my notebook and set off, giving my grateful thanks to Basil, who was killed shortly afterwards.

We went at top speed to Neuve Eglise and were within a mile of Division H.Q. when a shell burst right over the Humber. I was pretty good about shell noises and had ordered Tranter to stop and everyone to get out and take cover. But Chambres was a bit casual about doing so, as were two British soldiers on the pavement. The two latter were blown to bits and Chambres was badly wounded. The Humber looked in a very sorry state but by a miracle it still went.

At Division H.Q. Tim Moorhead had not returned and George Holmes and I had to get out detailed orders in great haste. 125 Brigade appeared to have become completely lost. They got attached to some other formation and we didn't see them again until we got back to England.

That night we had much more difficulty in breaking contact. The Germans were obviously very much on the *qui vive* and there was heavy shelling all along my front as the battalions started to withdraw. We had another all night slog with the men becoming absolutely exhausted. The roads were choc-a-bloc with troops and refugees, and Jonah and I had once more to abandon the Humber and take to our feet.

I set up an intermediate H.Q. at Poperinghe, close to where I had first been in action next door to the 1st H.L.I. in the First World War. There were no tanks then. Now we narrowly escaped being eliminated by some German tanks coming along the Hazebrouk–Poperinghe road.

A motor cyclist despatch rider arrived in a spurt of dust with a message from George Holmes to say that I was wanted urgently at Divisional H.Q. But how on earth was I to get there? The dispatch rider provided the answer. He was a dirt track rider in civil life and suggested that I should get on the pillion of his motor cycle. We set off amid the cheers of my staff. We skidded round slow-moving cars and lorries, under horses' necks, up banks and in between the ranks of weary marching men. I had not enjoyed myself so much for years. I kicked out this way and that to clear the way and keep us on an even keel. My pilot was so pleased with my performance that he attached himself to me and never left my side until we arrived at Dover. At last we found George Holmes at a wayside estaminet, where he had set up a temporary H.Q.

My orders were to be in reserve to the 48th Division which was already in position on the line of the Yser. I was to select rest billets in the Rexpoede area for my units. The trouble was to convey these orders to them. And here again my D.R. was an invaluable asset and got me back to Brigade H.Q. the way he had come. It was Wednesday 29 May. The men of my Brigade Group had been on the go continuously for two days and two nights, including two rearguards, each between twenty-five and thirty miles. Many of them were asleep on their feet.

The brigade pressed wearily but steadily on, and by noon I had them all settled down into the rest areas held by 48 Division. We were now only one march from the Dunkirk defences, and the wholesale destruction of all surplus transport, kits and offices was ordered. Only brigade commanders' and C.O.s' cars could go on from here.

I had hoped that my exhausted men would get some rest; but no sooner had we finished this organized destruction than we experienced a situation which might well have brought us down at the last hurdle. A small force of German tanks and motorized infantry had somehow got through, or round, the widely extended 48 Division front and proceeded to create all the havoc they could in our area. I had left Brigade H.Q. in the Humber to visit my battalions with Derek Kay, my brigade transport officer, at the wheel to give Tranter a rest. The other units of my Brigade Group had now reverted to divisional control. I was on my way to the H.L.I. when I heard firing and saw German tanks moving across country on a line that would cut our road back to Brigade H.Q. We decided to pass straight on to the H.L.I. and try to find out what was happening by means of their wireless. But suddenly we saw two German tanks coming straight down the road towards us. Quick as a flash Derek turned the Humber and we took the only road now open to us, which led to 126 Brigade H.Q. and then on to Division H.Q.

It was not until an hour later that I managed to contact my Brigade H.Q. and learned that it had been attacked by German tanks. Jonah was now dodging about the country but had so far not been able to contact any of the battalions. I told him to keep on trying and to move Brigade H.Q. back to Hundshoote, where the Divisional Commander and I would meet him, if we could. After a somewhat precarious journey, during which we ran into a minor tank battle and my brigade signal officer was ambushed and taken prisoner, we reached Hundshoote and had a joyous reunion with Jonah.

I learnt later that when the tanks had suddenly appeared at Brigade H.Q. Jonah and Wright, my batman, with two anti-tank guns, had had a sharp encounter in which one German tank had been knocked out and two others badly damaged. For this gallant little scrap Jonah was awarded the Military Cross and Wright the Military Medal.

Meanwhile all battalions had been contacted, and each was ordered to send a liaison officer to me at Hundshoote as soon as possible. They all reported that they had been suddenly attacked in their rest areas by tanks and motorized infantry. All three battalions had had a bit of a scrap, especially the H.L.I., and were now being closely picketed by German troops. Philip Kindersley, the liaison officer of the H.L.I., had had particular difficulty in getting through to me and was obviously going to have an even more dangerous job to get back. But he did it and gained a very well deserved M.C.

Clearly this was no time for detailed or complicated orders. I told all battalions, and the units in rest areas with them, to break out before daylight and join me at a named rendezvous inside the Dunkirk salient. I left the method and exact timing to C.O.s, as they were all in fairly widely separated areas.

At 3 a.m. the Divisional Commander and I, and our respective headquarters, set off from Hundshoote as quickly as possible, and in inky darkness, on our last journey. It was not a pleasant one as we were an easy prey for almost any body of German troops. But fortune favoured us and our road was clear. All my battalions broke through successfully – only the H.L.I. having any serious opposition. Having got well away, one of their companies bumped into a large party of Germans on the road and a savage fight in the dark took place, in which the H.L.I. suffered rather severely, but gave as good as they got. Once again I had the whole brigade under my hand, although quite a number of men were missing, many of whom joined up with me later.

It was now Thursday 30 May and some four divisions of the B.E.F. and many administrative units had already embarked from Dunkirk or from the beaches of Bray dunes. The situation within the Dunkirk salient has been described by many writers. It presented a scene of organized disorder. Although personal effects, offices and a good deal of transport had already been destroyed outside the salient, operational transport and weapons had been brought in and, except for those units manning the salient, they all had to be destroyed systematically before embarkation. Personal weapons, such as rifles and light automatics, were retained, although in some cases where men had to swim or wade deeply out to boats these were lost. On all sides lorries were being broken up and stores, guns and ammunition destroyed.

A French cavalry regiment rode in, dismounted and shot their horses, leaving a horrible mess and an increasingly disgusting stench. On the beaches large crowds of men waited patiently and quietly to be embarked.

Meanwhile an ever-increasing number of German troops were hammering at the salient; the artillery fire and the bombing became heavier. Suddenly I received an order from the Divisional Commander to say that I was to proceed at once to do a reconnaissance, with the commander of another division (General Curtis) to select a final lay-back position for the B.E.F. to hold when they retired from their present defences in the salient. I was amused to see that my companion was wearing the 'gong' that the French used to present to distinguished officers visiting the impregnable Maginot Line. It bore the words, 'On ne passe pas', and here we were almost in the sea!

It was getting dark when I arrived back at Division H.Q. with my report. There I received orders that my brigade was to move down to the Bray beaches at 10 p.m. that night. With the exception of my Humber brake all vehicles had now been destroyed, as had all personal kit and baggage. I stood on the steps of the little house which we had been using as Brigade H.Q. to watch the battalions file past. There was some desperate fighting going on in the salient that night and our sister brigade, 126, with whom we had shared so many adventures in the past few weeks, had gone into the defence line. They were not due to embark until the next day and during that night's fighting they gained one of the first V.C.s of the war. This was won by Captain H. M. Ervine-Andrews of the 2nd Battalion East Lancashire Regiment.

All round the salient the Verey lights were going up, just as they had done at Ypres in 1915. The din was terrific: a constant blaze of musketry punctuated by the crash of artillery fire, of bombs, of exploding ammunition and of our own guns being destroyed. Only in front of me was there a line of darkness and silence which marked the beach area, with the battered ruins of Dunkirk blazing from a hundred fires. When all the units were well on their way Jonah and I, Phil (the Staff Captain), Tranter and Wright drove slowly down to the Bray dunes. We left the car with Phil and Tranter, as Phil had some job to do, and the Humber, which had served us so well, was broken up by them before they embarked from the jetty at Dunkirk.

Once having arrived in the beach area we came under the directions of the Embarkation Commandant. Part of 127 Brigade were sent on a weary seven-mile tramp along the coast road to Dunkirk and the remainder, which included my own Brigade H.Q., and George Holmes with his Divisional H.Q., were ordered to embark from the shallow sandy beach of Bray dunes. Long narrow planks on wooden piles had been rigged up stretching some way out into the sea. We were shepherded on to these and there we stood for two hours waiting for boats to take us off, but none arrived. When we were ordered back on to the beaches a German battery opened up on us with such accuracy that a number of casualties were caused. This was a most unpleasant moment in the pitch darkness, with the groaning of the wounded and the pitiful cries of the dying. However, the firing was not continued, and the direct hits must have been a pure fluke.

I had hoped that we should be well on our way before dawn and the German bombers were up, but this was not to be. When it did get light we could see a mass of little ships of every kind lying off the beaches, whilst further out lay some naval destroyers and passenger craft of deeper draught. A small motor-boat was allotted to George Holmes and his staff and we were given a large sixteen-oared ship's boat which was lying well up on the beach. I took Jonah, Wright, one officer from Division H.Q. who had been left behind, and seventeen N.C.O.s and private soldiers. There was no difficulty about getting the boat into the water; it was only when we had done so that I discovered that none of the men could row and, curiously enough, none of them could swim. Just as we got the oars sorted out and I was giving a little elementary rowing instructions, with Jonah at stroke and myself at the tiller, the first morning flight of German bombers appeared. Conditions were not ideal for the rowing lesson; but the rudiments had to be mastered before we could make any headway at all. I was irresistibly reminded of a romantic novelist who wrote of her hero in the Oxford and Cambridge boat race : 'all rowed fast but none so fast as stroke'!

Whilst we went round and round like an intoxicated centipede the bombing really started and the din was terrific. However, my crew at last came to the somewhat painful conclusion that we must either proceed by some orderly method or not at all. So they grimly settled down to it. They had obviously fixed their eyes on some of the comfortable looking shallow-draught vessels which were lying close inshore, and I could feel them pulling against the rudder in that direction. But I had my eye on a long thin destroyer which was lying farther out, and it was quite a battle of wills and muscle to keep them on the course I had selected. The Divisional Commander had obviously had the same idea, and we saw his very overladen motorboat chugging slowly towards the destroyer.

In the end we got there first and I shall never forget the comfort we derived from the solid, cheerful and immensely efficient officers and men of the Royal Navy. They pulled us all aboard and stowed us wherever there was space, either above or below decks. The destroyer waited until every inch of deck space was filled and then, at 6 a.m., she up-anchored and started to zig-zag her way across the Channel.

The submarine menace was probably more serious than the bombers, but it was certainly a quieter one and soon the rest of our little party, the General's H.Q. and mine, had fallen into an exhausted sleep. But I had got beyond the stage of sleep and lay on my back, with my head on my haversack, thinking over the amazing events of the past three weeks. It was now about 7 a.m. on Friday 31 May, and almost exactly three weeks since the Germans had invaded Belgium. In those momentous weeks the Allied Armies had sustained a catastrophic defeat; the Belgian Army had laid down its arms; the British were re-embarking for home, and the French Army, thoroughly disorganized and demoralized, was on the brink of an even greater disaster.

I don't think any of us who made that journey back from Dunkirk will forget our arrival at Dover. The organization there was superb. And everything possible was done to make the B.E.F. feel that, though defeated, they had done their best.

We found our train was bound for Worcester, where the Centre Commandant, Colonel Rupert Lee, was an old Dragon School friend of mine. He sent me straight to his house; a phone call was put through to Frances and within a few hours we were celebrating a reunion which neither of us had thought could ever happen again. All over Britain these joyous reunions were taking place; in little streets, in country villages and in the great cities.

On Sunday 2 June, Colonel Lee held a Church Parade at which he asked me to take the salute. I stood at the saluting base in the lovely old red brick triangle of the depot of the Worcester Regiment while the troops marched past. Even in this short time they had cleaned and smartened themselves up, but they were a motley collection from every type of unit in the British Army. My arm raised at the salute began to feel like lead. And still more men came swinging past, over four thousand of them. Up to this moment I had no idea how tired I was. I felt very proud to have been privileged to take part in this great adventure with them; the very glorious disaster of Dunkirk which will be remembered as long as British history itself.

CHAPTER ELEVEN

Peril of Invasion

THE disaster, and yet the miracle, of Dunkirk had aroused and united the whole British nation and the inspiring broadcasts of Winston Churchill had stimulated every man and woman in the country, but the menace of a German invasion weighed heavily on the minds of the Government and the senior military commanders. It was true that an incredible number of men from the B.E.F. in France had been brought safely home, but they were now far from being a trained and equipped fighting force. Their guns, equipment, transport, tanks, ammunition and a large number of their small arms weapons had been left behind in the Dunkirk salient. We were very fortunate that Field-Marshal Goering was Hitler's chief adviser at this critical time. He of course was in charge of the powerful German Air Force: he was also a very conceited man and was absolutely confident that the Luftwaffe would defeat, and ground, Britain's Fighter Command and lay the way open for an overwhelming sea, land and air invasion.

And so in August 1940 the great German air offensive against Britain's Fighter Command was launched, which became known as the Battle of Britain – one of the most decisive battles in the history of our country, and indeed of the world.

The battle worked up to a crescendo until finally, on Sunday 15 September, 56 German aircraft were shot out of the skies over Britain. The Battle of Britain had been won, but by how narrow a margin no one will ever really know.

During these crucial months of July, August, September and October 1940, I attended many conferences and discussions on the possibilities of a German invasion; what form it might take and how we could best defeat it. Few informed people really believed that Hitler would not attempt it and I never came across anyone who really knew the inside situation and did not pray fervently that he would not try.

On their return from Dunkirk 127 Brigade was re-formed at Stokesley in Yorkshire. There was little I could do whilst the battalions were arriving and being re-formed and re-armed, so Frances and I went to London for a few days. There I lunched with General Pug Ismay, Winston's Chief of Staff and Secretary to the War Cabinet. Pug, who was an old friend of mine, had just returned with Winston from France, and on the day of our lunch the Reynaud Government fell and Pétain took over.

Back at Stokesley things were beginning to happen. George Holmes had been given command of the 10th Corps and 'Ulysses' Wilcox, a fellow student of mine at Camberley, succeeded him in command of 42 Division. I had received my sixth mention in despatches for Dunkirk and was one of the comparatively few brigade commanders to be thus honoured.

Air raids on Britain were now taking place on an increasing scale and the general official opinion was that invasion was certain. We began a series of intensive anti-invasion exercises and started to dig defence lines. By 6 July the Brigade had been completely reorganized and re-equipped with rifles, Bren guns, and anti-tank rifles; but we had no signal equipment, practically no transport, very little ammunition and no anti-tank guns.

On 8 July we were moved to Barnsley in Yorkshire, where we were visited by General Ronald Adam, who was now G.O.C. Northern Command. From there we moved to Penistone, where we had an extensive anti-parachute landing role on the Yorkshire moors. I was heartily glad that the Germans didn't attempt it. The area we had to watch was enormous for the troops at my disposal, and our mobility with antiquated London buses was so poor, and our communications were so inadequate, that we would have been lucky indeed to get information of an air landing and to get to it within hours of its happening.

All through July anti-invasion exercises continued and I kept my battalions constantly on the moors until they knew every inch of the ground and the roads and main roads in the area. The air raids on Britain increased in intensity and we watched with a great thrill some of the aerial combats between the German raiders and the British fighters. On 18 August twenty-four bombs fell in my brigade area (without any damage being caused) and there were damaging air raids on Sheffield and Manchester. On 26 August the Germans started night bombing.

The code word which meant that an invasion had started was 'Cromwell'. It was of course highly secret and was only disclosed to the more senior officers in responsible positions. I received the signal

'Cromwell' at 8.30 a.m. on 7 September, and then orders that the brigade was to move by M.T. next day to Wheatley, Oxford, where we were given a counter-invasion role on nine widely separated aerodromes on which parachute and air-transported troop landings were expected. However, 'Cromwell' had clearly been a false alarm and a few days later the emergency 'stand to' was cancelled. But what a flap it had caused.

At Wheatley 'Brooky' (General Sir Alan Brooke), who was then Commander-in-Chief Home Forces, came to inspect 127 Brigade. He had been one of my teachers at the Staff College and was to become Chief of the Imperial General Staff, Chairman of the Chiefs of Staff Committee, and one of the greatest Allied staff officers of the war. He had already commanded 2 Corps with great success in France and would, in my opinion, have also been a great commander if he had had the opportunity – but he was much more valuable as Chief of Staff. We had an enjoyable talk and he was complimentary with regard to the way I had conducted the operations of my Brigade Group in France. I had every prospect of getting command of a division at home, serving with all the officers with whom I had worked at the Staff College, Camberley – provided always that I was not recalled to India.

Shortly afterwards, when things had quietened down, General Sir Claude Auchinleck, who was in charge of the important Southern Command Defence Area of England, asked me to go down to his headquarters at Salisbury and spend a day with him looking round his defences. It was a tremendous feather in his cap that, as an Indian Army officer, he should have been given, first the very sticky job of commander of our troops in Norway, and then Southern Command in England at one of the most critical times in our history.

I arrived at Auchinleck's headquarters at Wilton House almost before he had finished his breakfast so that we could make the most of the day. It was a lovely autumn morning and we set off in his car, taking our lunch with us. We had had the same military upbringing, had both been teachers at the Staff College – he at Quetta and I at Camberley – and had both served in operations on the Indian frontier together, so we spoke the same military language and had learnt the art of soldiering the hard way.

During the day we saw much of his defences, walked miles over beaches and up and down sand dunes, checked arcs of fire, talked to local commanders and thoroughly enjoyed ourselves. He was gay and self-confident and gave out an aura of assurance to the troops. He fired questions at me all the time and I gave him frank answers.

At the end he asked : 'Well, what do you think?'

I replied : 'I think that with the men and equipment and the supporting arms at your disposal you have tackled the problem wonderfully well – but the distances are terrific, the troops very thin on the ground and communications stretched to the limit. I can only hope it never happens.'

With an infectious grin Auchinleck said : 'Between ourselves, Jackie, so do I.'

That night after dinner Auk let me into a secret, and also gave me some information which was to affect my own future fundamentally. In fact this was to be the next big milestone in my life, but again one over which I had no control. He told me that provided there were no untoward happenings in the next few weeks he would be appointed Commander-in-Chief in India and that when that came to pass one of the first things he intended to do was to demand my return to India at once.

I must say that this came as a douche of cold water to me. There was no one under whom I would rather have served than Auchinleck; but I was now in line for a divisional command at home and I had hoped that I would have been allowed to remain in the Western theatre, at least until the war was over. However, he was adamant that I belonged to the Indian Army and that all my previous training and experience had fitted me for high command with mixed forces of British and Indian troops. I was glad for his sake that he was about to attain his life's ambition, and flattered that he thought so highly of me, but at the same time I hoped that with all the important matters on his plate he would forget about me.

On 1 November the Brigade moved to East Anglia, where we took over a coast defence role. The Germans were now doing a lot of night bombing of selected sites and the invasion of Britain was still considered likely, but I felt somehow that Hitler had now missed the bus so far as that was concerned.

On 3 December H.R.H. the Duke of Gloucester again spent a very pleasant day with the brigade. I had not seen him since 1 May, when he showed me round the defence sector at Halluin. Since then we had both been through some exciting times. I liked him very much and he seemed to like me.

With the coming of winter our constant coast watching and anti-invasion exercises became very trying for all concerned. On 16 December a most important exercise was carried out at Felixstowe in my brigade area. Around long stretches of the coast, which were considered likely invasion approaches, miles of steel scaffolding had been erected at vast expense. It was believed that this type of obstacle would be proof against the impact of the Belgian barges which the Germans were thought likely to use, though no one knew for certain. A full dress trial was now to be carried out.

On this very cold and foggy winter's morning the sea front at Felixstowe was stiff with brass hats from all three Services, together with all sorts of high civil and political dignitaries. The demonstrations were run by the local naval authorities, so I had only a watching brief as the local brigade commander. There was a printed programme of events, heavily marked *Secret*, for the selected few, which described in detail the size, speed and weight of load of each of the two barges taking part, and the time they were to make their runs. The general opinion seemed to be that the barges would bounce back from the scaffolding and probably overturn, so all the crews manning them were wearing life jackets. I took up my position next to the naval officer in charge of the demonstration and the harbour master, both of whom were equipped with megaphones and field-glasses.

The cold grew bitter and the fog thicker. Only the importance of the occasion held everyone's attention. There was a long delay and then the first of the barges could be seen emerging from the fog. But it seemed to me that it was off course and making for Felixstowe pier instead of the beach in front of us.

I said in a still small voice: 'I think that barge is going to ram the pier.' I was favoured with glances of withering scorn from my two naval companions. The harbour master, however, took a look through his field glasses and yelled: 'My God, it *IS* going to ram the pier.' And, my God, next minute, with a sickening crash, it *DID* ram the pier. The contest was really a draw because although the damage inflicted on the pier was more severe than that done to the barge the latter was in no condition to take any further part in the demonstration.

There was a long and depressing pause. The fog thickened and visibility extended only to about two hundred yards beyond the scaffolding. Suddenly the second barge appeared, coming dead on course so as to hit the scaffolding just in front of us. Standing up in the bows was a blue-jacket with a boat hook. Everyone yelled at him through every megaphone: 'Get down, you bloody fool – look out – you silly idiot – you'll be killed.'

But the blue-jacket obviously didn't think that these rude remarks could be addressed to him, for he took not the slightest notice. Next moment the barge hit the scaffolding – and went through it like a knife through butter. All that could be heard was a faint metallic tinkling sound of falling steel – and there stood the blue-jacket scooping up the remains with his boat hook as the barge ran up on to the beach. There was no applause from the spectators, only a shocked and ghastly silence.

Frances and I spent a very happy Christmas together; we saw the

New Year in and returned to East Anglia. What with the snowy weather and icy roads the troops were getting fed up to the teeth with the constant strain of remaining in a state of instant readiness for something that never happened. On 27 February we were relieved in our coast defence role in Suffolk and moved to Chelmsford in the Southern Area, where we had an invasion counterattack role.

On 14 March I was informed that General Auchinleck, now Commander-in-Chief in India, had promoted me to full colonel with backdating to 1936, and requested my return to India immediately. This put me high on the list for promotion – in fact well above Bill Slim, who was two years older. I went up to London and saw General Muspratt in the India Office and Pug Ismay, but they both advised me to 'go quietly'! The Auk carried too many guns. My greatest consolation was that I should now be serving under him again. Little did I know that soon after I arrived in India he would have departed to relieve Wavell in command of the Desert Army, and I would fight my last and grimmest battle serving under completely strange commanders.

My next worry was about Frances. She was desperately anxious to come with me, but the Atlantic had become a battleground, with the Germans attempting, by submarine and surface raiders, to sink every ship in sight. But Frances is a courageous and determined person and in the end she had her way and we were allotted passages in the *City of Venice* which was due to leave Liverpool early in April. Although anxious for her safety we both felt that if we had to be drowned it was better to drown together.

I bade farewell to my beloved 127 Brigade on 1 April, with the pipers of the Highland Light Infantry playing me away, and the Divisional Commander and all the officers from the Brigade and many others there to say goodbye. In the fourteen months I had commanded them we had been through unforgettable times together – hard times, dangerous times and good times. My admiration for them was unstinted and my gratitude and affection for officers and men was deep and lasting.

CHAPTER TWELVE

Return to India

ON 13 April 1941 Frances and I embarked from Liverpool on the *City of Venice* and arrived in Bombay on 3 June, after an adventurous voyage lasting fifty days, dodging surface raiders and submarines. April 1941 was the height of the Battle of the Atlantic and we had to go almost to Iceland and halfway to America before we were able to adopt our proper course, which took us round the Cape. A wartime voyage under these dangerous conditions meant sleeping in one's clothes, and in the total blackout erected in the early evening, which was very trying in tropical waters. We were thankful to stop at St Helena, where we were able to visit Napoleon's tomb on the 120th anniversary of his burial and to spend a few days in Cape Town and Durban.

General Auchinleck thought that I must have been lost at sea and there was no immediate divisional command vacant for me. I was therefore posted temporarily to command the 36th Indian Brigade which was forming in a hutted camp at Baleli just outside the big military cantonment of Quetta in Baluchistan. The day after my arrival General Auchinleck visited the Brigade and gave me a very warm welcome. My Brigade Major was Captain Latif Khan. He was one of the first Indian officers to be posted to an important staff appointment and he proved most satisfactory.

As the only Indian Army officer who had held a command at Dunkirk I was in great demand to give lectures on the subject to the Quetta Staff College and to other audiences.

Suddenly misfortune fell upon me in a way I could never have guessed. Throughout the whole of my service in India I had always kept extremely fit and had managed to avoid all the plagues and fevers which afflict the white man in the tropics. Now, for no known reason I contracted a disability known in medical circles as an anal fissure, which is generally regarded as a most painful complaint. On top of this I developed a bad go of malaria which compelled me to enter the Quetta hospital. I came out a few days later feeling very weak and went back to my job in Baleli.

In the meantime General Auchinleck was appointed to relieve Wavell as Commander-in-Chief in the Middle East, and the latter took his place as Commander-in-Chief in India. I did not know Wavell and wondered what my future would be.

But my fissure trouble had now got so bad that I had to go into hospital again. The doctors discovered not only a fissure but an internal abscess and insisted that I should be operated on immediately. I had always sworn that I would never have an operation in India but now I had no choice. At this stage of the war many of the top surgeons, doctors and nursing sisters had gone overseas and those that remained were very overworked, and many of them were either elderly or inexperienced. It was the subsequent treatment even more than the operation which laid up for me so much trouble later on. I had had the operation and been in hospital a few days when Quetta was struck by a very severe earthquake which many people considered was worse than the disastrous one in 1935 which had caused such terrific damage and such appalling loss of life. Since then however Quetta had been largely rebuilt with earthquake-proof houses and the hospital was an entirely new building constructed on earthquake-proof lines.

Flagstaff House, where Frances was staying with the Commandant of the Staff College, 'Ozzy' Osbourne, was one of the newer buildings. She was having breakfast with the Commandant and his family when the 'quake started. She described it as a loud rumbling noise and then the floor started to rock and roll. They all realized as soon as the noise started that it was an earthquake and, gathering up the children, they rushed for the door to get outside. The floor was shaking so much that everyone fell in a heap in the doorway, but they managed to get out into the garden safely, to see the flagstaff rolling from side to side at an angle of 45 degrees.

The hospital began to shake and sway so violently that it was considered that the patients should be brought out into the open immediately and every patient who could possibly walk, which included me, had to rise from his bed and help to carry out those who could not help themselves. The result was that my wound broke out again.

Nevertheless, I was soon out of hospital and on the road to recovery when, on 2 October, I got a telegram from Army Headquarters in Delhi, offering me the appointment of commander of the 18th Indian Division which was due to form immediately in Secunderabad. This carried with it the acting rank of major-general. The decision I had then to make turned out to be one of the most important milestones in my life, and this time it was one that was entirely within my own control. Had the 18th been an active division I would have refused without hesitation on medical grounds, but the division did not exist as yet; it had first to be formed, and then trained, and would not be fit for active service for at least six months. I felt confident that well before then I would have become completely fit and ready to command the division in whatever theatre of war it might be sent. I discussed the matter with the head military doctor in Quetta. He was very sympathetic and said that as he had not been officially informed of my appointment and had not been called upon to give any medical report on me, he didn't propose to throw any spanner into the works. He considered, however, that the climate of Secunderabad was excellent; I would, to start with, have only a watching brief without any undue strain and there appeared therefore no reason why I should not accept. I therefore wired back accepting the appointment and said I would be arriving in Secunderabad immediately.

But things don't always turn out as one anticipates – particularly in war. Bill Slim said to me years later: 'Jackie, how silly you were to rush into action. Why not let others take the first shock and come in yourself when the early disasters, which Britain always has at the beginning of all her wars, have been overcome.' And of course, being wise after the event, I should have refused the appointment and taken two months' sick leave instead; in which case I might have become a Field-Marshal!

On 16 October I left Quetta with few regrets, largely because I had been so ill there. Secunderabad was a delightful part of India with which I was unfamiliar. The climate was good, there was wonderful training ground and every facility for sport. Flagstaff House was one of the most charming in the whole of India. Frances proceeded to furnish it with all possible speed, which was a considerable job as it was completely bare and we had no household goods of our own. The brigade commanders and their staffs had already arrived and the units were gradually arriving also, as were the members of my own divisional staff.

The brigades of these new divisions were numbered consecutively, thus 17 Division brigades were numbered 44, 45, and 46, and those of 18 Division were 47, 48 and 49. In 18 Division Brigadier Blight of the Royal Berks, commanded the 7th, Brigadier Hugh-Jones the 48th and Brigadier Whitehill the 49th. The battalions had of course all been 'milked' unmercifully to find drafts for the new battalions, but they did contain quite a proportion of their old pre-war personnel, and the traditions and background of these regular battalions were magnificent. Noel Hugh-Jones's 48th Brigade was composed entirely of Gurkha battalions, the 1/3rd, 1/4th and 2/5th, three of the finest regiments of the Indian Army. This division, composed of units disciplined and hardened on the North-West Frontier of India, than which there are few better training grounds in the world, was probably second to none in India. They were now required to fit themselves for mechanized warfare in the wide open spaces of the Middle East, and they had to assimilate mechanized transport and adapt themselves to a different method of warfare.

Obviously they would need more than anything else several weeks of basic training in the management and control of these new vehicles under their own commanding officers, and I had no intention of interfering with that. Then they would proceed to brigade training, and finally to divisional exercises. I set about holding a certain number of tactical exercises without troops for the more senior officers, so that we could weld the units and brigades into a corporate whole. I also set about getting to know as many of the regimental officers and senior N.C.O.s in the units as I could. In a short time we achieved an atmosphere of confidence and trust, which means so much to a fighting formation. Frances did a splendid job in getting Flagstaff House going and in giving a series of little cocktail parties at which everyone could get to know one another.

Every division, both British and Indian, had a divisional sign. At this stage of the war it was difficult to think of something striking yet simple which had not already been thought of by another division. I decided to have a competition in which anyone could submit his own suggestions. Frances asked if she could enter and I said she could provided her suggestion was anonymous. She submitted the striking 'Dagger' sign which was unanimously selected – and became so famous that the division was always known as 'the Dagger Division'. Meanwhile I was gradually getting fit and back to my usual form.

On 4 December only four days before the Japanese war started, a despatch rider arrived in Secunderabad with an urgent message. General Wavell wanted me to take command of 17 Division immediately. Only two days earlier I had received a wire from Army Headquarters saying that the number of my division must be altered from the 18th to the 19th in view of the fact that the 18th British Division was on its way to India and there might be some confusion; so in actual fact I did command three divisions in the same week – the 18th, 19th and 17th. And I don't suppose that has ever been done before.

The 17th Division were just completing their six months' training and were due to go overseas almost immediately. Their commander, General Lewis, generally known as 'Lewisa', had been the Indian Army teacher at Camberley a couple of appointments before mine and I knew he had not been too fit. Now he had sustained an accident to his knee just as his division was due to go on operations overseas. How lucky he turned out to be! He retired with a major-general's pension and lived happily ever after.

I was very sad to leave 19 Division, the Dagger Division, just as they were shaping so well. They were to make a great reputation a few years later under command of my friend, General Pete Rees, who had been one of my pupils at Camberley. In 1944, just after they had captured Mandalay, Pete sent me a signal in which he said: 'I wish you could have seen your baby 19 Division, Jackie. Even by your high standards I feel you would have given your approval. The chaps fought splendidly and now we have got to finish off the little yellow men altogether.' And they did.

Although I never thought of refusing this new assignment on medical grounds for a moment – that wasn't my creed – I could have done with another month or two in Secunderabad as I was still having a bit of trouble from my operation wound and the aftermath of the operation generally. And although General Wavell later criticized me severely for not having a medical board before accepting the appointment I don't believe that he would have done so himself if he had been in my place! In February 1942, just before the surrender of Singapore, he had a bad fall, broke two small bones in his back and became unconscious. But he absolutely refused to be hospitalized.

The 17th Division had suffered many interruptions to their training. Their infantry were all newly raised Indian battalions with a large proportion of very young soldiers. The Division had been trained and equipped with all possible speed for mechanized operations in the wide open spaces of the Middle East and their transport was all mechanized. They were now in camp near Poona engaged in their final manoeuvres and it was there that I found them on 8 December, the day the Japanese invaded Malaya.

It was soon obvious to me that they needed a good deal more training before they could be considered fit to engage a first-class enemy. I got my old friend, Brigadier 'Punch' Cowan, who was officiating as Director of Military Training, to come down from Delhi and have a look at them. He entirely agreed with me and arranged for them to have a further period of six weeks' training as soon as we arrived in Iraq. The last words Punch said to me as he left to return to A.H.Q. were: 'For God's sake get me out of here, Jackie.' And I very soon did.

In due course I saw off the 45th Brigade, under Brigadier Duncan, complete with their thick battle-dress against a winter in the desert. They were followed by the 44th Brigade, under Brigadier Ballantyne. I was then summoned to Delhi, on 28 December, for an interview with General Wavell at Flagstaff House. I had been informed previously by the General Staff that the 45th and 44th Brigades had been diverted at sea to Singapore and that I was to take my Divisional Headquarters and the remaining brigade, the 46th, commanded by Brigadier Ekin, to Burma where I was to form a new 17th Division. I shuddered to think what would happen to my two brigades in Malaya, completely un-equipped and untrained as they were for jungle warfare, and with their half tracked vehicle transport.

It was only some time afterwards that I discovered that the 45th Brigade had been flung immediately into a desperate engagement in which they had been almost completely annihilated. Brigadier Duncan had been killed while gallantly leading a counterattack, after his head-quarters had been hit by a bomb. The 44th Brigade had gone into the bag on Singapore Island.

I had only met Wavell once or twice whilst I was on the Directing Staff at the Staff College in 1931–3 and he was commanding a brigade at Aldershot. He was of course a leader of the highest repute who had already gained undying renown by his defeat of the Italians earlier in the war in the Western Desert. Since then however he had had a series of setbacks against the Germans and had eventually been re-moved from the Middle East Command and replaced by Auchinleck. Wavell had had to undertake vast responsibilities which no one could have surmounted. At the end he was a very tired man in urgent need of a long rest. Winston Churchill has recorded :

> At home we had the feeling that Wavell was a tired man. It might well be said that we had ridden the willing horse to a standstill. The extraordinary convergence of five or six different theatres with their ups and downs – especially downs – upon a single Commander-in-Chief constituted a strain to which few soldiers had been subjected. . . . General Ismay, who was so close to me every day, has recorded the following : 'All of us at the centre, including Wavell's particular friends and advisers, got the impression that he had been tremend-ously affected by the breach of the Desert Flank. His Intelligence had been at fault and the sudden pounce came as a complete surprise. I seem to remember Eden saying that "Wavell had aged ten years in the night".'*

* *History of the Second World War*, vol. 3, *The Grand Alliance* (Cassell, 1950), pp. 308–9.

This exchange of appointments between Wavell and Auchinleck was one of Winston's gravest errors, and it was his alone as he made it in defiance of the advice of the Chiefs of Staff and the earnest pleas of the Viceroy of India and Leo Amery, the Secretary of State for India. This is not to say that Auchinleck was not fitted for the North African Command nor that he did not carry it out brilliantly with the forces at his disposal at that time – he did. But Auchinleck was ideally suited for the post of Commander-in-Chief in India, particularly at a time when it was almost certain that Japan was coming into the war. And Wavell was essentially a Western soldier with little experience of the Eastern theatre.

General Dill, Chief of the Imperial General Staff, who was a friend and admirer of both Wavell and Auchinleck, was so firmly against the Prime Minister's proposed exchange of commanders that he wrote an immediate minute couched in the strongest terms and took it himself to 10 Downing Street. Dill was a farsighted strategist and knew full well that a war against Japan was imminent. He strongly advised that Auchinleck should remain in India, that a new commander should be appointed to the Middle East Command, and that Wavell should be given a good long rest which he so urgently needed, and for which he himself had asked.

Churchill however turned down Dill's request and said that he 'could not have Wavell hanging around London living in a room at his club and in India he could enjoy sitting under the pagoda tree'.

What Auchinleck and Wavell thought about it was their own affair;* they just had to do what they were told. But Auchinleck expressed in forthright and forcible terms his feelings about the Prime Minister's action. He realized however that it was an order which he must accept, and of which he must make the best. Wavell had made repeated requests for leave in the United Kingdom.

John Connell, who was Wavell's biographer as well as Auchinleck's, comments : 'The greatest statesman can be cruel and the most illustrious of generals can be tired and homesick. Wavell made no complaint : like the men he commanded he soldiered on. Five days after he had handed over to Auchinleck he flew to Delhi.'

On 12 December 1941 Burma was put under Wavell's direct command and on 30 December he became Supreme Commander of the Allied Forces in the South Pacific. What an impossible assignment !

For me personally the exchange of generals was a disaster. Instead of the general who knew me well and who had promoted me high on the Colonel's list and brought me back to India to command a division, I had someone who never really made contact with me at all. Apart

* *Auchinleck* by John Connell (Cassell, 1959), p. 241.

from his lack of knowledge of the Eastern theatre Wavell had another disadvantage: he had a very low opinion of the Japanese as soldiers, from which view he never deviated right up to the fall of Rangoon, and even after. He had therefore refused Generalissimo Chiang Kai-shek's offer of two Chinese divisions for the immediate defence of Burma when the Japanese war started, to be followed by more. Two months later Wavell was screaming for Chinese support, and General Hutton, the Burma Army Commander, was sent by air in a vain attempt to obtain it. The Americans were highly critical of Wavell's decision and maintained that it was the chief reason for the loss of Burma.

Field-Marshal Slim also criticized Wavell's decision in his book, *Defeat into Victory* (Cassell, 1956); and Wavell himself said in his Burma campaign despatch, written in 1942, and published in the London Gazette of 11 March 1948: 'I had every reason to suppose that I should have ample British, Indian and African troops available to defend Burma *which did not seem immediately threatened*' (the italics are mine).

These last words are uppermost in my mind when I look back on my interview with Wavell in his study at Flagstaff House, New Delhi on Sunday 28 December 1941. On that date the war against Japan had been in progress a bare three weeks but already the shadows of coming disaster were only too apparent. The American fleet had sustained a crushing blow at Pearl Harbour; Hong Kong had already capitulated; things were going badly for the Americans in the Philippines and with our own forces in Malaya; and Burma was obviously in grave and imminent peril of invasion.

In his review of the war situation which Wavell gave me in his study that day in Delhi he maintained that the Japanese had been over-rated and he did not consider they imposed any immediate threat to Burma. He had given Brigadier Taffy Davies exactly the same impression a few days earlier when he was on his way to Rangoon as Chief General Staff Officer to the Army Commander (General Hutton).

Opinions may vary as to Wavell's place among the British commanders of the Second World but I should very much doubt whether he could yield pride of place to any of them for sheer toughness of body, mind and spirit. His mental fatigue at this time, however, showed itself to his staff at A.H.Q. Delhi in his unwillingness to come to the office and give decisions on vital matters of policy, and to his subordinates, like myself, his unwillingness to consider – or even to ask – their opinions with regard to the operations in which their troops were engaged. Besides his unwisdom in under-rating the Japanese he never really understood the great difference in fighting value between the

4th and 5th Divisions he had had under his command in the Middle East, which were the elite of the Indian Army, and the new hastily raised Indian divisions which were being sent into action entirely untrained and unequipped for jungle fighting.

After a talk in which he hardly mentioned what I was supposed to do in Burma, Lady Wavell summoned us down to a most enjoyable tea, at which Wavell talked enthusiastically about pig-sticking, the new and thrilling sport in which he had lately become intensely interested. He could not have been more cordial to me personally, nor could he have shown more confidence that I would dispose of any little local difficulty with regard to the Japanese in Burma. As he saw me off he said: 'The General Staff will tell you the form. Look after Burma for me.' And he wrung me warmly by the hand.

As it turned out these were almost the last words that Wavell ever spoke to me. On his two fleeting visits to my division in Burma his complete silence indicated his strong criticism of my having had to withdraw from the frontiers of Burma in face of 'the despicable Japanese'. Major-General Billy Key, who had commanded the 11th Indian Division in Malaya, wrote to me (on 29 December 1969): 'Wavell had been a wonderful soldier and I had the greatest regard for him, but in Malaya he hardly uttered. He was inclined to adopt the attitude that the Japs were a rabble – why couldn't we stop them? But you and I know they were fine soldiers and fanatics.'

When I went to see the General Staff at A.H.Q. India they told me that Wavell had sent General Tom Hutton, the Chief of Staff, to Rangoon as Burma Army Commander. This was a great mistake from two standpoints: Tom Hutton was an excellent C.G.S. and his presence at A.H.Q. India was much missed: but he was no commander of troops in battle and Brigadier (later Major-General) Taffy Davies, Chief General Staff Officer of Burma Army, wrote to me after the war: 'To do him justice Tom Hutton had begged Wavell not to give him an executive command.'

The Chiefs of Staff in London were extremely critical of the appointment and very soon began to bring pressure to bear in various directions to get Hutton removed. But it was their own fault; they should have sent Alexander to command the Burma Army much earlier and not waited until Burma was almost lost. I am not trying to make out that any commander could have saved Burma at that time, with the quite inadequate troops available; but with Alexander in Burma and Auchinleck in charge of India there could not have been a Sittang disaster and the Japanese conquest of Burma would have been much more difficult and far more costly for them.

The General Staff at A.H.Q. had not much comfort to give me.

There were precious few reinforcements available. The Japanese had already started to infiltrate into Burma but their main line of advance was problematical, though their objective would obviously be Rangoon. My job would be to do the fighting. That suited me. It was the job for which I had been trained all my military life. Fighting was my business and I was the only general in India who had already had experience of modern war against the Germans.

Frances was an ideal soldier's wife. She got an apartment in New Delhi (not an easy job as Delhi was choc-a-bloc), and a job at A.H.Q. and faced whatever might befall with her usual courage. 46 Brigade were preparing to embark as soon as shipping could be provided. I flew out from Calcutta in the early hours of Friday 9 January 1942.

CHAPTER THIRTEEN

The Japanese Invasion of Burma

THE period from December 1941 to May 1942 was the most disastrous six months in the Second World War for the Allied cause, and particularly for the British. When the Japanese launched their aggression in the Far East it was plain to the Chiefs of Staff in Washington and London that, with the resources available there would have to be a period of 'make do and mend'; some stern rearguard actions would have to be fought and almost certainly some setbacks suffered before the tide in the Far East could be turned. The American and British commanders in the field in the Philippines, in Malaya and in Burma, were very unlucky in having to bear the brunt at this particular period of the war when the British were already stretched to the limit against Germany and Italy in the Western theatre.

During January and February 1942 the eyes of the world became focused on my so-called 17th Division, as they were the only troops available in Burma to stem the invasion of the highly trained Japanese divisions, backed by a superior air force, dead set to capture the Sittang bridge and advance quickly on Rangoon.

Burma's complete unpreparedness for war must be laid at the door of the British Government and the British Chiefs of Staff, who had been responsible for the defence arrangements of that country since 1935 when it was separated from India. When Japan struck in December 1941 the War Office in London, with almost indecent haste, planted their Burma baby in India's lap. At that time the defence forces of Burma were trained, organized and equipped purely as a police force with the primary tasks of maintaining order internally and controlling the frontier tribes. The air component was negligible. A very serious deficiency was the absence of any intelligence service. Consequently, when operations started there was nothing on which to build and the complete blindness which resulted remained a grievous handicap throughout the short campaign in which the fate of Burma was decided.

As soon as the war with Germany began India was pressed to provide everything she could find for the Middle East and Iraq. The result was that in December 1941 all India's trained divisions were overseas and only brigades and divisions in process of formation remained. The late Major-General H. L. Davies, C.B., C.B.E., D.S.O., M.C., was one of the finest fighting soldiers in the Indian Army. He was C.G.S. to General Hutton, and then to General Slim, in the 1942 Burma campaign, and later commanded a division with great distinction. The operations of my 17th Division at that time can best be summarized in his words:

The 17th Indian Division was a very young unit, only partially equipped and completely untrained as a division. Having been earmarked for the Middle East it was on a mechanized basis and its battalions had had no experience of jungle warfare. Moving and fighting in the jungle needs special techniques, special equipment and pack transport. To put a mechanized division into the jungle means that you tie it irrevocably to a road because only by means of that road can you supply it.

But in the absence of anything else the 17th Division had to serve and it was, therefore, with the dice heavily loaded against it that this young and untried formation was despatched hurriedly to reinforce the tenuous defences of Burma.*

The 17th Division's state was even worse than this description implies. If 17 Division had gone to Burma as a division it would at least have had some cohesion. But Division H.Q. arrived in Burma with only one brigade and the formations tacked on to it when it got there were even more untrained than the brigades it had lost. General Davies continues:

At this time there was no real appreciation of the formidable character of the foe we were facing. General Wavell himself regarded the Japanese as a second-class enemy. This illusion persisted even after we had lost Malaya and Burma and after the experience of the Americans in the Philippines and elsewhere. In fact the Japanese Imperial Army, with its savage; hardy and completely fanatical infantry element, constituted as formidable an enemy as has ever been faced by any British Army. In addition, the Japanese armies

* In his foreword to my book, *Before the Dawn* (Cassell, 1957).

Winston Churchill comes to support me in Central Wandsworth on the eve of the poll of the General Election in 1945

Congratulating my opponent, the great Labour leader Ernie Bevin, on his victory in Central Wandsworth in the 1945 Election

Frances and myself after I had become Conservative M.P. for Norwood in the 1950
Election

had been specially trained in ideal training areas, for the type of campaign on which they were setting out.

Field-Marshal Bill Slim entirely agreed with General Davies. He wrote as follows :

The strength of the Japanese Army lay, not in its higher leadership but in the spirit of the individual Japanese soldier. He fought and marched till he died. If 500 Japanese were ordered to hold a position, we had to kill 495 *before it was ours* – and then the last five killed themselves. It was the combination of obedience and ferocity that made the Japanese Army, whatever its condition, so formidable, and which would make any army formidable. All armies talked of fighting to the last round and the last man. The Japanese alone did it.*

General Davies continues :

General Smyth, commanding the 17th Division, was unfortunate enough to find himself in the position which so often confronts senior British commanders at the beginning of most of our campaigns. He was fighting on a shoe string with inadequate, ill-equipped and semi-trained troops against a formidable enemy. He was ordered to gain time at all costs and to attempt to regain control of huge areas of territory. These orders compelled him to disperse his forces in widely separated forward localities without mutual support. Moreover, on some occasions he was not permitted to withdraw from an untenable position without orders from higher authority. While all his military instincts urged him to concentrate well back and to fight on ground of his own choosing, the political pressure being excercised on his Army Commander (General Hutton) enforced a forward policy with which, in loyalty, General Smyth had to conform.

Throughout the nightmare campaign which started on the Burma–Thailand border in the Dawna Hills, east of Moulmein, and ended over 500 miles further north on the Assam frontier. I was Brigadier General Staff, first with General Hutton, the original Army Commander, and then, after the evacuation of Rangoon, with General Slim, commanding the makeshift Burma Corps.

In this capacity I was in close touch with the formation commanders in the field. Our great anxiety was always lest the continuous series of reverses and rear-guard actions, fought in generally unsatisfactory tactical conditions, allied to the absence of supporting arms,

* *Defeat Into Victory*, W. Slim (Cassell, 1956).

of air support and of many of the essentials of life, let alone any luxuries, should sap the morale of the fighting troops to such an extent that they become unreliable. That this never happened must go to the everlasting credit of the divisional, brigade and unit commanders who led and encouraged their men with unfailing resource and courage.

It is I suggest comparatively easy to be a good leader when our troops are on the offensive and things are going well; it is a very different kettle of fish when everything is going badly, when the troops are strained and discouraged and when one's own mind is full of foreboding and anxiety. If in such circumstances a commander can maintain his own and his troops' spirits and by his personal will-power and determination inject renewed confidence into his command, then he must be a real leader. We had such leaders in Burma and Jackie Smyth was one of them. I never saw him other than composed, cheerful and radiating confidence, whatever his real feelings may have been. I know it always did me good to visit him. Every moment of the four months' operation was a test of guts and discipline. It is my personal opinion that the army in Burma, by its grim defensive tactics and by its refusal to surrender its freedom of action, saved India from invasion in 1942 when all the dice were loaded in favour of the Japanese.

In the Supplement to the *London Gazette* of the 11 March 1948, General Wavell said, speaking of the situation in Burma as he saw it in January 1942 :

I admit I did not at this time consider the threat to Burma serious. I overestimated the natural difficulties of the wooded hills on the Burmese frontier. Nor did I realize the unreliable quality of the Burmese units, nor the lack of training of the British and Indian troops. I was certainly guilty of an error of judgement in minimizing the danger to Burma, but it is doubtful whether, even if I had appreciated it thoroughly, I could have done much to help Burma.

This of course is a handsome apology from General Wavell but it did little to compensate 17 Division for all the obloquies which were heaped upon it over the operations in early 1942 which led up to the Japanese capture of Rangoon. Nor did the apology excuse the complete apathy at A.H.Q. India in the early days of the operations, when the Japanese war machine was working in top gear and the British in bottom. There was, for example, plenty of pack transport in India but none in Burma. Although it is true that India had no modern air force Britain could have sent to Rangoon (up to the end of February 1942) squadrons of modern fighter and bomber aircraft; but no urgent demands were made for anything of this nature. It is also true that when the Japanese captured the aerodromes of Mergui and Tavoy in Lower Burma in the middle of January 1942 they cut the air route from Britain to Singapore and prevented air reinforcements being flown to Malaya. But Rangoon airport remained open until the end of February and reinforcements could have been flown in which could have been of the greatest assistance to my 17 Division. The light tank brigade which was asked for by General Wavell in early February should have been demanded two months earlier. Just as Rangoon was on the point of falling a fresh infantry brigade arrived by sea from India. It could have been sent two months earlier.

As regards Burma's unreadiness on the civil side. Field-Marshal Slim, in *Defeat into Victory*, had this to say :

> Up to December 1941, even the military regarded the likelihood of invasion as remote, so it was not surprising that the Civil Government did not take any measures to educate and prepare the population for it. As a result no one was prepared for war and the series of British reverses came as a stunning surprise. The Burmese fighting forces themselves were affected in much the same way as their civilian brothers. They were hurriedly expanded with new recruits who had no military tradition and had incorporated in them civil armed corps such as the Burma Frontier Force and Burma Military Police, who were neither equipped nor trained for full scale war.

Apropos Bill Slim's remarks regarding the Burma Rifles, having seen them in action I, and all my brigadiers, came to the conclusion that they were quite unfitted to stand up to the Japanese in a regular role. Used in this way they were not only a weakness but a danger to other troops with whom they were co-operating. I therefore recommended to General Hutton that I should be allowed to use them as mobile, lightly armed guerrillas, operating well forward and on the flanks of my regular brigades. They could have lived on the country and been completely independent of the lorry transport which so limited the operational scope of my regular brigades. In this role they could have been invaluable and made a decisive effect on the outcome of the operations. But this very vital proposal was turned down flat by General Hutton. He replied to me in his DO/13/23/G of 2 February 1942 :

> I am quite clear that your proposal must be dropped. Instead of being a method of utilizing the special qualities of the Burma Rifles, it will

be regarded as a method of destroying them. They have certain good qualities and certain weaknesses and by putting one battalion in each infantry brigade [as he ordered me to do] we shall be able to use them to the best advantage. Anyway if you let it be known that you consider troops useless they will be useless and the result is very unfair to the officers who are in my opinion a very fine lot.

I had always felt that in this decision and in many others affecting the fighting efficiency of my troops Hutton was apt to be influenced by the views of the Governor with whom he lived in such close proximity in Rangoon. Very seldom during the operations did General Hutton come to my battle headquarters. He did however control the movements of my division by rigid orders made from the map and was not prepared to discuss any alternatives.

Taffy Davies tried in all loyalty to support his commander's decisions, whether he agreed with them or not. But he certainly had not agreed with this one, about the role of the Burma Rifles, as he confirmed in a letter to me years later (dated 29 December 1955): 'Your views on the unreliability and unsuitability of the Burma component of the Army were completely proved by events. They were never good at anything except patrol work. To employ them as regular infantry was murder.' Putting a Burma battalion in each of the regular Indian Infantry brigades and a regular battalion in a Burma brigade, as Hutton ordered me to do, merely weakened the regular brigades to no useful purpose, and after one trial I managed to avoid doing so.

This decision of General Hutton's with regard to the Burma rifle battalions was one of the comparatively few important ones he made himself, and would certainly not have had the support of his chief, General Wavell. The latter had written in his despatch on these operations submitted to the Secretary of State for War on 14 July 1942:

The Burma Rifles who composed practically half the available force were of doubtful fighting quality. The inhabitants of Burma have shown themselves brave and tough fighters in defence of their country, *but as irregulars in guerilla fighting. Regular soldiering and discipline made no appeal to them* [my italics].

I would emphasize here that I did not intend to use the Burma Rifles in 'patrol work', but as something much more important and offensive as *guerrilla fighters*. In this capacity they would have laid ambushes and attacked lines of communication, advanced aerodromes etc. I am in entire agreement with General Wavell here.

General Hutton, in his own despatch on the operations in Burma from 27 December 1941 to 5 March 1942, said:

The fighting troops consisted mainly of Burma Rifles. This force was in the process of expansion. It was soon discovered that while these units were of considerable value for reconnaissance and patrol work in the jungle they were not as a whole fit to stand the test of serious operations against an enemy like the Japanese.

Famous last words! The Burma Rifles would have been of 'considerable value for reconnaissance and patrol work' if they had ever been given a chance – but they were not. How generous it would have been of Hutton if he had added: 'General Smyth, the 17 Division commander, had wished to use them in an irregular role from the beginning of the operations but I had not allowed him to do so.'

My arrival in Rangoon on 9 January was not propitious. As my flying boat came to rest on the wide reaches of the Irrawaddy river the air raid warning sounded. Rangoon had already experienced two very unpleasant air raids, against which they had little protection. In this densely populated oriental city, with its mixture of races – Burmese, Indian and Chinese – its narrow streets and flimsy houses, it was almost impossible to put into practice any scheme for civil defence. As a result of their experience of air raids, which had resulted in heavy casualties, the native inhabitants of Rangoon City, and of the crowded dock area, had worked out a method of procedure for themselves. When the sirens went all those who possessed cars jumped into them and drove madly for the open country with all possible speed. The remainder downed tools and hid themselves in the nearest ditch or drain. There was complete pandemonium as the 'carriage folk' shrieked their way through the main streets, hooting their horns; then there was a still and deathly silence through which the noise of the engines of the approaching Japanese bombers obtruded ever more loudly like the voice of impending doom.

Now, at the sound of the sirens, the boats which had been on the point of coming out to take us off, put hastily back. The flying boat lay on the water in the bright afternoon sun like a sitting duck. It appeared impossible that the Japanese could miss seeing us, but they were dropping their eggs on the docks.

With the sounding of the All Clear things slowly began to come to life again. I thought: so this is the lovely Burma in which my father had spent all his service, the glamorous land of the pagodas about which

Kipling had written, 'Come you back you British soldier, come you back to Mandalay'. And I was coming. But what a welcome! General Hutton's A.D.C. was there to conduct me to Army Headquarters.

There I met the General for the first time. Tall, tough and wiry, with a rather droopy moustache; Brigadier 'Taffy' Davies, Brigadier General Staff; and Major-General Eric Goddard, the very capable head of the Army Administrative staff, who worked in the closest co-operation with my Colonel Gerald Thompson throughout the operations.

In my first conference with General Hutton in Rangoon he gave me a short but perfectly clear and correct appreciation of the situation. The Japanese had already advanced from the south and captured Victoria Point, with its airfield, in the southernmost tip of Lower Burma. But General Hutton quite rightly did not consider that the real threat would come from this direction. As their objective would certainly be Rangoon it appeared obvious that their main thrust would be likely to come from the direction of Raheng via Kawkareik–Paan–Kyaikto and Sittang. To block this immediate threat the 16th Indian Brigade, under Brigadier J. K. Jones, had already been despatched to Kawkareik right on the Siam border. The 2nd Brigade, under Brigadier Bourke, consisting of Burma Rifle battalions, stiffened by the 4/12th Frontier Force Rifles, attached from 16th Brigade, was spread over 300 miles of jungle country, and was also responsible for the defence of airfields of Mergui and Tavoy. It was actually a bad decision on General Hutton's part to give Brigadier Jones a vitally important task and then take away his best battalion to boost up the unreliable Burma Rifles.

There was also another possible line of approach in the north from Papun on to Sittang, so my area of responsibility extended from Papun in the north to Mergui in the south and eastwards to Reheng and the Three Pagoda Pass. This was an enormous area of jungle country extending for anything between 500 and 800 miles, depending on how the area is measured.

For this task I had at the time only two brigades, the 16th Indian and the 2nd Burma, although my own 46th Brigade was expected to arrive in Rangoon from India within a few days.

The Governor of Burma, Sir Reginald Dorman-Smith, had invited me to have a drink at Government House before dinner. He had been a subaltern in my battalion, the 15th Sikhs, and gave me a warm welcome. I think Government House Rangoon was one of the most hideous buildings I have ever seen. From the outside it looked like an enormous barracks or lunatic asylum; inside it was full of vast rooms and long slippery corridors. As I arrived at the gates I met General Lance Dennys, our liaison officer at Chunking, whom I knew well and was delighted to see again. He was killed shortly afterwards in an aeroplane accident. The Governor was full of confidence and appeared to think that the Burmese would rise up in wrath against the Japanese. In this he was sadly astray. I was not to see him again until Rangoon was on the point of falling and he had been forced to move his Government to Upper Burma.

The day after my arrival in Rangoon, Saturday 10 January, General Hutton and I set off at crack of dawn in the one Blenheim bomber the Air Officer Commanding could provide, to visit my detachments at Mergui and Tavoy. The Army Commander sat in the front seat with the pilot whilst I lay in the bomb rack. The Air Officer commanding did not much like the idea of this trip. He reckoned at that time that there were about 150 Japanese fighter and bomber aircraft within striking distance of Rangoon and it was more than likely that we might run into some of them on the way. The airfields of Mergui and Tavoy were now so close to the advanced Japanese airfields that they were only being used for emergencies and the principal role of their garrisons was to deny them to the enemy. The A.O.C. was so short of aircraft in Rangoon that he could only supply one Blenheim bomber and two antiquated fighters as escort.

We arrived at Mergui across the Gulf of Martaban after about three hours' flight. I was delighted to find there in command an old friend, Lieut.-Colonel Denis O'Callaghan, with his 2nd Burma Rifles plus two companies of the 3rd. Denis was a well-known Wimbledon and Irish Davis Cup Lawn Tennis player, with whom I had won the Delhi Open Doubles Championships three years running in happier days. His 2nd Battalion were quite the best Burma battalion in my command. His first responsibility was the airfield, although he had other responsibilities as well.

It took us another hour to reach Tavoy, flying along the coast of Tenasserim. Tavoy was the centre of the local mining industry which was still working at full pressure, but here again the main responsibility was the aerodrome. Tavoy was under closer threat than Mergui as it was within 300 miles of Bangkok, the main Japanese base in Thailand, and much easier to get at. The garrison consisted of the 6th Burma Rifles, a police battalion only just converted to a regular role and very raw and untrained.

I hate unnecessary detachments, particularly when our main force was so small, but these airfields were of the greatest importance to the Japanese and I agreed with the Army Commander that we had to try to hold them, although the garrisons were woefully inadequate and they fell to the Japanese like ripe plums.

We arrived at Moulmein, where my Divisional Headquarters was to be located, at 4 p.m. on 10 January. I then left General Hutton to continue his journey to Rangoon alone. The senior members of my divisional staff had already arrived by air. My G.S.O.1, 'Simmy' Simpson, Tommy Thompson, A.Q.M.G., 'Tuffet' Armitage, C.R.E., and 'Mac' Mackenzie, my A.D.M.S., were not only extremely efficient officers but my loyal and wholehearted supporters in good times and in bad – and there were not many of the former.

Colonel Raymond Pelly, the Commissioner, who had known my father well when he was in the Indian Civil Service, had kindly invited me to stay in his bungalow and he and his delightful family remained my lifelong friends, and I their lifelong admirer. Although Burma was as unorganized for war on the civil side as it was on the military, I have never met a more helpful, efficient and gallant group of civilians than those with whom I had to deal in Moulmein.

The Pelly family were typical of many splendid British civilians who had to face danger, captivity and possibly death in those very critical times, against a brutal and barbarous enemy. Their daughter, Fleurette, and her cousin, Pamela Gage, did invaluable work in my depleted Divisional H.Q.; Raymond Pelly was a stout-hearted colleague and adviser and his wife, Kathleen, red-haired, Irish and unconquerable, was a tower of strength, keeping open house in the evenings, organizing people to work in the hospital and much else. She had a delicious Irish tongue and didn't always understand the military situation. On one occasion she said to Fleurette: 'Don't tell anyone, but I think Jackie is moving his hindquarters across the river tonight!' a *mot* which never ceased to make us laugh.

Every British, Anglo-Indian or Anglo-Burmese woman was employed to the full and wanted to stay on to the last. But having heard reports of Japanese brutality to women in Hong Kong and Malaya I decided that they must all get out while they could. I felt sorry for Mrs Pelly having to leave her lovely house on the ridge in which she and her family had lived for years and jettison nearly all her belongings. About ten days later a Japanese bomb hit the house and destroyed it completely. The Pellys had many adventures in the next few weeks and were lucky to get away in one of the last civil airline planes.

I shall always remember the first air raid on Moulmein when I was staying in their house. It was at daybreak on 17 January when fourteen Japanese bombers with an escort of five fighters came over. From our slit trench up on the ridge in the Commissioner's garden we gazed in impotent rage at the raiders. The household presented a very comical sight, clad in night clothes and tin hats, whilst mosquitoes devoured exposed ankles – but not mine as the pair of Colonel Pelly's pyjamas he had lent me trailed on the ground, he being over six feet tall to my five foot seven.

The aircraft circled slowly round in the bright early morning sun and then dropped their bombs at leisure. Considering the lack of opposition they failed to do much serious damage but the effect on the local population was devastating. All the shops in the bazaar put up their shutters and a steady exodus of people into the surrounding country began. In some ways it was a good thing as it was becoming more and more difficult for us to feed the civil population in addition to my own troops, and the Burmese civilians could subsist quite comfortably on the rice of the country. But it did result in a great shortage of civil labour, on which we depended in many mays.

The Pellys (Raymond, Kathleen and Fleurette) are still alive and we keep in touch. I often wish the British people knew more about the very splendid behaviour of such people in Britain's darkest hour.

From the start of the campaign General Wavell had been insistent that my 17 Division should fight as far forward as possible and this objective was passed on literally by General Hutton. Both generals liked to see on their maps each day in far away Java and Rangoon the red line depicting the situation of my division as far in advance of Rangoon as possible. One reason for this was that even General Wavell had at last realized that the existing strength of my division might not be sufficient to stop the two Japanese divisions opposing me, with their superior air support, and that outside help, in the shape of Chinese and Australian divisions, might be necessary. The Australians would obviously not consider landing in Rangoon unless my division was shown as holding the Japanese well in advance of that city. The great danger in this remote control was that, by not allowing the fighting commander (myself) to choose his positions and decide how long he should hold them, a disaster might occur which would put the whole defence of Burma in jeopardy. This is what I warned might happen, and despite my warning it was allowed to happen.

On 12 January I set off in my car to visit 16 Brigade in the Dawna Hills, in the position the Army Commander had ordered them to hold. It took us the whole day to get there and the journey included the crossing of two rivers by ferry. It was not difficult to imagine what would happen if troops had to get across in a hurry, even if the ferrymen remained on the job, which was hardly likely. Within a few days that was what actually happened.

Brigadier Jones, whom I had never met before, was a first-class Indian frontier soldier, and although over fifty was as fit and active as many officers half his age. I took to him at once and my admiration for him increased as the operations progressed, but he certainly had been handed a very raw deal. Later, under Alexander's command, he was awarded a well-deserved D.S.O.

His brigade had just arrived in Burma and he had only taken command of them in India a few days before embarkation. His three battalions had been 'milked' to the last drop to send reinforcements to other newly formed units and had been made up to strength with a large batch of raw recruits three days before embarkation. They were therefore completely untrained and unequipped for jungle warfare. Their main transport was a small pool of lorries. They only had two battalions, the 1/7th Gurkhas (less a company detached watching the Three Pagodas Pass) and the 4th Burma Rifles, who were in the main position on the top of a thickly clad ridge, from which there was no visibility at all. The third battalion, the 1/9th Jats, had not yet arrived from Moulmein. When I visited the Burma Rifles I found they had four hundred cases of malaria (mepacrine was not yet available) and so far as fighting value was concerned they were useless for that reason alone.

No one could possibly have felt happy about Brigadier Jones's dispositions, least of all himself, stuck right out in the blue, with a couple of rivers behind him, but they were conforming with General Hutton's orders of fighting well forward – in fact they were right on the Siam border. If I had had the Army Commander with me, or there had been a corps commander, I would have advocated most strongly a withdrawal behind the rivers with a screen of Burma Rifle skirmishers well out in front. We should at least have been saved one disaster. But Hutton's orders were strict and rigid.

Burma Army had no Intelligence Service, and Taffy Davies wrote to me: 'I will accept any criticism you care to offer on the complete absence of intelligence about the enemy at A.H.Q. Rangoon. We possessed no intelligence organization and were completely dependent on you for our information.' It was a case of the blind leading the blind.

Before leaving next morning I got hold of the local forest officer, and he told me that the Japs might attack any day now. Hutton had, as he states in his despatch, ordered Jones 'not to get so involved as to render withdrawal impossible'. But this was easier said than done. When the Japanese assault came the ferry boat was sunk and after a hair-raising operation 16 Brigade arrived back in the Moulmein area having lost most of its mule transport, many of its weapons and all its M.T. Brigadier Jones received an imperial raspberry from the Army Commander for having withdrawn too soon. On the other hand if he had delayed any longer he would have lost his whole brigade. As it was this brigade really never recovered from its initial disaster.

Wavell, in his own despatch, comments on this operation as follows:

On 20th January, fighting began in Northern Tennasserim with an attack on the 16th Indian Brigade near Kawkareik. These engagements are described in General Hutton's report. It is quite clear that the enemy were allowed to gain cheap initial successes through bad handling by the local commanders, lack of training, and in some instances lack of fighting spirit on the part of the troops. It was an unfortunate beginning to the campaign and had serious results in raising the morale of the enemy and depressing that of our own troops. *It became clear that the battalions of Burma Rifles, which formed so large a proportion of the Army in Burma, were undependable* [my italics].

In all fairness General Hutton might have mentioned the grave disadvantages under which 16 Brigade were suffering and how completely raw it was.

I had now seen enough of my troops and the country in which we had to fight to come to some very definite conclusions as to how best we could engage the rapidly advancing Japanese in conditions most favourable to us. I did of course realize that the reason General Wavell wanted me to fight as far forward as possible, was in the hope that substantial reinforcements might be forthcoming. But it was obvious to me that we should not attain this object by holding widely scattered bits of Burma 'as long as possible', which was General Hutton's constant demand, but by concentrating our strength and giving the Japanese a real knock. Our present action was merely inviting defeat in detail, and was unsound from every military point of view.

The general pattern of the Japanese advance had now become clearly apparent. My distinguished and highly trained commanding officer, Lieut.-Colonel W. D. A. Lentaigne (later Major-General, C.B.E., D.S.O.), 1/4th Gurkha Rifles, who had just completed a period as instructor at the Quetta Staff College, and who was one of the most highly thought of officers of his rank in the Indian Army and certainly a whole-hearted supporter of mine, wrote with penetrating clarity in volume III of his regimental history :

The Japanese knew that we were tied by our transport to the roads. They, on the other hand, could carry what they needed on their backs or in light carts that could traverse any jungle track or byway. Rice was their staple diet and rice was everywhere abundant. It was reaped in Burma in December and, at the turn of the year every granary was full; rice with a modicum of fish and green stuff – to be had in any jungle village, almost in any jungle clearing – was the Japanese soldiers' whole diet.

He avoided our dangerous front therefore and pricked us in our vulnerable tail. He side-stepped and re-appeared behind us and our first inkling of his whereabouts would be a road-block in our rear, astride our communications, our life-line upon which we were completely dependent for food, fuel, stores and ammunition.

Sometimes these road blocks were simply well sited weapons, and the Japanese certainly knew how to site their weapons; sometimes they were strongholds thoroughly prepared and almost unbreakable. If we did succeed in breaking one it was set up elsewhere. The road therefore was denied to transport; and our forward forces could not be maintained.

Added to this frugal way of life, which made these simple tactics possible, the Japanese was physically tough and enduring. Moreover he was, if not fanatically eager to die, at any rate always ready to give his life for a cause.

He had, in short, all the first qualities of a soldier.

How very different from General Wavell's opinion of him !

I lost no time in submitting to General Hutton my first appreciation of the situation, the gist of which was that unless I was reinforced at an early date by two additional divisions, it would be unlikely that we should be successful in stopping the Japanese. As a first reinforcement I asked for the 48th Gurkha Brigade from my old 19th Division to be sent to me immediately.

My appreciation must have been passed on to higher quarters, as things began to happen. Orders were given for the 48th Brigade to be sent. (There was no reason why the whole 19th Division should not have been sent. They were sitting in Secunderabad merely training for desert warfare where they would never be required.) Wavell then made frantic efforts to obtain the two Chinese divisions he had so foolishly refused; and Churchill and Roosevelt both pressed Mr Curtin, the Australian Prime Minister, to send at least one division to Rangoon. But time, which had previously been our servant, was now in danger of becoming our master, and the servant of the Japanese.

The only position which offered a really good opportunity for protracted defence, followed by some action, was Sittang, where the broad and swiftly flowing river provided a really formidable obstacle and the open ground on the west bank of the river was suitable to the operation of our troops as opposed to the thick jungle which favoured the Japanese. There was only one bridge over the Sittang River, the steel railway bridge which the Army Sappers had been planking to take troops and transport.

There could be no doubt whatever that the possession of this bridge was a first priority objective of the Japanese in their thrust on to Rangoon. With their superior air force they could have destroyed the bridge any day they liked. Whatever else we did, in the absence of very substantial reinforcements, we must get the whole division across the Sittang River in sufficient time to give us a week to prepare a really strong position on the other side. When General Wavell set on foot steps to provide us with a regiment of light tanks my plan assumed even greater importance as the ground west of the river was ideal for their use.

But before further consideration could be given to this matter an important decision had to be taken with regard to Moulmein, which the Army Commander wanted to hold. It was of course an important Burmese city but of no military value whatever.

On 23 January Brigadier Taffy Davies came up to get my views on the defence of Moulmein. I recommended holding it with a skirmishing force of not more than one battalion. But unbeknownst to me General Hutton had already informed Wavell, and A.H.Q. India, that 'in spite of its disadvantages he intended to hold Moulmein as a bridgehead with one infantry brigade as long as possible'. This had Wavell's strong support. My last remaining brigade of the old 17 Division – 46 Brigade under Brigadier Roger Ekin – had now arrived, and they were a welcome reinforcement. Roger Ekin was a first-class commander.

I objected strongly to being compelled to hold this old pagoda city, which I knew well as I had had my headquarters there. And I considered it to be quite inexcusable that I, as commander on the spot, should have been forced to risk the loss of a third of my whole force in this very foolish operation. In effect, owing to the skill of Brigadier Ekin and the very courageous performance of his brigade, I managed to extricate them with the loss of 600 men and a great part of their arms and equipment. Ekin himself recorded in a letter he wrote to the official war historian in September 1955: 'Throughout the operation General Smyth was never given permission to withdraw in time. At Moulmein, Martaban and Thaton, we only got through by the skin of our teeth.'

However, the stream of signals coming from Wavell in Java to Hutton in Rangoon, showed how completely out of touch the former was with the situation of 17 Division and the two Japanese divisions which were attacking us. But Wavell's signals made Hutton tighten his instructions to me. Instead of my having to hold bits of Burma 'as long as possible', I was now ordered 'not to withdraw from them without the permission of the Army Commander'. And as the Army Commander was way back in Rangoon and often had to be away for several days in pursuit of his other extensive responsibilities, that made a nonsense of my command, which could not be carried out effectively under such rigid restrictions.

Wavell cabled Hutton on 22 January: 'I have no resources with which I can assist you. India as usual is providing all possible help. Cannot understand why, with troops at your disposal, you should be unable to hold Moulmein and trust you will do so. Nature of country and resources must limit Japanese effort.'

I did not of course know about these messages until I read Connell's excellent book, *Wavell, Supreme Commander* (Collins, 1969), many years afterwards – but the last sentence of the above cable is almost farcical.

CHAPTER FOURTEEN

The Disaster at Sittang

THE next defensive front which the Army Commander ordered me to hold was on the line of the Salween river from Martaban northwards. The main front from Martaban to Paan was some fifty miles in extent and we also had to hold Papun, a further 100 miles to the north. Our line of communications, which was also my responsibility, ran back by rail and road through Thaton via Bilin to Kyaikto and thence to the Sittang river.

To hold these enormous frontages battalions had to be given certain key points to hold while at the same time endeavouring to watch the intervening country by means of patrols. This meant that in many cases battalions were as much as forty miles apart. This policy gave no opportunity of any concerted offensive action on our part. General Hutton recorded in his despatches: 'Although the Divisional Commander was still anxious to withdraw to the Bilin I issued orders that the division was to fight hard to hold the line of the river Salween – and give no ground.'

On 3 February I motored back along the whole length of my lines of communication from Martaban to Sittang, about 100 miles as the crow flies. The road ended at Kyaikto and from there to Sittang it was just a rough track feet deep in mud and dust. The Army Sappers were busy making the steel railway bridge fit for road traffic and there was also the boat ferry, though this of course was a very archaic method of transport in a crisis, particularly as the boatmen disappeared at the first sign of danger.

I spent my whole time visiting the troops and morale raising in every way possible. Everywhere the Japanese were making contact with our troops and their air force was active – mostly on reconnaissance at this stage.

On Friday 6 February General Wavell flew over from Java and drove round my divisional area with me and the Army Commander.

He was obviously furious at the loss of Moulmein and never once spoke to me about my troops, my plans or my dispositions. In fact, for several hours he didn't utter at all. However, he did ask me one very important question : whether there was any scope in this type of country for the use of light tanks. I replied 'Yes' without any hesitation. He said he would cable to the Middle East for an armoured brigade. He could have asked me the same question weeks before over the telephone and we could have got this valuable reinforcement very much earlier. This was the 7th Armoured Brigade consisting of two regiments of light cruiser tanks, one R.H.A. battery and one anti-tank battery. They were due to disembark at Rangoon about 21 February and could arrive up at the Sittang some three or four days later, provided the dock labour was still functioning.

The only thing I asked Wavell to do was to say a few words to my staff and the brigadiers. However, in his short talk to them he reverted to his old theme that the Japs were no good and their fighting ability had been grossly exaggerated, and then astonished us all by saying that I was going to take the offensive and drive the Japs out of Burma. It wasn't the sort of talk I had hoped for and it depressed them deeply as it made obvious that he was quite out of touch with realities.

On Sunday 8 February I had a great acquisition in the arrival of 48 Gurkha Brigade from my old 19 Division, under command of Noel Hugh-Jones, for which I had asked almost as soon as I arrived in Burma. They were composed of the 1/3rd, 1/4th and 2/5th Gurkhas. Although, like the other troops I had, they were without training or equipment for jungle warfare, they were in my opinion better fitted for close jungle fighting than any other troops in India. Unfortunately they arrived with untrained mules and without pack saddles or leading ropes, but this was no fault of theirs. The Gurkhas came up into reserve bivouacs near my Division H.Q. at Kyaikto and I spent some hours of Sunday going round all the battalions and chatting with old friends. They certainly gave me a heart-warming welcome.

On the next day, 9 February, the Japs captured Martaban and were everywhere infiltrating between the extended and isolated positions I had been ordered to hold, and crossing the Salween river in small parties by boat. The Japanese air force was active all along the front.

On this day I had another welcome reinforcement in the shape of Brigadier Punch Cowan whom I had asked for as a reserve brigade commander. However, as I was responsible for such a very extended front and had so many odd units and was also getting the Armoured Brigade, I asked the Army Commander if I could keep him for the time being as my chief of staff. Punch was a tough and resolute fighting soldier in whom I had the greatest confidence and I was delighted to have his robust support at this critical juncture. He certainly gave it me in full measure, both during the operations and in the controversies which arose over them afterwards.

On the 10 and 11 February I had conferences with Punch and my other brigadiers, as a result of which I phoned to A.H.Q. to say that I was sending Cowan in to Rangoon with an important request for the Army Commander. Punch Cowan (and all my brigadiers) and I had all come firmly to the conclusion that unless I concentrated my division on the Bilin river immediately and then, *without further delay,* proceeded to withdraw behind the Sittang river we might well be risking a very grave disaster.

I should make it clear that the so-called Bilin river, which was marked as such on Wavell's and Hutton's maps, was at that time of the year, an almost dry ditch running through thick jungle country, which one could jump over. But it was at least a clear co-ordinating line, both on the map and on the ground, although quite unsuitable as a defensive position.

The official history records : 'Smyth told Cowan to impress on Hutton the grave danger in which 17 Division stood of being cut off from the Sittang bridge and to urge that he might be allowed to withdraw the division behind the Bilin river immediately and that there should be no delay in the next stage of the withdrawal which should be behind the Sittang river.'[*] Now nothing could be clearer than that and I confirmed it in a personal telegram to General Hutton.

Punch Cowan returned with a firm negative from the Army Commander to my making any withdrawal whatsoever from the Bilin, but agreement that he should stay with me as my Brigadier General Staff. In later years when Punch Cowan had to give his account of his interview with the Army Commander for the war history, he wrote to me on 8 October 1055 as follows :

I know that the Sittang disaster is laid at the door of H.Q. 17 Division and I have objected to this distortion of the facts. I was completely of your way of thinking. I am not likely to forget my ghastly journey to Rangoon as your emissary. I did convey your views most strongly [to General Hutton]. You will remember as a result of my visit I became your B.GS.

As a result of the Bilin delay we were doomed. We withdrew much too late, over a ghastly 'dirt track'. We were bombed to hell by our own aircraft as well as the Japanese and were already surrounded

* Major-General S. Woodburn Kirby, *The War Against Japan,* Vol. 2, *India's Most Dangerous Hour* (H.M.S.O. 1958), p. 41.

by Japs. The operations never had a chance from the word 'go'. The slogan was that Rangoon must be protected at all costs and we were sacrificed for that slogan!

But the sacrifice was quite useless. It neither deterred the Japanese nor did it do anything but disastrous harm to our cause. As both Hutton and Wavell made clear in their despatches on the operations, the destruction of my two brigades at Sittang made the loss of Rangoon and Burma inevitable. They both however maintained that it was my fault.

My chief administrative officer, Colonel (later Brigadier) W. G. N. Thompson, makes the position perfectly clear from his point of view in a letter to me dated 3 October 1955. He says:

> You were perfectly clear and decided from the first moment you had had a look at the troops and their dispositions, their transport and their equipment, that our only chance of putting up a real battle against the Japs was to concentrate your scattered division well back towards the Sittang, which was the only real obstacle. Naturally I supported you most forcefully because the supply and medical difficulties were made almost impossible by the forward isolated defensive policy which you were ordered to carry out.
>
> I must say you obeyed most loyally the Army Commander's orders for a forward defence; much as you disagreed with them. But the final stupidity was making you stand those four days on the Bilin which was no defensive position but only a co-ordinating line. That really did upset the apple cart. It completely exhausted the troops, resulted in heavy casualties which we found very difficult to evacuate, and stretched the transport and supply services to the limit when we could have been getting transport back.
>
> If we had got back to the Sittang ten days earlier how different things might have been. Even so you managed to get all the transport which could possibly be spared from the forward area back across the Sittang on 22nd February, and to the best of my recollection the only vehicles left with the fighting units were those essential to the tactical situation.

When the matter was under discussion during the writing of the official history in 1955 General Davies (Hutton's Chief of Staff) wrote to the historian, Major-General Kirby, on 4 February 1955, as follows:

> Wavell's misjudgement of the Japanese and his insistence on holding them up in fronts hundreds of miles wide, undoubtedly influenced

General Hutton. It was in the light of Wavell's constantly expressed views that Hutton turned down Smyth's very much sounder proposal to concentrate and fight a divisional battle on ground of his own choosing. I think I must mention that in discussing Smyth's appreciation with General Hutton I made it quite clear that I agreed with Smyth's conclusions.

The deductions I make are :
  (i) General Wavell's false ideas about the Japanese led him to force Hutton into unsound decisions
  (ii) Smyth, whose appreciation was absolutely sound, was placed in a series of impossible tactical positions
  (iii) The decisive battle for Rangoon, which had to be fought at the Sittang river, found 17 Division placed at the maximum disadvantage.

General Kirby was unable to find a place for this letter in the official history.

The official history, pp. 45–6, says :

On 13th February, after having interviewed Brigadier Cowan and seen Smyth's telegram reviewing the state of his troops Hutton sent the Commander-in-Chief in India an appreciation of the position. He said he had every intention of fighting it out east (the Japanese side) of the Sittang, but it was possible that the exhaustion of the available troops, and continued infiltration might eventually result in 17th Division being driven back to the river. Withdrawal of transport across the river would be very difficult since, except for the vulnerable rail-road bridge, communications consisted of boat ferries of which only one had a road connection. . . .

On 15th February Hutton heard that Smyth had withdrawn from the Duyinzk–Thaton position. From the information available to him at Rangoon at the time there seemed to be no reason for this withdrawal for there was little indication of the danger to the division's left flank and the line had not been attacked. He therefore wrote to Smyth expressing his disapproval of his action which he considered to have been premature. The same day, reporting the situation to Wavell, General Hutton said : 'I shall endeavour to stop this withdrawal but Thaton has already been evacuated'. . . .

It is easy to understand how, to Hutton, this withdrawal appeared at the time to be unnecessary, though afterwards he agreed it was justified and carried out only in the nick of time.

By 15 February the whole division, less the small detachments which were laid back to defend the Sittang bridgehead, was concentrated on the Bilin. One Japanese division was pressing us in front and another rapidly turning our flanks. Behind us was the single road, flanked by thick jungle on either side.

There were amusing interludes in these rather grim operations and we remained quite a cheerful crowd at Divisional H.Q. We were running the railway as part of our supply service but had to man it entirely by soldiers as all the railway personnel had disappeared. I was having a conference with my brigadiers after we had withdrawn to the Bilin when to our horror we saw the afternoon train from Rangoon to Thaton puff past into territory which was now held by the Japanese. British soldiers were driving the engine, the Indian military guard was admiring the view and the passengers, British, Indian and Burmese, were sitting looking out of the windows. They had obviously not been advised of the new situation, but they were past before anyone could stop the train. The question was what were we going to do about it. Some of my staff were convinced the train would return loaded with Japanese; so we laid on a warm reception accordingly and preparations were made to blow it up.

A few hours later however the train came puffing back still with the British soldiers, the Indian guard and a new load of passengers. The Japanese had been so flabbergasted by the unexpected appearance of the train that it had been loaded up with supplies and new passengers and had started off on the return journey before they had gathered their wits.

The next evening I had a telegram from A.H.Q. Rangoon to say that an important American war correspondent was visiting my headquarters. This seemed very peculiar as no war correspondent had visited us since the operations started. At one time Bill Slim's 14th Army of 1944 had been referred to as 'the Forgotten Army'. We might have been termed 'the Army no one had ever heard of' !

The divisional staff were billeted in a couple of old bungalows and my A.D.C. produced a camp bed for the war correspondent in a room occupied by four other officers. He went down to meet the train, which was due to arrive about midnight. Imagine his astonishment when out of the train stepped an exceedingly elegant young woman. All women had been evacuated from this area some weeks earlier. The visitor turned out to be the well-known Miss Eve Curie. She was reporting for the British Kemsley newspapers as well as for American newspapers. How she had managed to get there remained a mystery but she was a most determined young woman.

The A.D.C. hastily woke up the sleepy staff officers and told them not to wander around in the nude. I was naturally quite astonished when he brought her round to see me after breakfast next morning. I have met a great many war correspondents but never one with a quicker grasp of a somewhat complicated situation. Her book, *Journey Among Warriors* (Heinemann, 1943), was excellent. She was only allowed one day with us and my A.D.C. took her around all day in an armoured carrier. Despite all my instructions for her safety she captivated my A.D.C. to such an extent that she went a good deal further forward than I had intended. However, she escaped any trouble and was back to dine with the Commissioner and myself before catching the midnight train to Rangoon.

The only criticism she made of me in her book was that I smiled too much and changed into trousers for dinner. Later on, when I met her in London, she agreed that in that particular situation there was nothing else to do but look as cheerful as possible and a change from one's sweaty bush shirt and shorts into a long-sleeved shirt and slacks for dinner not only made one feel better but kept the mosquitoes from biting one's legs!

On 16 February General Hutton came up from Rangoon to visit me. He had just returned from an abortive air trip to the Chinese with his A.D.C. The pilots of the two Lysander aircraft had lost their way over the thick jungle country and run out of petrol. The pilot and A.D.C. in one plane made a fairly successful landing by parachute but the General's plane crashed into the jungle and burst into flames. The pilot was concussed and remained strapped in his seat. The General, though very bruised and shaken himself, managed to get the pilot out, but he died some hours later. General Hutton made light of this incident but it had naturally shaken him badly and he was obviously in pain. He looked ghastly and was really in no fit state to face the ordeals of the next few days. General Wavell, having refused Chiang Kai-shek's offer of two Chinese divisions earlier on, when they might have saved Burma, was now making frantic efforts to get Chinese assistance but it was now much too late to save Rangoon.

However, as the official history records (p. 60): 'Before returning to Rangoon Hutton reminded Smyth that the Bilin position must be held for as long as possible and *that there was to be no withdrawal without his permission.*' (The italics are mine though the emphasis was Hutton's.) This very definite order is confirmed in John Connell's book, *Wavell, Supreme Commander* (p. 180). Without risking a court-martial it was an order I could not disobey, disastrous though I knew it to be. General Hutton also informed me that Singapore had fallen, which would obviously free further Japanese air formations for the Burma front.

For the next four days the brigades and units of 17 Division gave everything they had to obey the Army Commander's order to stand fast on the Bilin. Even in this thick jungle country they showed what they could have done if the battle had been fought in an infinitely stronger position on the west bank of the Sittang. As I had no idea what the Army Commander's plans were it was impossible for me to make any of my own. I could have laid back troops or transport had I been taken into his confidence (I realized afterwards he had no plan), but I never was. All I could do was to keep A.H.Q. Rangoon clearly informed of what was happening on the Bilin by our daily situation reports. No intelligent commander could fail to read the Japanese intentions. The longer they could hold us on the Bilin with one division the more time they would have for enfilading troops of their second division to intercept us at Sittang.

The official history has this to say of the Japanese plans: 'General Iida ordered 33rd and 55th Divisions to take the offensive as early as possible without waiting for the arrival of their rear echelons. Both divisions, acting in co-ordination, were to drive the enemy away from the line of the Salween and Sittang Rivers and advance on Pegu' (p. 39). And as to the next step (p. 59):

On reaching Thaton 55th Division was to wait until 33rd Division had cleared the town and then cross the Bilin river estuary to Zokali and advance on Taungzun and Kyaikto [my Divisional H.Q.] so as to turn the right flank of any British position on the Bilin river. The 214th Regiment had reached the Bilin before 16 Brigade and portions of its two leading battalions had crossed the river to Danyingon. Thus, when early on 16th February 2nd K.O.Y.L.I. (the left battalion of 16th Brigade) was moving into position it found it had been forestalled.

This shows how very closely 17 Division was engaged on the Bilin and how right I was in reporting that the Japanese were turning my flank. The official history (pp. 60–1) goes on to describe the bitter fighting which ensued during the next three days until at 4.45 p.m. on 18 February I sent a signal to Hutton that the troops were fought to a standstill and I had put in my last battalion to try to stop Japanese flanking movements.

The description of further Japanese movements given in the official history (p. 64) makes it clear that the Japanese and General Hutton were of one mind; that 17 Division should be closely engaged on the Bilin as long as possible. But I was well aware that every day we remained on the Bilin was a good day for the Japanese.

It must also be remembered that in Singapore on the night of 10 February General Wavell, having issued a very wounding farewell message to General Percival's troops in Malaya, had a very heavy fall as he was about to depart by air from the Malayan scene. He had broken two small bones in his back and became unconscious. With his usual bulldog courage he had refused to be put on the sick list and he remained in control at his Java headquarters. The stream of ill-judged and ill-informed directives which he fired at General Hutton during the next fortnight and the unwise decisions he made could only have been the vagaries of a very sick man. I certainly was shocked at his appearance on his last visit to my headquarters in Burma. I had always wondered why Wavell, at this critical time, had not flown up to see me at my battle H.Q. and stayed long enough really to understand the situation. I am sure Auchinleck, Alexander or Slim would have done that – and sacked me immediately if they thought I was doing the wrong thing; but I realized afterwards how sick Wavell was at the time.

Lieutenant-General Sir Henry Pownall, Wavell's Chief of Staff, records in his diary (*Chief of Staff*, Leo Cooper 1974) on 15 February 1942: 'It hasn't been easy to keep the show running as Wavell has been in bed for the past four days as the result of his accident in Singapore on 10th February when he fell some six feet off the pierhead on to rocks and barbed wire. Wavell was still not fit to travel on 20th February.' He also records how powerless Wavell's A.B.D.A. Command were with no reserves to influence the battle.

On 23 February A.B.D.A. received orders to pack up and Pownall's last remark is: 'There is no doubt that we have under-estimated the Jap. He is far more efficient, a far better fighter than we ever thought.' Of Wavell he wrote: 'Wavell is not easy to serve. His silences are hard to interpret. Whether they mean "yes" or "no" or "wait" it is almost impossible to tell.'

The A.B.D.A. Command only lasted six weeks and achieved absolutely nothing. I have always thought that, as Malaya and Burma were their two vital responsibilities, they would have done better to establish an operational H.Q. first in Malaya and then in Burma, where Wavell could have kept in close touch with the operations and that Pownall should have been appointed Burma Army Commander. He was completely wasted in A.B.D.A. It is clear from Pownall's diary, as it was to me, that in the last days of February Wavell, in addition to being a very tired man, was also a very sick man and should have been in hospital.

Towards the middle of February the Viceroy of India had sent Churchill a signal expressing his alarm at the way things were going in Burma and severely criticizing Hutton as a commander but giving him credit for having been an excellent C.G.S. in India. Churchill had sent this chilling telegram on to Wavell, saying that if Wavell concurred he would send out Alexander to replace Hutton. Churchill also asked after Wavell's state of health.

Wavell replied on 18 February saying he had great confidence in Hutton and was 'reluctant to make the change'. He did however ask to be informed what would become of Hutton if he was replaced and how quickly Alexander could get to Burma. He also asked if the whole of the Australian Corps could be landed in Burma. As regards the state of his health he said that he had 'ordered himself out of hospital somewhat to the scandal of the doctors and was making a rapid recovery'. Wavell was very loyal to Hutton, whom he had appointed to the Burma Command, and continued to be so to the very end; in his despatch in the operations, he absolved him of all blame. On this day, 18 February, Sandy Reid Scott, Wavell's A.D.C., recorded that he looked 'tired, worried and tucked up, though considering the severity of the fall he had at Singapore he had made a remarkable recovery'.

Churchill cabled Wavell on 20 February saying that the A.B.D.A. Command was to be broken up and he would again become Commander-in-Chief in India and 'from this centre you would be able to animate the whole war against Japan from our side'. He was sending Alexander to command Burma Army immediately. Wavell then informed Hutton of Alexander's arrival and that he, Hutton, would be his C.G.S. Alexander, however, soon made other arrangements.

Not until 19 February did we see Hutton again up at the battle front and then his stay was brief indeed. As he says in his despatch, 'Finding the troops very weak and exhausted I gave permission for Smyth to withdraw across the Sittang.' But why wait until they were weak and exhausted when he could have withdrawn six days earlier, fit and unimpeded – except of course from air attacks which we would have had to stomach anyway?

Hutton had flown to Lashio to confer with the Chinese and returned to Rangoon to find that, in his own words, 'a very serious situation had arisen at Sittang'. And how right he was. I had been reporting this to A.H.Q. Burma every day since General Hutton's last visit five days earlier.

The troops at Bilin were so closely engaged that it would have been most unwise to try to break contact in daylight, and indeed this very tricky operation needed a lot of detailed planning, although skeleton orders had been prepared. Considering how tired the troops were and how closely they were engaged, the disengagement and the actual withdrawal under cover of darkness was carried out brilliantly. The brigades leap-frogged back through one another and by the next morning we had got clear of the Japanese division on our front. But my chief worry was with regard to the formations which had been turning our flanks : two Japanese Regiments had done so and were moving well ahead of us by cross-country tracks to intercept us at Sittang. Tired as my 17 Division troops were I had to keep them going through the night of the 19th, all through the 20th and into the following night.

The one big question in the minds of myself and my staff was : had we still got a chance of getting the division, or at least a part of it, over the Sittang bridge with all the odds of time and space and superior Japanese ground and air forces against us? There was obviously no chance now of our getting time to prepare an organized defence across the river. We had sent back all the transport and impedimenta we could but as so much of our fighting and medical transport was on wheels, and we had no idea how long we would be kept in action on the Bilin, we still had to keep a great many vehicles with us.

The utter weariness of the troops, the appalling state of the dusty track and the slating we got from the air – from our own air force as well as the Japanese – weighted the scales heavily against us. The troops had put in their last ounce of energy to hold the Bilin line intact and were utterly exhausted. We had expected to be heavily bombed by the Japs during our withdrawal but the bombing by our own air force was the last straw. Air support had to be arranged by Rangoon as we had no wireless set which could reach that distance.

The official history describes the bombing :

The 21st was very dry and hot and dense clouds of thick red dust and a shortage of water added to the trials of men and beasts alike. During the day the column on the main track, which was flanked by thick jungle on either side, and the troops in the Bayagi Rubber Estate were repeatedly bombed and machine gunned, first by Japanese aircraft and later by aircraft carrying Allied markings. As a result vehicles, including ambulances full of wounded, were ditched and destroyed; mules carrying weapons and wireless sets broke loose and vanished with their loads into the jungle; casualties were numerous, the march was delayed, considerable disorganization was caused and morale suffered. (There were also many cases where the Burmese ambulance drivers, frightened by the bombing, disappeared into the jungle, leaving their ambulances, full of wounded on the track.) Most of the persistent attacks which caused havoc were owing to a grievous error, made by British and American Volunteer Group aircraft. Air reconnaissance in the morning had falsely reported an enemy column of three hundred vehicles moving through Kyaikto to

Kinmum. All available aircraft at Rangoon were ordered to attack and given the Kyaikto–Mokpalin road instead of the Kaikto–Kinmun road as the western limit for the bombing operations.

Although the 17th Division could by no possible stretch of the imagination be blamed for this grievous and damaging error, it was at the time, and for many years to come, charged against us as part of the whole Sittang disaster bill.

During the day of 20 February I was able to interchange the brigades. All day long and far into the night the troops plodded steadily along. At dawn the Japanese made an attack on my Division H.Q. which was beaten off by the timely arrival of a company of the 12th Frontier Force Regiment. It was reminiscent of my subaltern's days in the 15th Sikhs in 1914–15 to be standing on the perimeter with drawn revolver – but somehow I didn't like it so much as a major-general as I had as a second lieutenant; the old careless rapture had departed!

On the 21st the march continued without cessation. All three brigades were making good progress but the condition of the track was now appalling, ankle deep in dust, and the Indian troops marched with their pagris over their faces. I impressed on the brigadiers that they must keep the men moving despite their weariness, but they had to have food and water. Dense jungle extended right down to the east bank of the broad Sittang river. The Sittang bridge itself had been built entirely for rail traffic but for some time now all the engineers who could be made available from Army resources had been engaged in planking the bridge to make it useable for road traffic and marching columns. This was by no means an easy business and necessitated the cutting and laying of thousands of wooden planks and sleepers. There was in addition a boat ferry which might be used in an emergency for small bodies of troops, but this was a slow and unsatisfactory procedure and all the boatmen had fled.

Some time beforehand I had laid back a bridgehead defence consisting of odd units, some of which had been too knocked about in action to be capable of mobile operations. That evening of 21 February I had a good look at the bridgehead defences. By nightfall 48 Gurkha Brigade were bivouacked with Division H.Q. about two miles east of the river. The troops could now have their first few hours' much needed rest and some food as the transport started to cross the bridge in a steady stream.

A staff officer from A.H.Q. Rangoon arrived with important news. First, information had been received at A.H.Q. which indicated that the Japanese might make parachute landings next morning on the open ground to the west of the river, to try to take the bridge from that side.

Second, 7 Armoured Brigade had arrived in Rangoon. All the dock labourers there had fled and they had had to unload all their tanks, stores and petrol themselves. They would, however, be sent up to join me as soon as possible, though it was unlikely that they could arrive within the next twenty-four hours. That was good news but how very much better it would have been if we had been in a strongly entrenched position on the other side of the Sittang.

It was now dark and not an easy business for the transport to cross without lights, but it had to be done. At 3 a.m. I stopped the transport to get the 1/4th Gurkhas across for the anti-parachute task. Everything was deathly quiet; the men's feet made no sound on the dusty track; they were just shadowy figures moving steadily along. Not a shot was being fired anywhere, nor was there a single aircraft in the sky. I ordered Brigadier Hugh-Jones to get his Brigade H.Q. across the river and take charge of the bridgehead defences.

Suddenly there was a check in the moving stream of troops and transport which developed into a long halt. I made my way on foot up to the head of the column and found that a lorry had overturned right in the middle of the bridge. My indefatigable C.R.E. and his Sappers were at once on the job but there was nearly two hours' delay whilst the obstruction was being removed. Nevertheless, by daylight on the 22nd the 1/4th Gurkhas were across the river and taking up their anti-parachute landing positions. The rear portion of Division H.Q. had crossed the river and were en route to their new location, which was a small railway station where we could get signal communication with Army Headquarters.

Brigadier Hugh-Jones had established his own brigade headquarters across the river, just behind the bridgehead, and my staff set up a small Division Operational H.Q. within a short distance of him. I put Hugh-Jones in charge of the bridgehead defence.

Up to this point it really seemed as though, owing to the superhuman efforts made by the troops, we might be able to get at least a part of the division across the river. But I somehow smelt danger. Everything was unnaturally quiet. Soon after daylight I decided to cross the bridge to have a look at the 1/4th Gurkha dispositions. At the near end of the bridge Colonel 'Mac' Mackenzie, my good Assistant Director of Medical Services, had spent the night with one of his field ambulances. He hailed me and asked me to stop and have a cup of tea with him. But after we had had a few words I decided to push on. I was half-way across the bridge when there was a great burst of firing and the Japs, who had been lying up in the jungle, ready to pounce when the time was ripe, swarmed in to the attack and interposed the best part of a division between our bridgehead defence troops and the rest of 17

Division. All the medical personnel with whom I had been talking only a moment before were either killed or captured. Three and a half years later, Colonel Mac, who had spent those years in Rangoon jail, hobbled into my study in London with a long white beard and crippled with beri-beri. With his usual broad smile he said: 'Well now, Jackie, to continue what I was saying to you on the morning of 22nd February 1942 when we were so rudely interrupted . . .'

A great deal has been written about this engagement and the blowing of the Sittang bridge became one of the most historic and controversial episodes of the war. The only people who were concerned and had to make the vital decision were myself, my Chief of Staff, Brigadier Punch Cowan, and Brigadier Hugh-Jones and his commanding officers. There were no staff officers from Army Headquarters, no war correspondents and no reporters of any sort. And a lot of the things that were cabled and written afterwards, by people who were not there, were quite inaccurate.

At this time, the morning of 22 February 1942, all I knew was that my troops across the river were engaged in a dog-fight in the jungle and that the bridgehead defence troops under Brigadier Hugh-Jones were all too few to resist for very long the attacks on the bridge which would certainly be made in increasing strength by a superior force of Japanese. Otherwise the oft-quoted 'fog of war' was complete. I was well aware that if the Japanese succeeded in capturing the bridge the fate of Rangoon – and of Burma – would be sealed immediately and the 7th Armoured Brigade would be caught on the march and blotted out.

Throughout the 22nd anxious queries had been coming from the Army Commander in Rangoon, who requested me to meet him and his staff for a conference next morning at a point halfway between Rangoon and Sittang. No time could have been more inconvenient for me to leave my H.Q., but I could leave Punch Cowan in charge and would have to see what the night brought forth. I fully realized how critically the result of the action at Sittang would affect Burma, with big responsibilities but no troops – except mine. I thought how Hutton must now be regretting that my division was not across the Sittang and holding strong defensive positions, as I had planned. But neither then, when the disaster I had foretold had occurred, nor even in the after years, have I ever heard General Hutton, in speech or in writing, acknowledge that any blame could be attached to him or General Wavell: all the blame was on me.

As darkness fell and the firing from across the river died down I left Noel Hugh-Jones's H.Q. at the bridgehead, leaving my G.S.O.1 with him, and moved back with Punch Cowan to my Ops H.Q. Before leaving I ascertained that there was no sign of any of our troops across the river being able to break through. There was however every sign that Japanese pressure on the bridgehead defences was increasing, and I impressed on Hugh-Jones that at all costs they must not be allowed to capture the bridge. I had the fullest confidence in him, as he had in me.

I would have to make an early start next morning if I was to make my rendez-vous with the Army Commander, so Punch and I had a quick snack and hoped to get a few hours' sleep – of which neither of us had had much during the past three days.

At 4.30 a.m. next morning Punch Cowan woke me to speak to Hugh-Jones on the telephone. During the night pressure on the bridge had increased, and it was continually being swept by fire. He could not guarantee to hold the bridge against a dawn attack, and if it was not blown now, under cover of darkness, he couldn't be sure he could blow it at all. He therefore wanted my permission to withdraw the bridge-head troops and blow the bridge immediately. I just wanted to make certain that he had consulted the C.O.s of the 1/4th Gurkhas and 4/12th Frontier Force Rifles, both of whose opinions I valued. I then had five minutes' discussion with Cowan.

I had all the pros and cons clearly in my head. If we blew, it was in the knowledge that two-thirds of my division was left on the far bank of the broad Sittang. If we did not blow, a complete Japanese division could march straight on to Rangoon, and my troops on the far bank would still be cut off from the bridge and at the mercy of another Japanese division. There was no alternative but to give the order to blow, and the bridge was most gallantly destroyed under heavy fire by our Indian Sappers at 5.30 a.m. after the remnants of the bridge defence troops had been withdrawn.

In after years I received much commiseration regarding the appalling difficulty of the decision I had to make, but no educated soldier could have made any other. It was a very distressing one, and I realized that there would be a storm of uninformed criticism which would do me no good at all. General Joe Lentaigne, who had been commanding the 1/4th Gurkhas in the bridgehead at the time, wrote in his Regimental History:

All day of the 22nd and through the night of the 22nd/23rd very heavy firing could be heard from beyond the river. It was a soldiers' battle with great confusion and no control possible. At 03.30 on the morning of 23rd, the enemy brought machine-gun fire to bear along the whole length of the Sittang Bridge. Pressure was increasing. A dreadful decision had to be taken – whether or not to blow the bridge.

The prime factor was that it must not fall into Japanese hands intact. It was becoming more and more clear that it could not be destroyed in daylight, when it would be under observed fire. It was doubtful even whether it could be held until daylight. To destroy it meant to sacrifice the division but all the indications were that in any case the division could never now reach the bridge. The matter grew more urgent, the decision was taken and the bridge was blown.

General Taffy Davies, Hutton's Chief of Staff, wrote in his memoirs; which he committed to my care :

A terrible decision had to be made by Smyth. If he blew the bridge he sacrificed the bulk of his division. If he failed to blow the bridge and it was secured intact by the enemy, the way to Rangoon lay open with nothing interposing. General Smyth blew the bridge. In my opinion an heroic and inevitable decision.

Although informed soldiers like General Davies, great commanders like Alexander, Slim and Auchinleck, and my own brigadiers, have all agreed that in the circumstances which existed there was no other course which any commander worthy of the name could have taken then – to blow the bridge to prevent the Japanese taking it, even though two-thirds of my division was on the wrong side – world opinion at the time accepted the initial report made by Generals Hutton and Wavell that the Sittang disaster and the inevitable loss of Burma which followed, was entirely the fault of myself and my staff in our mishandling of the withdrawal; and it was only natural that the troops thus cut off, even though a large number of them were subsequently able to swim and raft themselves across the broad and swiftly flowing Sittang river, should have been bitterly critical of me and Brigadier Hugh-Jones, who actually blew the bridge. I could not possibly explain to these men, first, that the unbelievable mad scramble to cross the Sittang bridge, which could have been achieved ten days earlier with comparative ease, was utterly at variance with my own plan for this vital operation. Nor could I explain to them that, from the time the Japanese got there first and interposed the best part of one complete division between them and the bridgehead defences, there was never a time when the troops across the river ever looked like breaking through. Indeed the two brigadiers were hiding up in patches of jungle surrounded by Japanese.

It took the best part of seventeen years before I could explain these things. The *Economist*, in reviewing my book, *Before the Dawn*, in December 1957, said :

However late in the war it was, the newcomers to the 17th Indian Division would be told almost at once about the disaster at the Sittang bridge in the 1942 retreat. There were few survivors left to tell the story, but the horror of it lived in the collective memory. The stories were confused, exaggerated, contradictory, bitter and angry.

It was only natural that a lot of the criticism should have been directed against Brigadier Hugh-Jones, who actually blew the bridge, despite the fact that from the very first moment I had insisted that the blame, if blame there must be, was mine alone. If a disaster occurs when the senior commander is consulted then he must always carry the can, and not his subordinates. Incidentally I never heard Wavell or Hutton accept any blame for Sittang, even though the disaster resulted from the plan they had forced me to accept.

But this criticism affected Hugh-Jones more and more as the years passed. He was a great admirer and supporter of mine and his chief concern was that my reputation had been ruined by his action. I simply replied that he had referred the decision to me, that I had fully agreed with his advice, and the decision was therefore entirely mine. The strain he had undergone started to affect him both physically and mentally and when he last came to see me I was shocked at his appearance. He finally requested that I should approach Bill Slim, then Chief of the Imperial General Staff at the War Office, and demand that he, Noel Hugh-Jones, should be tried by court martial – for something he didn't do, all those years ago. I tried to reason with him but I was not surprised to hear that a few days later he had walked out into the sea and was drowned. He was a Sittang casualty if ever there was one.

CHAPTER FIFTEEN

Aftermath of Sittang

THERE was hardly a shot being fired as I had a hasty breakfast and, leaving Punch Cowan in charge, I set off to keep my rendezvous with General Hutton way back on the Rangoon–Mandalay road. He had with him all his principal military officers of Burma Army, together with some of the senior officers of the Burma Government. I had not a very cheerful story to tell them, but at least a Japanese division was not treading hard on my heels – and indeed it was some ten days before they started to cross the Sittang river. I forebore to say to Hutton 'I told you so'; subordinate commanders are not allowed to say things like that.

I did not see the immediate report he sent to Wavell, whose cable to the Chiefs of Staff in London merely said that Burma had been lost when three retreating British brigades had been trapped and destroyed owing to the premature destruction of the Sittang bridge by the Commander of 17 Division. That is recorded by the Chief of Staff, Field-Marshal Alan Brooke (later Lord Alanbrooke) in his diary (*The Turn of the Tide: Based on the Diaries of Viscount Alanbrooke*, Collins, 1957, page 311), and went right round the world.

The actual report which went to Prime Minister Winston Churchill is recorded by him on page 136 of volume 4 of *The Hinge of Fate* (Cassell, 1951) as follows: 'By February 20th it was obvious that a further retreat to the Sittang river was imperative if the whole force was not to be lost.' This of course is Hutton's version and the date is important. It may only have become obvious to him on 20 February but it had become obvious to me, the 17 Division commander on the spot, on the 12 February. And it was obvious to me and all my brigadiers and staff that 20 February was much too late.

Churchill continues:

Over this swift-flowing river, five hundred yards wide, there was only one bridge. Before the main body of the 17th Division could reach it the bridgehead was attacked by a strong Japanese force, while the marching columns retiring upon it were themselves beset by a fresh enemy division newly arrived, which caught them in the flank.

This part is correct. But he goes on :

Under the impression that our three retiring brigades were greatly weakened, scattered and beaten, and were in fact trapped, the order was given by the commander of the bridgehead, with the permission of the divisional commander, to blow up the bridge. When the division successfully fought its way back to the river bank it found the bridge destroyed and the broad flood before it. Even so, 3,300 men contrived to cross this formidable obstacle, but with only 1,400 rifles and a few machine guns. Every other weapon and all equipment were lost. This was a major disaster.

As I informed Sir Winston (as he had then become) in later years, he had been completely misinformed. I was not 'under the impression' that the three retiring brigades were weakened, scattered and trapped. I *knew* they were. But the bridge was blown for one reason and one reason only, that the bridgehead commander could not otherwise prevent it falling into the hands of the Japanese. And the idea that the three brigades 'successfully fought their way back to the river bank only to find the bridge blown' was a complete myth. But of such myths history is sometimes made. Even as late as 1972 General Tulloch wrote in his book *Wingate in Peace and War* (Macdonald, 1972) that Burma had been lost 'owing to the premature demolition of the Sittang Bridge'.

From the time the Japanese attack started on the bridgehead there was never any sign of any formed bodies of our troops across the river making any contact with the bridgehead defences.

Brigadiers Ekin and Jones had hair-raising experiences lying up in patches of jungle surrounded by Japs. The dog-fight in the jungle which took place across the river during the twenty-four hours before the bridge was blown is told in the war diaries of the units concerned and which I have recorded briefly in my book, *The Valiant* (Mowbray, 1970).

Winston Churchill in *The Hinge of Fate*, describes the efforts he made towards the end of February 1942 to persuade the Australian Government to land a division in Rangoon. He wrote in his letter to Mr Curtin of 20 February 1942 : 'It can begin to disembark at Rangoon about the 26th or 27th February. There is nothing else in the world that can fill the gap – and Save Burma.' Churchill also cabled President Roosevelt to the same effect and asked for him to bring his own pressure to bear on the Australian Government. The President then cabled to Mr Curtin saying :

> If Burma goes it seems to me our whole position, including that of Australia, will be in extreme peril. Your Australian division is the only force that is available for immediate re-inforcement. It could get into the fight at once and would, I believe, have the strength to save what now seems to be a very dangerous situation.

General Wavell had, quite independently, made a similar request a few days earlier. He had indeed asked that the whole Australian Army Corps should be transferred to Burma.

But these urgent proposals came too late. No substantial reinforcements had been received from India; no Chinese divisions were in action in Burma; and several days before the British Prime Minister considered that the Australians could be landing in Rangoon, my 17th Division, on which the resistance to the Japanese depended, had been destroyed whilst crossing the Sittang river. The landing of substantial reinforcements at Rangoon was therefore no longer feasible. It would only have been possible at that stage had my division been securely entrenched on the west bank of the broad Sittang river.

The real tragedy was that the main battle, on ground favourable to our troops and with the tanks which were very shortly arriving to support us, was never fought at all – and the battle for Burma was lost in the broad waters of the Sittang.

Wavell's despatch on the operations says :

> These engagements are described in General Hutton's report. It is quite clear that the enemy were allowed to gain cheap initial successes through bad handling by local commanders, lack of training and, in some cases, lack of fighting spirit on the part of the troops. The battle at the Sittang River bridgehead on 22nd and 23rd February which is described in General Hutton's report, *really sealed the fate of Rangoon and Lower Burma* [my italics]. In the withdrawal from the Bilin River to the Sittang and the action east of the river the whole of two brigades was lost.

And Wavell's 'uncensored opinion of the battle,' quoted in John Connell's biography of him, says :

The battle of the Sittang River bridgehead on February 22nd and 23rd, which is described in General Hutton's report, really sealed the fate of Rangoon and Lower Burma. From reports of this operation which I have studied I have no doubt that the withdrawal from the Bilin River to west of the Sittang was badly managed *by the headquarters of the 17th Division, and that the disaster which resulted in the loss of almost two complete brigades ought never to have occurred* [my italics].

It will be noted that Wavell based his strictures on myself and 'the Headquarters 17th Division' on reports given to him by General Hutton. The report by General Hutton covers the period 27 December 1941 to 5 March 1942. It is remarkable for the things it leaves out. He says that, 'It was soon discovered that the Burma Rifle Battalions were of considerable value for reconnaissance and patrol work but were not fit to stand the test of serious operations against an enemy like the Japanese.' What he leaves out is the fact that I had realized this early in the operations and had asked leave to use them as guerrillas and not in a regular role. Hutton had not only turned my request down flat but had censured me for making it on the grounds that it would show my lack of confidence in them. On the contrary I wanted to relieve them of a role which they knew they could not carry out (and in which they were a danger to the regular brigades) and employ them as guerrillas, in which role they could have had a really effective influence on the battle.

But the most serious omission from both General Hutton's report and General Wavell's despatch is that they both omit entirely that on 12 February 1942, eleven days before the Japanese attacked my division in process of crossing the Sittang River, I had sent my Chief of Staff, Brigadier Cowan, back to Rangoon to make one more urgent appeal to Hutton to allow me to move back to the Sittang immediately. This I could have done quite comfortably and then had at least a week in hand to prepare a strong defensive position on the far bank. I was quite positive that we would be risking total disaster if I remained for a week forty miles on the Japanese side of the Sittang River on the Bilin ditch, during which time the two Japanese divisions opposing me could turn both my flanks and get to the Sittang before me.

By refusing my request, and even saying that there must be no withdrawal from the Bilin without Hutton's personal permission, with Wavell's strong support Hutton had created a disaster which resulted in the loss of Rangoon and Burma. Of course the loss of Burma was inevitable anyway, but it need not have resulted in a military disaster which depleted our forces and left so many dead or prisoners of the

Japanese. It was inconceivable to me that these two big guns could possibly have arrived at such completely nonsensical conclusions in face of an utterly clear military situation. But if you don't trust the man who is fighting the battle, nor come up to the battle front to see what is really going on, then you deserve all the trouble you will surely get.

Sixteen years later – eight years after Wavell's death – I myself, General Taffy Davies and my brigade commanders forced the author of the official history to acknowledge these vital facts of 12 February 1942 and put them in all their stark significance into the final draft of the official history of the Burma Campaign. Wavell's despatch on the operations in Burma from 15 December 1941 to 20 May 1942 was submitted to the Secretary of State for War on 16 July 1942. It was not published until 5 March 1948, and it was another ten years before the grave omissions in Hutton's report and Wavell's despatch were brought to light. And during all those years, with the assistance of the Official Secrets Act, no contradiction was made to the idea that I and my staff were the villains of the piece. Wavell made a big contribution to this opinion by his dramatic removal of me, not only from my command, but from the Army altogether. This gave the impression that I must have been guilty of some very grave military offence.

I have always appreciated the great pressure which was brought to bear on Hutton by Wavell, who was even more out of touch with the battle in distant Java than Hutton was in Rangoon. On 21 February, the day on which 17 Division was struggling against hopeless odds to force its way through to the Sittang bridge, Wavell cabled to Hutton:[*] 'You have checked enemy and he must be tired and have suffered heavy casualties. No sign that he is in superior strength.' (The Japs had two highly trained and mobile divisions to our untrained and most immobile one and were greatly superior in the air.) 'You must stop all further withdrawal and counter-attack wherever possible. Whole fate of war in the East depends on most resolute and determined action. You have little air opposition and should attack enemy with all air forces available.' Wavell then sent Hutton another signal on the same day, 21 February, which read:

> You should draw up at once plans for counter offensive with Armoured Brigade and all available troops. If at all possible Sittang River must be re-crossed and counter offensive made east of the river. In any event plans must be made to hit enemy and hit him hard if he ever succeeds in crossing. He will go back quick in face of determined attack. Have your organized armoured train for railway.

[*] John Connell, *Wavell, Supreme Commander* (Collins, 1969).

This was back seat driving with a vengeance. On the day Wavell sent this extraordinary signal the 7th Armoured Brigade was just arriving in Rangoon, whence all the dock labour had fled. It was not until several days later that the brigade arrived to join me – and very useful they would have been if, as I had planned, 17 Division was then disposed in strong defence positions on the west bank of the river to fight the major battle, which never took place.

Wavell did stress the importance of not allowing the Japanese to cross the Sittang bridge, which at least we achieved by blowing it, though in very different circumstances to those envisaged.

The armoured train question must have been a fast one for Hutton. Even if such a train had existed it could only have crossed the river at the Sittang bridge into thick jungle country held by strong Japanese forces.

Had the bridge not been blown and fallen into Japanese hands, my troops across the river would have been killed or captured, and a complete Japanese division would have marched straight on to Rangoon. The Armoured Brigade would have been caught on the march from Rangoon. The 63rd Infantry Brigade from India could not have landed at Rangoon and there would have been no Alexander–Slim fighting withdrawal towards the frontiers of India. Alexander and Slim might well have gone into the bag with Hutton and his headquarters. The fact that Sittang was not an even greater disaster was due to the coolness of my staff, especially Brigadier Hugh-Jones, who was in charge of the bridgehead, and the incredible endurance of the troops. It was thanks to them that the Japanese were not at the gates of India before the rains had broken.

On my arrival back at my 17 Division H.Q. after my conference with General Hutton on 23 February, I found a most unexpected state of affairs. Almost immediately after the bridge had been blown the firing had died down and the Japanese pressure was relaxed. They had failed in their object of capturing the bridge and had suffered heavy casualties, particularly in the bridgehead area, and at once they started to withdraw and move up river to effect another crossing, but the Sittang river was broad and swift and I realized we had gained an invaluable respite.

Unhindered, except for a little desultory rifle fire at long range, some 3,000 of our men on the far bank were able to swim or raft themselves over. I was able to drive my divisional car close to the river bank without a shot being fired at me. But alas my beloved 1/3rd and 2/5th Gurkhas who were unable to swim were mostly killed or captured.

There was of course a colossal job ahead to get these exhausted (and in many cases unclothed) men recreated into fighting soldiers. It is a wonderful tribute to the survivors, both officers and men, that they so quickly recovered, physically and mentally, and were ready to play such a worthy part in the withdrawal back to India.

As John Connell writes quite correctly in *Wavell, Supreme Commander*: 'General Sakurai had won an overwhelming victory. He was now strategically placed to cut the land communications of Hutton's force in the Rangoon area, and the 17th Indian Division had virtually ceased to exist as a fighting formation.'

It was a curious coincidence that the two divisions I had commanded, part of the 19th and the 17th, who were together when the Burma campaign started in 1942 and suffered grievously at Sittang, should have been in at the death and got their own back on the routed Japanese at Sittang in July 1945. General 'Gertie' Tuker, the Corps commander at that time, write: '17 Division, who, with one brigade of 19 Division attached, had been here in February 1942, now repaid the debt in full. The Sittang River was simply flowing with Japanese corpses, all bobbing along, making their way to the sea. I was very glad I did not have to cross the broad, fast-flowing river with no bridge.' 'But why was there no bridge?' some simpleton asked. And the answer was that some unknown soldier had blown it up on 23 February 1942!

Back at Pegu on the main road we started to refit and reorganize covered by the 7th Armoured Brigade, which had now arrived, and was soon to be joined by the 63rd Indian Infantry Brigade from India, the last formation which was able to land at Rangoon. The change from the din of battle to a period of complete quiet was almost uncanny.

Nevertheless it was now obvious to Burma Army H.Q. that the days of Rangoon were numbered, and they therefore most wisely went ahead full speed with their preparations for the total demolition of the docks, oil tanks and so forth in Rangoon and for the withdrawal of the force into Upper Burma. Had Taffy Davies and his staff not looked well ahead and laid back supplies, ammunition, petrol and oil along the Mandalay Road, the army would indeed have been in an impossible predicament.

I had literally run myself to a standstill in this campaign, where my own commanders were as much worry to me as the Japanese. I was also having a recurrence of my fissure (or fistula) trouble. On 7 February, before the crucial battle had been joined, Major-General Treffry Thompson (later Lieutenant-General Sir Treffry), who was Deputy Director Medical Services to Burma Army, visited my H.Q. and insisted, despite my protests, that I should have a medical board immediately. Fortunately, the President of the Board, which was fixed for the 11th, went sick himself, and my own A.D.M.S., Colonel Mackenzie, was appointed President. I had a word with him beforehand and begged him to let me carry on, anyway until the critical battle for Sittang was resolved. Colonel Mackenzie gave me some arsenic and strychnine injections to keep me going. The Board was duly held on the 11th and I was pronounced fit to carry on provided I took two months' rest at the first available opportunity. This was entered on the Board proceedings. My A.D.M.S., Colonel Mackenzie, was taken prisoner a few days later and the actual Board report was only seen by Hutton and General Thompson before it and most of the other documents at A.H.Q. were lost in the hasty withdrawal from Rangoon. After Colonel Mackenzie came out of captivity he wrote to me as follows:

> You were of course involved in a most critical stage of the operations and were most anxious that there should be no suggestion of your being unfit, and were equally emphatic that you were perfectly capable of carrying on.
>
> We found nothing organically wrong with you but I did warn you that it was essential for you to have two months' complete rest at the first opportunity. In the meantime we gave you a course of injections to carry you along for the time being. There was also a recurrence of the old fistula which we recommended could be dealt with at a later date.

On 25 February therefore, not knowing that Hutton had been sacked and his successor was on the way, I wrote to him (Confidential D.O. No 4095/East/35), as follows, referring to the medical board's recommendation.

> As my division has now been so much reduced in numbers I am writing to ask if I could have the leave recommended as early as you could spare me. I should have hated to have asked for it whilst active operations were in progress or had there not been a really efficient substitute in Punch Cowan ready to step into my shoes.
>
> I have however had rather more than an ordinary strain and do feel very much in need of a rest.
>
> I have also had to conduct a series of withdrawals since I have been in command of the division which are always lowering to the morale of troops and I feel that they would perhaps do better under new management.

I said I was convinced that with a bit of a rest I should be absolutely fit for active service again. I had no answer to my letter, but my request was strongly recommended by General Thompson and Hutton had taken immediate action on it; and I was informed on 1 March by A.H.Q. Burma that I had been granted one month's leave in India; Punch Cowan would take over the remnants of 17 Division with acting rank of major-general. (The Secret Decipher No. 0097 said: 'Smyth 31 days war leave sanctioned from date of arrival in India. Chief approves Cowan taking command 17 Division.')

General Hutton then informed me that Wavell, who had arrived in Rangoon on 1 March, would take me back to India in his plane next day. Wavell cabled on 1 March to the Chief of the General Staff in London: 'Arrived Rangoon this evening and visited 17 Division near Pegu. There has been report of Japanese advance in force but so far unconfirmed. Cowan succeeds Smyth, who is definitely sick man, in command of 17 Division.' Wavell also says in his despatch on the operations: 'The Divisional Commander (General Smyth) was obviously a sick man and I replaced him by Brigadier Cowan, who commanded the 17th Division with success for the remainder of the campaign.' Hutton makes no mention of my departure in his despatch but merely says: 'On 1 March Brigadier Cowan assumed command of 17 Division.'

In the circumstances in which I had had to operate the strain of the campaign was of course considerable. But the far bigger strain was the constant battle in my own mind between what my military instincts knew to be right and the orders I had been forced to carry out. It was very galling to be making my troops carry out orders which anyone with any military sense on the spot could see were futile – and not to be able to explain, out of loyalty to Hutton, that it was not my plan but his. My whole reputation as a fighting soldier was going down the drain and lives were being lost to little military purpose. The Burma Campaign of 1942 was hard enough without these added conflicts.

John Connell, in *Wavell*, published twenty-seven years later (1969), says: 'Smyth, whose illness (against which he fought with the utmost courage) was so severe that, after eight months treatment in India, he was sent home and retired, was in process of handing over to Cowan.'

During his short visit to Burma on 1/2 March, Wavell had made it abundantly clear to Hutton that the danger to Rangoon had been greatly exaggerated and that it must not be given up without 'the most aggressive battle that our means allow'. I had made it clear to the staff at A.H.Q. before I handed over to Cowan that unless the remainder of the Burma Army got well clear of the Rangoon bottleneck before the Japanese had crossed the Sittang and returned to the attack they would be in danger of total destruction. I was accused by Wavell of being an alarmist.

On Monday 2 March, I took off with Wavell from Mingladoon airport, Rangoon. General Hutton had informed me that we were bound first for Lashio, where Wavell was going to confer with Generalissimo Chiang Kai-shek. Wavell and I sat at opposite ends of the plane. He had had no converse with me since his visit to my H.Q. on 6 February, nor did he ever speak to me again during his lifetime.

I realized what a shattering blow yet another defeat had been to him and I respected his silence. He was a very exhausted and most embittered man. But I had as yet no idea of the very deleterious report that Hutton had given him about me. I was shown this report later by the India Office in London. I had been their blue-eyed boy and they were shocked and unbelieving.

At Lashio I was most interested to see Chiang Kai-shek in person. The Generalissimo was at that time a powerful world figure in the Allied cause. He was certainly an impressive personality: very quiet and still in repose, his eyes were remarkable and he radiated vitality. He and General Wavell were closeted together for some time with an interpreter in a small round building with wide open windows. As there seemed to be no security precautions for this important summit conference, I appointed myself an unofficial watchdog. I walked slowly round the building, glancing in occasionally at the two 'Supremos'. They appeared deep in thought and apparently desirous of keeping their thoughts to themselves: so far as I could see neither of them uttered at all. Later I was amazed to read in their communiqué that everything in the garden was lovely.

However, one very important thing which did emerge from the conference was that Wavell cabled Hutton from Lashio: 'Hang on hard – Rangoon must not be given up without battle, and most aggressive battle that our means allow on ground and in the air.'

It must be remembered that it was Chiang Kai-shek who more than anyone else in December 1941 (with the exception of the far-sighted General Sir John Dill, C.I.G.S.) had realized the imminent danger to Burma and had offered two Chinese divisions, and more, for its defence, which Wavell had refused. Chiang was now very naturally deeply disturbed at the prospect of the loss of Rangoon and the cutting off of all land communications between China and the rest of the Allied world.

We stayed one night in Lashio and the next day flew to Calcutta – still at opposite ends of the Blenheim bomber! Almost as soon as our aircraft had landed another aircraft wheeled up alongside, out of which stepped the unmistakable figure of General Alexander, looking spick and span, calm and unruffled as always. I of course knew him well but we were not allowed to have any converse as General Wavell hurried him away to the rest house.

The next twenty minutes were fraught with the lives of many soldiers and no one knew it better than I did – but I could do nothing about it. Whatever General Wavell's feelings about me may have been I shall always think that it was quite inexcusable of him not to allow Alex at least to hear the opinion of the man who had been fighting the battle and knew ten times as much about the situation as did Wavell who had only descended from his faraway headquarters for a bird's eye view. I paced up and down on the tarmac, whilst seated up in Alex's big aircraft, all unbeknownst to me, was Major-General W. E. V. Abraham, (later Sir William) who was going out to Burma (which he knew well) on a special assignment. Later he became one of my greatest friends and we often discussed that moment of fate, concerning which at the time he was just as puzzled as Alex was.

After a brief conference Wavell and Alex emerged and Alex boarded his plane and departed. Knowing as I did Wavell's views of the situation and his low opinion of the Japanese, I felt very apprehensive as to what instructions Alex had been given.

As soon as Alex's aircraft had taken off for Rangoon Wavell cabled the C.I.G.S. in London : 'Have given instructions that Rangoon is not to be given up without a battle as aggressive as our means will permit.' It was these two cables and the briefing Wavell gave to Alexander on Calcutta aerodrome which so nearly caused the loss of the remainder of Burma Army and might even have resulted in a Japanese invasion of India.

I heard the rest of the story later from Bill Slim, Taffy Davies and others. On his arrival in Rangoon Alexander had shocked them all by announcing that there was no immediate threat to Rangoon. He cancelled all arrangements for the demolitions and for moving northwards via Prome, which were already in train. On the next day he attempted to stage a counter-attack against the rapidly advancing Japanese, intending to use the 7th Armoured Brigade and the newly landed 63rd Indian Infantry Brigade. But it didn't even get started. Alex had by then realized the very great danger of his position. He therefore ordered that the original arrangements for the withdrawal should proceed immediately. But it was too late. Both the roads leading out of Rangoon were blocked by strong Japanese forces which the strongest counter-attacks failed to shift.

Field-Marshal Slim, the newly appointed Burma Corps Commander, wrote in *Defeat into Victory* (p. 14) : 'General Alexander escaped from Rangoon by sheer luck. The whole British force and with it General Alexander and his H.Q., would have been destroyed had it not been for the typically rigid adherence to his orders by a Japanese divisional commander.'

Wavell, in his endearing way, apologized to Alex for the jam he had got him into. He cabled on 11 March when he heard of Alex's escape : 'Well done. Responsibility for position in which you and troops were placed is wholly mine and I congratulate you all on determination with which you have extricated yourselves. Much regret casualties.' Alexander was immensely loyal to Wavell and took the blame himself – merely writing in his memoirs, published in 1962 : 'This delay in evacuating Rangoon resulted in the whole of our forces in the south of Burma being encircled and gave the Japanese the chance to destroy them as organized formations – and they missed their chance.'

Whilst Wavell had been in conference with Alexander on Calcutta aerodrome the aerodrome commander had informed me that the Commander-in-Chief wished to continue his journey to Delhi alone and he was to fix me up with another plane. My baggage was removed from the Blenheim and piled on the tarmac. Wavell strode past me without any sign of recognition. What the Station Commander thought of all this can be imagined. Here were two general officers, who had travelled together in one large aircraft from Rangoon, en route for Delhi. Now the Major-General was removed. Obviously he was so very *persona non grata* with the C.-in-C. that he mustn't even be seen in his company. There was a great shortage of aircraft at the time and the only plane the Station Commander could offer me was a rather antiquated two-seater 'Camel'. I was very surprised to see that the pilot was a Sikh. He saluted and said : 'Smyth Sahib bahadur, it is a great honour for any Sikh to pilot you.' I made some appropriate reply and got myself aboard – he in the front seat and me in the back. The plane started to taxi across the broad Calcutta aerodrome, roaring along ever faster and faster but never getting off the ground. It overran the aerodrome into some thick bushes, lost one wing and eventually ended halfway up a tree. Mercifully it did not catch fire.

For a minute or two I did not know whether I was alive or dead, but having felt myself all over, came to the conclusion that I was all in one piece. The front part of the plane was a mess but the pilot was miraculously unhurt, and having extricated himself from the cockpit he came round to get me out.

'Not to worry, General,' he said cheerfully. 'We have plenty more of these old camels in the hangar.'

The station commander rushed over in a car and was very relieved to find me still intact. As we drove back in the car he said : 'I can't give you a different plane but I will give you another pilot.'

I replied : 'No, I will stick to my Sikh, you can give him a better Camel.'

After we had dusted ourselves down another Camel was wheeled out. This time I thought it was my turn to make a little speech. So I said to my Sikh : 'Now take out the back seat, do away with the parachute and put down a couple of army blankets. I am going to take a sleeping pill and you will wake me up in Delhi. O.K. ?'

'O.K., General,' he said with a broad smile.

He woke me up in Delhi.

I had a wonderful reunion with my beloved Frances, who had been warned of my arrival. She had got herself a job at A.H.Q. so that she would have news of me and be on hand if I ever came back in one piece. By this time I was completely drained and exhausted.

Next morning I received by express messenger an official letter from the Military Secretary at A.H.Q. informing me that by General Wavell's order I was to be deprived of my major-general's rank forthwith and immediately retired from the Service. The Commander-in-Chief requested me to report the country in which I intended to reside. This was a kindly thought! I only realized afterwards the point of the speed of my rank reduction. I was within a few days of becoming a substantive major-general, and would now be deprived of both rank and pension. On 6 March I was requested to forward immediately to General Wavell my reasons for applying for leave when my division was in action.

To say that I was completely shocked would be an understatement. I had no staff, no office, no papers and was very much in need of a rest, and actually much more in need of medical attention than I had realized. Frances, as always, was a tower of strength.

I made my explanation although I realized that nothing I could say was going to be accepted. I was then, by stern and official decree, dated 23 March 1942, charged with the following offences: Firstly, that I had proceeded to Burma (at General Wavell's urgent request) whilst still suffering from the effects of an operation which had not entirely healed. In doing so I had totally disregarded the provisions of Regulations (India) para 86, which (apparently) required that only personnel passed fit by the medical officer will be permitted to proceed from their mobilization station. And secondly, His Excellency the Commander-in-Chief considered that my applying for leave during a a lull in the operations when I had been passed fit by a medical board was calculated to have a detrimental effect on the morale of the troops. The charge was so worded that if I was not guilty of one part of it I must be on the other. Hutton was of course fighting for his military life. He had already reported to Wavell that Burma had been lost through my premature blowing of the Sittang bridge. He had obviously not told Wavell that my medical board had been emphatic that I must have a rest as soon as possible nor that his chief medical officer and he himself had recommended my leave. So Wavell, faced with yet another defeat – which no one could possibly have avoided – could be excused for feeling rather sore.

I requested to the Military Secretary that as my service in the Army over a period of thirty years had not been entirely undistinguished I should be allowed to have an interview with the Commander-in-Chief. General Hartley however strongly advised me not to seek an interview with General Wavell as nothing I could say would influence him in his current state of mind.

A lot of people were very shocked at all this, particularly General Hartley himself, the Deputy C.-in-C. at A.H.Q., my subordinate commanders in 17 Division when they heard of it later, and my friends at the India Office in London. The latter laid all the blame for it on Hutton, who had not only put the whole responsibility for the loss of Rangoon on my shoulders but had given Wavell a very adverse report on me personally.

General Treffry Thompson, Hutton's Chief Medical Officer, was absolutely furious. In his first letter to me he referred to it as being 'quite shocking'; and in a further letter dated 17 June 1942, he said : 'I am awfully sorry to hear of the way you have been treated. I have handed in a very plainly worded letter, showing exactly how it came about that you were recommended for two months' leave. I have not minced my language and hope that this letter will scotch the silly remarks which have been made about you.' He also informed me that at the first opportunity he went personally to A.H.Q. to protest at the way I had been treated but was not allowed to see General Wavell. However he handed in a letter of protest to the Military Secretary. Although General Wavell refused to see General Treffry Thompson and made no reply to his letter, he was forced to take note of what he said and also of the reports of the medical boards I had had since my reduction in rank and peremptory retirement, none of which would pass me fit for active service. And when Wavell came to write his despatches on the 1942 Burma campaign in Delhi on 14 July 1942 (it was not published until after the war) he was forced to admit that I was 'definitely a sick man' when I had asked for short leave as recommended by my medical board of 11 February 1942.

My own senior Medical Officer, Colonel Mackenzie, who had been President of the medical board, had been taken prisoner at Sittang and spent three and a half terrible years in Rangoon jail. When he returned and found what had happened his language was unprintable.

General Sir Alan Hartley, the Deputy Commander-in-Chief, a very old friend of mine, asked me to come and see him, which I did. He could not have been more distressed at his Chief's action and had done his best to get him to change his mind, but had received no response at all. He offered to do everything in his power to get me some suitable employment as a retired officer.

I suddenly began to see that a scapegoat would be required for the Burma disaster and it would be very convenient for General Wavell and Hutton if I could be made out to be the villain of the piece and removed from the scene altogether. How right that turned out to be.

Although my month's leave was given as a result of the recommendation of a medical board I was given no medical treatment from Service doctors and my health steadily deteriorated. Soon I was confined to bed. Two civilian doctors in Simla considered my condition to be so serious that Frances wrote to General Hartley, the Deputy Commander-in-Chief. Things then began to happen and I was medically boarded on 6 June 1942. The Board found me to be suffering from (a) paroxysmal tachycardia, (b) after effects of a fissure operation, (c) acute dyspepsia, and (d) malaria, and they insisted on a further three months' sick leave, after which the next Board placed me in category B, this was not good enough for an active service job which was all I wanted, but perhaps better than I could have expected. My great consolation was that all my military colleagues, from Bill Slim downwards, came to visit me on my various beds of sickness, to give me their support. And this I appreciated very much.

Meanwhile my retirement from the Service, though not my reduction in rank, was postponed until after my sick leave. On 17 September I had a final interview with General Alan Hartley, who had continued to do his best to get Wavell to change his mind, but to no purpose. Meanwhile I had to face a complete breakdown in health and the vital necessity of finding a job as soon as possible, and it was many years before I completely recovered.

However, out of evil came good and I was given the opportunity to make an entirely new and exciting career in journalism, authorship and politics, and in many other spheres which would otherwise never have been open to me.

Frances and I sailed from Bombay in the troopship *Malaya* on Sunday, 27 September 1942, to fresh woods and pastures new. I never knew I had so many friends.

Wavell's secret report on his reasons for giving me the sack was of course never shown to me. It was shown to a limited number of people I know, but I was never able to discover what became of it. However, unknown to me, Wavell had been taking steps to undo the harm he had done, though he could never take back his written strictures. On 8

March 1943 I was surprised to get a letter from the India Office saying that 'the commander-in-chief has recommended that you should get the rank of major-general and the necessary steps are being taken' : but I was not surprised to hear, on 23 April, that the Army Council could find no regulation by which this could be done. Nevertheless a regulation was found whereby I could be made an honorary Brigadier for specially distinguished service and this was done from the date of my retirement.

In later years, not long before his death, when I was a Member of Parliament, Wavell lunched with Lord Kemsley and when the latter asked him his opinion of me, he replied : 'Oh, splendid fellow. He dodged the doctors to get on to the Burma campaign. I'm still trying to get him restored as a major-general.'

I could certainly have done with the pension but the rank would have been an embarrassment. It was bad enough being a brigadier in the House of Commons. And when Winston made me a junior minister in his government I said I would like to give up the rank. He wouldn't hear of it. 'I like you being a Brigadier,' he said, 'and what's more the honorary rank was given to you as an honour which you certainly can't renounce.' So a brigadier I remained, though I seldom use the title.

Professor Michael Howard, the well-known military historian, in reviewing John Connell's *Wavell* for the *Sunday Times* on 13 April 1969, mentions how, in 1942, Wavell had returned from his A.B.D.A. Command to be Commander-in-Chief in India after the loss of Rangoon and Burma and had mounted the first offensive in Arakan which, by the following spring, had turned out to be one of the most discreditable failures in the annals of British arms :

Wavell could expect little sympathy on his return from the irate Prime Minister [Winston Churchill] and the impression he made on the impatient Americans was disastrous. Return to his command was out of the question. He remained disconsolately enjoying the improbable hospitality of Chips Channon in Belgrave Square until he received another titanic and impossible assignment, the Vice-royalty of the disintegrating Indian Empire.

Wavell died in 1950, famous always for his victory over the Italians in 1940–41 but never having another success. He was really a Churchill casualty as he was completely worn out in 1941 and needed a long rest, as Field-Marshal Sir John Dill had advised. His final impossible burdens were too much for any human to bear, let alone an already exhausted man.

It was not until September 1955 that I heard anything more about the Burma campaign, when I received from the late Major-General S. Woodburn Kirby the first draft of volume 2 of his *War Against Japan* (generally referred to as the official history) which I was asked to endorse. General Kirby was in a difficult position with regard to this book. He had served under General Wavell and Hutton at A.H.Q. India before and during the 1942 campaign and it was perhaps only natural that, as their accounts of the campaign differed strongly from mine on several important points, he should have accepted theirs and disregarded mine. Nor did he accept General Davies's opinions when they agreed with mine and differed from Hutton's.

The general slant of Kirby's manuscript was to make Hutton out as the hero of the campaign and myself and my troops as the villains. I did not so much object to being made the scapegoat myself, though naturally I wasn't too pleased, but what I did object to very strongly was that certain vital facts were entirely omitted from the history. The most important one was that on 12 February 1942, ten days before the Sittang bridge disaster, I had sent Brigadier Cowan back to Rangoon to make one more urgent appeal to General Hutton to allow me to concentrate my division and to withdraw it across the Sittang river *immediately* – otherwise I was certain disaster would follow.

Now I had given this information to Kirby, as had Cowan, but he completely disregarded it. He also disregarded a report from Brigadier Davies, General Hutton's Chief General Staff Officer, which not only confirmed my request but said that he, Davies, had warmly supported my plan, but Hutton had over-ruled him. And nothing was said of Hutton's refusal to allow me to use the Burma Rifle battalions in a guerrilla role.

Major-General H. L. Davies (as he had then become) wrote to Kirby on 12 October 1955:

> Smyth has approached me on the subject matter of some of your chapters in which he feels that he has been most unfairly portrayed as the person responsible for the unhappy events culminating in the loss of Rangoon and indeed of Burma in the 1942 campaign. I can only say I am in complete agreement with Smyth when he protests bitterly at the implications.

There were a number of other statements in Kirby's draft which shocked and infuriated my brigadiers and chief staff officers of 17 Division. As we could get no change from Kirby, as a result of a closely reasoned correspondence, which continued for over a year, I finally approached Lieut.-General Sir Henry Pownall, who was acting in an advisory capacity over the history; and at his suggestion I requested an interview with Professor J. R. M. Butler, the Editor in Chief, who had tea with me in the House of Commons on 15 November 1956. As a result of this interview and the long correspondence which had preceded it certain important corrections were made in the final draft of the official history, which put the record straight to a considerable extent.

But what shocked me was that had I not been in a position, as a Member of Parliament, to contend with this matter, and had not had the facilities to collect the facts and opinions of the people concerned, the true story of this very controversial campaign would have been completely distorted in the official history.

CHAPTER SIXTEEN

Wartime London

A VOYAGE home in a troopship at that stage of the war was no picnic. The ship was full of wounded men and married families; and I knew, and the ship's officers knew, that a torpedo attack could be expected at any time, in which case the outcome didn't bear thinking about. I formed a great admiration for the Merchant Navy, who remained calmly impervious to all these dangers – at least when anybody was looking! Just as on the outward voyage, the blackout was a great nuisance, both for the crew and the passengers. We had our adventures: we narrowly escaped running into the U-boat pack which sank the *Orcades* just off Cape Town, and indeed took her Captain, Captain Fox, back to England; and later we sailed, all unknowingly, right through the middle of the British landing in North Africa.

Nineteen months previously I had left Liverpool with the military world at my feet and as fit as a fiddle. I returned a sick man, compulsorily retired on a Colonel's pension and with no disability pension to help out. The latter was my own fault as I had continually begged the doctors to pass me in as high a category as possible in the hope that I could get back to the war in a front line capacity. A doctor in Cape Town on the voyage home had told me that it would take seven years and every ounce of determination and courage to recover from my very serious breakdown in health. I didn't believe him at the time but in fact it took twice as long as that.

This breakdown included paroxysmal tachycardia, a functional disorder that is an irregular beat of the heart. At any time of the day or night I would suffer an attack. The pulse began either to beat very slowly or alarmingly fast. In either case the world went black; one felt very ill and on the point of passing out. It was a frightening sensation. A side effect was what the doctors called a 'mild effort syndrome' which meant that I could no longer play any games and even walking was sometimes troublesome for the rest of my life.

Frances was a tower of strength. Both her parents had been doctors and she had been brought up with a working knowledge of how the body functions, so she understood my condition pretty well; and whilst being sympathetic, she remained completely robust and confident that the attacks would pass.

Fortunately I found a wonderful doctor in Harley Street who specialized in nervous disorders and if it had not been for him and Frances, who remained certain all the time that I would make another successful career, I might have given up and retired to the country to grow cabbages. Our financial situation was very pressing and it was imperative that I should make some money. But first I had to get fit.

Remembering how General Dick O'Connor had been saved from premature retirement before the war owing to his acute arthritis by a period at a Nature Cure Clinic, I went for a month to Champneys, where I did a fast of seventeen days on water, followed by fourteen days on milk. Both Frances and I had some faith in fasting for certain complaints; but I don't think this was one of them and I would have recovered quicker without it.

When we first arrived back in England we had absolutely no place to go. We arrived at Euston station, with piles of luggage, and told the taxi driver to take us to some hotel where we could find a room. London was choc-a-bloc and it was almost impossible to find anywhere to stay. The taxi man drove round and round and eventually we landed up at the Park Lane Hotel in Piccadilly. After my time at Champneys we stayed for a little with some friends until we found some miserable digs in Gloucester Road.

I then set myself a steady regime of physical exercises which I stuck to, day in and day out, no matter how ill they made me feel. Later I started to swim every day before breakfast. At the same time I set myself a routine of intense mental activity. Gradually, but terribly slowly, my debilitated body and nervous system started to respond.

I didn't waste time brooding on my wrongs and we set about flat hunting and then job hunting. We were lucky to find a small furnished flat in Dolphin Square, where we have lived happily ever since, though not in the same flat. Then I was lucky to come across my old Staff College instructor, General 'Boney' Fuller. He had retired from the Army before the war as a major-general and had made a considerable reputation as a military writer. He had rated me as No 1 of all his students at Camberley and had a flattering opinion of my writing ability. He was convinced that I should become military correspondent of a national newspaper. None of them at that time had correspondents with any personal experience of the Second World War.

Boney Fuller introduced me to Henry Newnham of Kemsley Newspapers who became a great friend and supporter. I was interviewed by Lord Kemsley on 2 May 1943 and he engaged me as military adviser to Kemsley Newspapers. I became military correspondent to the *Manchester Daily Despatch* and the *Glasgow Daily Record*, for whom I wrote regular feature articles every week until I was transferred to Lord Kemsley's two chief national papers, the *Sunday Times* and *Daily Sketch*. I had an office in Kemsley House and became a full-time military journalist. The *Sketch* gave me a whole page for my commentary at least once a week and I also wrote for other newspapers in the Kemsley group. The *Sunday Times* was of course a great newspaper and I remained with them, first as military, and then as lawn tennis, correspondent for seven years, until I became a Minister in Winston Churchill's Government in 1951.

I attended meetings of all the leader writers of the Kemsley Group each evening under the Editor-in-Chief, H. N. Heywood, and on important occasions, was asked to write a 'guide' leader which editors use or translate into their own words.

From time to time I was summoned by Lord Kemsley – a splendid and kindly man for whom to work – to discuss the war situation. James Gomer Berry, 1st Baron Kemsley, later created a Viscount in 1945, was then aged sixty. He had had a remarkable career in newspapers, and was at that time Chairman of perhaps the greatest chain of newspapers in the world. He had two other national Sunday papers in addition to the *Sunday Times*: the *Sunday Empire News* and the *Sunday Chronicle* for both of which, particularly the latter, I also wrote.

Lord Kemsley often invited me to his lunches where he entertained celebrated political and military personages, and it was in this way that I was later invited to stand for Parliament in the first election after the war. I found my own military contacts of immense importance, the officers who had been with me at the Staff College, and particular friends such as Auchinleck, Alexander and Slim, who had become some of our most prominent war leaders.

Hard work, always my favourite hobby, was far the best cure for my condition, though I found going up and down stairs in Kemsley House a strain to start with – which few of my colleagues realized. I became a fanatical newspaper man, and have remained so.

Lord Kemsley took the greatest personal interest in his papers and the first editions of the London papers were sent up to him each evening and he sometimes made alterations for the later editions. There is a story that one evening a whole front page of one paper was taken up by a prize bull. Lady Kemsley thought it was much too bullish and insisted that its male parts should not be so prominent in the final edition. The rather emasculated bull duly appeared, and the irate owner sued the paper for damages!

The accredited military correspondents were briefed and assisted in every way possible by the Ministry of Information. Later in the war I and Liddell Hart were instrumental in the formation and expansion of the Military Commentators' Circle. I became the first Vice-Chairman of the Allied Circle in Green Street, where many Allied nationals employed or living in London could meet and discuss matters of common interest, and where lively lectures and discussions took place. I became a Councillor of the East India Association, a member of Chatham House, the Royal Central Asian Society and many other organizations where I met Allied representatives.

Besides my work for Kemsley Newspapers I wrote ever more extensively for British, French and Russian publications and for the Ministry of Information. I was naturally much in demand to write and speak about India and the Far East. By July 1943 I was having anything up to twenty full feature articles a month published in Kemsley Newspapers alone, and that meant a great deal of hard work.

My life and work with Frances were ideally happy and fulfilling. She too was a tremendous worker and utterly dedicated to me and our life together. She had done a crash course in shorthand-typing during the phoney war period, and was able to get a job in the War Office, which though not very well paid was a help to us. Admittedly life in war-time London had its drawbacks and difficulties; the air raids, the blackout, the everlasting queueing for food and drink; but there was a vitality and unity of purpose everywhere, and of course the constant irrepressible humour of the ordinary Londoner was infectious.

My eldest son, John, had made a great reputation for leadership at Ampleforth and had achieved a notable success as Master of the Beagles. He had joined the 1st Battalion, Queen's Royal Regiment in India in July 1941 and went with them to the Arakan in August 1943 for one of the grimmest campaigns of the war. Julian was still at Ampleforth when the war started but later joined the Royal Navy as an Ordinary Seaman. Robin was also at Ampleforth and was about to join the Rifle Brigade. Jill was only ten when the war started and was at school at the Convent of the Sacred Heart, Roehampton.

I heard glowing reports about John and many people told me that he was the life and soul of the party, rallying his men with his hunting horn, which he always carried in battle, and making light of every danger. In February 1944 he was sent, suffering badly from jungle sores, to the ill-fated hospital at the foot of the Ngaklindauk Pass, where he had hardly arrived when the Japanese broke in and butchered all the sick and wounded with the exception of John and a few soldiers of the Queens who managed to fight their way out and rejoin the Battalion.

It was not until I received a letter from someone saying that he might get a V.C. any day that I became really alarmed. The 18 May (1915) was the day we always remembered as V.C. Day. I tried to convey to him in my letters a remark that had been made to me at an even younger age, that 'it was much better to be a live donkey than a dead lion'. But his letters to me were so happy and carefree that I was lulled into a sense of false security. He seemed almost immortal, as I had been, and the war in Burma appeared to be nearing its close. April gave place to May and then, on the 7th of that month, he was killed leading his company in an attack on Jail Hill at Kohima.

Bill Slim cabled me at once. I had some wonderful tributes to John from officers and men of the Battalion and his Commanding Officer, Lieut.-Colonel Duncombe, came to see me. John's batman, who brought home his hunting horn, wrote: 'Captain Smyth was an officer whose example we strive to follow – words cannot tell you what he meant to me.' On his death his brother Robin wrote, thinking of their days together at Camusdarach between Morag and Arisaig, with its exquisite views of the islands of Rhum, Eigg and Skye, where the boys fished in drifters from Mallaig:

> *What if the sun should rise above those eyes*
> *And be no longer seen. If rain at night*
> *Comes silently to where his body lies*
> *Unmindful of the passing of the light.*
> *If he should never hear the winds rejoice*
> *Or on the grey crowned moors at break of day*
> *Should listen to his hounds unhurried voice*
> *Yet he has cheated death in his own way.*
> *For surely these strange rocks will not forget*
> *The one who loved them, and who cast his net*
> *Between the isles, among the magic seas?*
> *Surely this love will all our lives outlast?*
> *For I remember how, in summers past*
> *His horn awoke the sullen Hebrides.*

By the spring of 1944 all our thoughts were centred on the coming invasion of Hitler's Europe by the Allied forces. No one was in much doubt that it would take place in the summer, the only question was when and where.

Towards the middle of May the National Broadcasting Company of

America were deciding on their team of radio commentators to cover the coming invasion of Europe. They decided that it should contain one British commentator, and their choice fell on me. This was not only pleasing, but lucrative. I was engaged to broadcast on a two-way conversation with an American commentator in New York on D Day and the two following days. I don't think that anyone at the time realized what a delicate and difficult assignment this broadcast would be.

Although the War Office had given sanction for this broadcast, when it came to the point they had considerable misgivings. The questions to be put to me from New York were very pointed. Did I think the first landings were a feint? If so, where did I think other landings would be made? and when? And so on. Although my answers were made without any inside knowledge I was a highly trained soldier and I knew a lot of the *dramatis personae* and how such operations were likely to develop. I was interviewed by our own Military Intelligence and the American Intelligence, both of whom were worried about it. I was quite prepared for the whole thing to be called off, but it wasn't.

Lord Kemsley of course was tickled to death that his military correspondent was engaged on this assignment, and Frances and I were invited to dine with him at the Dorchester that evening.

I was most amused and interested at the very different approach and methods adopted by the B.B.C. and the N.B.C. on such an occasion. The B.B.C. liked to get you there hours before the assignment and much rehearsing took place beforehand, in which a number of their staff took part. In this case, a very smart American girl arrived at our flat at what seemed an incredibly short time before I had to go on the air. She had a huge American car down below, in the front of which sat a man who was to play Judas Iscariot in a radio nativity play. The girl drove the car, delivered Judas Iscariot to his playmates, clocked me in at the broadcasting room, gave me a run through of my script and then, herself, got through to New York. Frances and I gasped in amazement at the sheer slickness of it, and the casual 'do it yourself' attitude. But as I took my seat at the microphone two formidable American G.I.s with white gaiters and enormous revolvers stood on either side of me in a menacing sort of way. I gathered that I would have to stick to my script – or else!

It was a very hot night and the studio was like an oven. It was full of people snapping out sentences in broad American. I had answered the first two questions from New York when a very excited announcer snatched the microphone from my hand and rapped out : 'News flash – American troops have captured such and such a place.' My girl friend was furious and, by the time we had got back to my opposite number in New York, the two-way transmitter had ceased to function and I could no longer hear the questions. However, my girl friend said in a flattering sort of way: 'Go ahead, you can do it. They can hear you even though you can't hear them.' So, as I knew approximately what they wanted from me, I gave a one-way broadcast on my own. But the two G.I.s were teetering about like nobody's business as I had gone right off the script. However, at the end, everyone was smiling and saying 'Well done'.

I was dripping with sweat but my condition was nothing compared to that of poor Judas Iscariot, who had been pushed around in this excited military atmosphere and told eventually that his play had been postponed. My girl friend took it all very calmly and drove us back home in her car as if nothing had happened. Things had calmed down for my next two broadcasts and everything went according to plan.

During the succeeding weeks I wrote extensively on the operations across the Channel and in Italy, and of the doings of Bill Slim's 14th Army in Burma and on the great Russian counter-offensive.

The attacks of the V1 flying bombs and the V2 rockets which followed were no fun at all and tried the nerves of the people of London very severely. If Hitler could have launched these weapons a year earlier, as he had hoped the war might conceivably have taken a different turn.

However, by the time our D Day offensive was ready, a large number of launching sites had been completed in northern France and the Low Countries facing Britain, and Hitler had planned to counter our invasion by hurling thousands of these robot weapons against London. Top priority was given to this project and it was intended to launch 10,000 robot projectiles on London a day: but the timing and success of our Normandy landings upset the programme.

So London escaped, by only a few months, from an ordeal which it would have been very hard for the people to bear – particularly as we had no counter to the V2. Coming as it did after nearly five years of total war, with its depressing blackouts, severe rationing and heavy casualties on all the battle fronts, this V2 attack was the last straw.

The first flying bomb to reach London went over Dolphin Square. It made a quite new and peculiar sound, and Frances and I rushed to the window to see it go over. At the time of course we didn't know what it was but that it was something new and strange we had no doubt. Dolphin Square, being so near to Battersea power station, was very much in the danger area from the bombers and we slept with our mattresses on the floor with the beds lying on their sides between us and the windows to protect us from flying glass. From then on until the troops overran the launching sites London had to endure a spate of these flying bombs.

My closest escape from a V1 occurred during a visit to my dentist in

Park Lane. I was seated in the chair in his window overlooking Marble Arch when the sirens sounded. The dentist and I considered whether we should proceed with the drilling or retire to the corridor. Fortunately we decided on the latter course. There was an earth-shaking explosion and when we returned to the surgery the long front window had been blown in and my chair was a mass of glass.

On 18 June I seemed to be pursued by the so-called bumble bombs. Two fell across the river opposite Dolphin Square; one landed in Vincent Square and, as I was walking across St James's Park, one fell on the Guards Chapel during the Service, killing the Colonel, Lord Edward Hay, and killing or wounding over a hundred officers and men. This was a terrible tragedy.

The V2 rocket was a much more alarming and formidable weapon and we were extremely fortunate that it had to be used prematurely at an early stage of its development. The moral effect of the V2s was greatly increased because they fell without warning and we had no defence against them, except to speed our advance on the rocket sites across the Channel. It would have been of considerable encouragement to the Germans if they could have known the full physical and moral damage these weapons were causing.

The last part of 1944 was an intensely busy time for me, with the doings of Bill Slim's 14th Army in Burma added to the mounting offensive of Eisenhower's forces in Europe. In November 1944 Kemsley Newspapers gave a big lunch for me at the Midland Hotel, Manchester, to which they invited some of my old friends in the Manchester Brigade.

Frances, as always, was an enormous help to me. She wrote well herself and was an invaluable assistant and sub-editor, and my sternest critic. How she managed to get up at crack of dawn, make the beds, get the breakfast, do a full day's work at the War Office, cook the dinner and at the same time comfort, advise, criticize and praise I shall never know. Strong and courageous as she was, the end of 1944 saw her fine drawn and living on her nerves, as were so many other wives at that time. My paroxysmal tachycardia still continued, though the attacks were less frequent and not so frightening. But, without Frances's encouragement I would never have survived the war. My good doctor was always there in the background but he quite rightly encouraged me to stand on my own two feet. Fortunately I enjoyed my writing so much that I had little time to think too much about myself.

I also did a lot of speaking on all sorts of platforms. One of these was on 13 February 1945 when I spoke in aid of the newly formed Ex-British Prisoners of War Association. This was a momentous occasion for me as it was the forerunner of my close connection with the Far

Eastern Prisoners of War Federation and my exciting battles on their behalf in and out of the House of Commons.

The end of the war came with the historic V.E. Day (Victory in Europe) celebrations on 8 May 1945. Every newspaper of course carried a tremendous victory article and I was very honoured to be asked to write the one for the *Daily Sketch* when Arthur Bryant dropped out.

Frances and I went out into the streets to join the throngs of happy people, who surged up Whitehall to acclaim Winston Churchill, the man of the hour, the man of the war, the greatest Englishman of his generation. He had led them through their darkest hour, through defeat and tribulation, for nearly six long years, to victory. How they cheered him! And within exactly fifty-eight days they flocked into the polling booths to vote him out of the premiership.

Outside Buckingham Palace hordes of cheering people waited for the King, eager to convey all the joy and loyalty they felt as this momentous hour. I was so glad that Frances and I had been in London together when the war started, that I had taken part in Dunkirk and the dark days that followed; and that we had been in London again together, through the bombings, the V1s and the V2s, and had shared in its vicissitudes. We rejoiced that the war had been won at last; that we were still alive and more devoted to one another than ever. And the premature end of my military career, which had seemed such an irretrievable disaster, now appeared to have been the intervention of divine providence.

CHAPTER SEVENTEEN

I Begin My Political Life

1945-1950

TOWARDS the end of the war my thoughts had turned to politics. I had never had any affiliations with a particular party and I had never been in a position to use my vote at a general election. Lord Noel-Buxton did his best to persuade me to accept a safe Labour seat and, had I done so, I might have entered Parliament in 1945, which would have been a great advantage as I was already fifty-two.

Having been duly accepted as an official Conservative candidate (one of my sponsors being William Temple, Archbishop of Canterbury, in spite of the fact that he himself was a Socialist), I set about getting myself adopted by a constituency. That was much more difficult than it would have been in the Labour Party at that time as the latter were making efforts to enlist more people who had no strong party affiliations, but with general experience such as I had. Hugh Gaitskell, Lance and Per Mallalieu (all Dragons and public school boys), General Mason-Macfarlane, and others of the same type, were being found Labour seats for this first post-war general election.

To my great surprise I was short-listed for the Wirral in Cheshire, one of the safest Conservative seats in the country. I was told afterwards by one of the Wirral Selection Committee that my final adoption had hinged on my answer to one question : Would I take a house there and live in the constituency? Had I merely answered 'Yes' the seat was mine. But at that time the war against Japan was still in progress and there was no indication of its early conclusion. I had a very busy job in London as military correspondent and I couldn't in all honesty agree to leave London until the war was over. By a very narrow majority therefore the Committee decided to adopt a distinguished local candidate. His name was Brigadier Selwyn Lloyd, whose career in politics and as Speaker of the House of Commons has made him one of the most distinguished men of our time. But, had I known as much about politics as I do now, I think I could have worded my answer rather differently! In which case my life might have taken another turn.

Soon after this the Conservative Central Office asked if I would allow my name to go forward for Central Wandsworth, at that time a small and very compact constituency, which was the seat of the great Labour leader, Ernest Bevin. No one thought for a moment we could win this seat, but lost causes have always appealed to me, so I accepted, and was duly adopted on 21 April. Right away this contest caused tremendous interest and the spotlight of the Press was continually turned on it. Bevin himself declared that Central Wandsworth would be a test fight, but the Labour Party had arranged for him to conduct a nationwide speaking tour; and it was this that the Conservative Central Office were anxious that I should interrupt. In this at least I succeeded, and gained a good deal of kudos in so doing and in running Bevin to a narrow majority. *But I did not get into Parliament.* So this was definitely a milestone in my life where I took the wrong turning. However, my first election against such a redoubtable opponent was a great and thrilling experience.

The Central Wandsworth Conservative Association was in a bad way. The office had been bombed and most of the records destroyed; there was no register, no organization, few known helpers and very slender funds, and most disastrous of all, no agent. However, Lord Beaverbrook, whom I had got to know during the war years, managed to find me one and was immensely helpful. On 18 June he and I were billed to speak in Battersea Town Hall in support of the Battersea candidates. This turned out to be, for me, the rowdiest meeting of this or any other election. The Beaver spoke first and got such a battering that the police had to be called in to escort the speakers out before I had spoken at all. But he was determined to finish his speech and I much admired his courage in doing so, though the last part of it was drowned by hecklers.

My plan of campaign had to be a simple one. As we had so few canvassers I had to spend most of my money on my election address, which had to go out by post, and this took a large chunk of the funds allowed. It was vitally important as it was the only means I had to reach the bulk of my electorate. It had been a considerable job to get it addressed and stuffed by my small band of helpers. The night before it was due to go out all the election addresses were stacked in an upstairs room in the office.

In the middle of the night, in our flat in Dolphin Square, Frances, who had taken to politics like a duck to water, woke me up and said that she had just dreamt that a man had broken into our Wandsworth office and set fire to all our precious election addresses. She insisted that I should ring the office at once.

But I said: 'Don't be silly. Who would be in the office at two o'clock in the morning?'

However, I did ring, and the phone was at once answered by my agent, who said that the police had seen a man on a ladder trying to climb in at the top window. He had made good his escape and no damage had been done!

Having spied out the nakedness of the land in Central Wandsworth I had decided to base my campaign on an intensive personal canvass, and very effective it was. Every day Frances and I set off and tramped the streets, knocking on doors and talking to all and sundry on doorsteps and in the streets. Within a week the local Labour Party had become thoroughly alarmed. Bevin was recalled from his nationwide tour and battle commenced.

The Labour Party fought the election on a programme of massive nationalization and State control. But they also managed to convey that they were the party of new blood and new ideas, and held out the ideal of a land where social justice would be done. This policy appealed to the electorate who, after six years of war, wanted something different.

A unique feature of this election was that, after polling day on 5 July, there was an interregnum of twenty-one days to allow men in the Services overseas to record their votes, and the count and declaration of the result did not therefore take place until 26 July. The task of carrying the ballot papers and election addresses to and from these widespread overseas stations was performed by R.A.F. Transport Command and the loss in transit of completed papers was negligible. It was a curious feeling, after all the hurly burly, to sit back and wait.

Although the war in Japan was continuing at the time of the election, on 25 June Winston Churchill, still Prime Minister and Minister of Defence, but as leader of the Conservative Party, began an extensive tour of the constituencies. His last two visits before polling day were made to me in Central Wandsworth and then to his son-in-law, Duncan Sandys, in Norwood. Alas, in neither place did his support bring us success. I had a word with him in his car when he arrived and he then made a short speech. He was grey with fatigue, and no wonder. He had a good reception, which had not been the case in some of the other London constituencies, as his personal attacks on some of his late Labour colleagues in the National Government were much resented.

There was a record poll in Central Wandsworth, with the odds heavily on Bevin. Frances and I were absolutely whacked and we went off for a short holiday at St David's Hotel, Harlech. The election had been a great strain for me as I was still suffering from bouts of heart trouble; but I got through it somehow.

On 25 July the Service votes were counted and showed a big swing to Labour. The men on Service overseas not only voted Labour themselves but asked their relatives at home to do so also. They had been persuaded that a Labour Government would get them home quicker and that nationalization would give them jobs and houses and a life fit for heroes. When I heard the Service vote I was quite convinced that the election was lost. But Ernie Bevin was acutely nervous at the count and much more doubtful, even about the Wandsworth result, than I was. He was like a cat on hot bricks, his face and hands twitching, and he was unable to remain seated. However, as the count neared its conclusion and it became obvious that he was home and dry, he heaved a sigh of relief and relaxed. He then started to look through the various ticker tape results which had been piling up on the table. Suddenly he turned to me with a look of incredulity on his face and said: 'By God, we're going to get in.'

At last it was all over. Bevin had a majority of 5,174. By that time it was certain that the Labour Party were in power. We duly made our speeches to the assembled multitude. Bevin said: 'This has been a clean fight, and I have been lucky to have such a clean opponent.'

The nationwide result of the election was a landslide to Labour which increased its representation in the House of Commons from 164 to 393, while the Conservative representation fell from 358 to 189. A notable feature of the election was the elimination of the smaller parties. The Liberal Party suffered a shattering defeat and their 307 candidates only secured twelve seats. Out of the eighty-seven women candidates only twenty-four were elected; and as the years went by the constituencies selected remarkably few women to represent them; in the October 1974 election only twenty-two women were returned to Parliament, fifteen Labour, five Conservatives and two Scottish Nationals.

The Conservative Central Office were extraordinarily complacent and over-optimistic over the 1945 election. Winston Churchill records in his last volume of the Second World War, entitled *Triumph and Tragedy*, that on the eve of the poll: 'The latest view of the Conservative Central Office was that we should retain a substantial majority.' That was in the days before the Gallup Polls.

I have never admired Winston more than at that hour of crushing and unexpected defeat. Bevin and I retained our liking and respect for one another. Some time after the election, when he was Foreign

Secretary and we were both guests of Civil Defence at a big Victory rally at the Albert Hall, he asked me to share the private room which had been reserved for him. Over a plate of sandwiches and a succession of very strong whiskies Ernie really let himself go over some of the matters of high policy which were worrying him, knowing that I would respect his confidence. Even then it seemed to me that he was a very sick man, driving himself hard by an indomitable will and the assistance of a very big ration of alcohol. But he was a great man and a trade union leader the like of whom we shall probably never see again.

There was no point in my remaining in Central Wandsworth. I was anxious to become prospective Conservative candidate of a winnable constituency in London which I could 'nurse' and possibly win back at the next election. Norwood, in Lambeth, had been represented since 1935 by Duncan Sandys. His defeat in 1945 at the hands of Ronald Chamberlain had been one of the biggest upsets of the election and Labour now held it with a majority of 2,023 votes. Duncan Sandys had left and they were looking for a candidate. There were about a hundred applicants, including several eminent ex-Members of Parliament, and I was lucky to be adopted in November 1946.

Norwood was a so-called dormitory seat with few vested interests, where the candidate had a real opportunity of making his presence felt. It was only about twenty minutes by car from my flat in Dolphin Square. The constituency had altered very greatly during the war years. It had been badly bombed and the old Victorian houses, which had been owned and occupied by a very solid type of middle-class family, now housed several families in a much less well-to-do way of life. There was a considerable Liberal community and the Norwood Liberals had gained 3,944 votes in the 1945 election. There was a great housing shortage and a growing coloured immigration problem. The Lambeth Borough Council was completely Labour, and indeed Lambeth was one of the strongest Labour boroughs in London.

In addition to all this I had a really strong opponent in the new Labour M.P., Ronald Chamberlain. He was on the extreme left of his party, an indefatigable worker with a personality, appearance and strong religious convictions which appealed strongly to a very large number of the post-war constituents of Norwood. I could well understand how it was that he had been able to win Norwood for Labour against such long odds and I knew he would hang on to it with all his might. He had a great initial advantage over me because he knew the constituency inside out. I never underestimated him for a moment.

In the sixteen months which had followed the 1945 election the Conservative Association in Norwood had sunk into a slough of despond from which Mr Aubrey Stapleton, my most excellent and great-hearted Chairman, considered they could only be rescued by a strong Conservative candidate around whom the organization could be rebuilt and morale and confidence restored. Frances and I threw ourselves wholeheartedly into the job and the twenty-one years I spent in Norwood were very busy, very happy, and very successful.

We aimed to take on Ronald Chamberlain at his strongest point – to get right into the life of the people. But most important of all we embarked on a personal canvass lasting three years. We canvassed in all weathers, and where we led others followed, particularly the Young Conservatives, which soon grew into a strong and lively branch. Frances was a very good canvasser. She knew most of the answers and was a good mixer; she was utterly fearless; she would knock up a houseful of coloured immigrants in a bad area without batting an eyelid. And such was her sympathy with people that she nearly always made friends with them.

We also attacked the seemingly impregnable strongholds of Labour in the Borough Council and the L.C.C. We not only put up a lot of candidates, but at last started to get some elected. Those people who said in 1945 that Norwood would be Labour for all time began to wonder, and some of them began to join the Conservatives. When Harold Macmillan came to speak for me on Friday, 24 September 1948, he said: 'It seems to me that you are winning your election now.'

I replied: 'That's what I'm aiming to do because I know it is going to be very tough when the election comes.'

Lord Woolton said to me on one occasion: 'You could make Norwood a bastion from which we could win other seats in South London.'

I said: 'Yes, but I've got to *win* Norwood first.'

On the journalistic side, 1946 found me still with Kemsley Newspapers as military correspondent to the *Sunday Times* and *Daily Sketch*. One day, however, early in 1946, at an editor's conference of the *Sunday Times*, an urgent matter was brought up by the Sports Editor, which was to have a profound effect on my life. He reported that the very well-known referee and sports writer, Hamilton-Price, who had been the *Sunday Times* Lawn Tennis Correspondent, had died and lawn tennis tournaments were starting, including the Davis Cup competition and the first post-war Wimbledon. These events must be reported in the *Sunday Times* at once. All the other papers had already appointed their correspondents.

In the gloomy silence which ensued, I found myself saying: 'Well, I have played quite a lot of first-class tennis, both at home and in India, and have been a member of the All England Club since 1938 and a member of the International Lawn Tennis Club of Great Britain. I have never written about the game but I think I could and there is little for me to do on the military side at the moment.'

As no one could think of a better solution I was invited to write an anonymous article for the *Sunday Times* of 3 February on the coming Davis Cup match between Britain and France! It was printed in the smallest possible type and was tucked away in an inconspicuous corner of the sports pages. Two other anonymous articles followed. As these met with general approval I was given the green light and on 14 April quite a big article appeared under my own name. I had arrived as a lawn tennis writer.

Towards the end of 1947 I accepted the appointment of 'Comptroller' of the Royal Alexandra and Albert School for orphan and necessitous children. The appointment was for six months, and I remained in it for seventeen years! The school was an amalgamation of two famous schools for orphans, the Royal Alexandra and the Royal Albert. The former was a City of London school for 240 boys and girls which, in 1939, had been evacuated from London and moved to the hutted Bishopswood camp near Reading. The Royal Albert, with just over 100 boys, was situated at Collingwood Court, Camberley. The Chairman of the Royal Alexandra, a Methodist school, was James V. Rank, brother of Arthur Rank, and the Chairman of the Royal Albert, a Church of England school, was Sir Noel Mobbs.

Both schools were maintained entirely by public subscription, but under the Education Act of 1944 the children were educated by the local authorities in county schools. When I was invited to become Comptroller the two schools had decided to amalgamate and had purchased Gatton Hall at Reigate, formerly the seat of Sir Jeremiah Coleman, and some of the surrounding parkland. This historic and lovely place provided an excellent site for the new school. But the problems which confronted us were legion; there was an enormous financial problem – to keep the two schools going and, at the same time, raise the money to build the new school.

Royalty had always taken the greatest interest in these two royal orphan schools. The new school had Her Majesty Queen Mary as Patron, the Duke of Gloucester as President, and the Duchess of Kent and Lady Patricia Ramsay as Vice-Presidents. James Rank was the first Chairman, Sir Noel Mobbs Vice-Chairman, and Marshal of the Royal Air Force Lord Portal was Hon. Treasurer. Eric Corner was a first-class and dedicated Secretary.

The school suffered a severe blow when the Chairman and chief financial supporter, Jimmy Rank, died. He was a rugged but delightful Yorkshireman of whom I was very fond. We were rescued in the nick of time by the tremendous efforts of our new Chairman, Sir Frederick (Albert) Minter and the generosity of the Rank family and many others.

The object of the school was to give boys and girls who, through no fault of their own, had met with family or other misfortunes, as good a start in life as possible. Old boys and girls of both schools who came down to Gatton to see the new school, were quite amazed at the change which had been wrought in the character and status of the school.

But a school cannot be created in a day and this one was no exception. It became one of the greatest interests in my life, and that of Frances too, to see the school grow and unfold after all the difficult problems which had beset its infancy. We felt that we had helped to create something of true value for the future.

The bicentenary was celebrated at Gatton on 10 May 1958, when our President, the Duke of Gloucester, arrived by helicopter and was joined by our Vice-President, the Duchess of Kent. Gatton had never looked more beautiful in the clear spring sunshine, and our royal visitors were indefatigable in seeing everything and talking to many of the children. As one small girl said to Frances: 'This is a day we will remember all our lives.'

These five years after the war, with the Norwood constituency, the *Sunday Times* tennis, and the Royal Alexandra and Albert School, were certainly years of great endeavour; but none of my jobs brought in much cash and we remained as always, just solvent, but no more.

But I had largely recovered my health and our marriage was a very blessed thing.

CHAPTER EIGHTEEN

I Become a Member of Parliament

THE 1950 general election was about the most dramatic in British parliamentary history and it provided the closest result for a hundred years. In 1945 a Labour Government had been elected on a policy of all-out nationalization and had been given an overall majority of 150 to carry it out. The Labour leaders had made it clear that this first five years of Socialism was only an hors d'oeuvre; the meaty part – the full nationalization of all the means of production, distribution and exchange was still to come. The electorate had to decide in 1950 whether it liked what the Government had already provided and whether they were happy about the second course. The 1950 vote showed that the British people didn't much like either and the enormous Labour majority of 1945 was reduced to seven.

The Times reported on 15 February 1950:

The most marginal constituency in Lambeth is the dormitory area of Norwood where in 1945 Mr Ronald Chamberlain converted a Conservative majority of 12,456 to a Labour majority of 2,023. The Conservative organization in this 'safe' seat suffered a jolt which has shaken it into brisk activity. Since then it has won all three seats on the L.C.C. and has swept the board in the Borough Elections. And it reposes high hopes in its candidate, Brigadier J. G. Smyth, V.C., a gallant soldier and a redoubtable political campaigner, who ran Mr Bevin to a narrow majority in Central Wandsworth in 1945. The Liberal intervention here may affect the Conservatives more than Labour, as the candidate, Mr R. Fredericke, is the daring young man who, as Chairman of the Chelsea Young Conservatives, challenged his leaders at the Party Conference and rebounded into the Liberal camp.

I personally have never worked so hard at any election nor would I ever contemplate doing so again. I walked hundreds of miles during the campaign and talked to many thousands of people in their homes, or in the streets. For over a year before the election Frances had been canvassing the Tulse Hill and other big blocks of new flats. When the election started she was joined by my brother, Bill, who was then Assistant Secretary of the Middlesex Hospital; he continued his canvass in all my subsequent elections in Norwood. The dwellers in these big blocks of flats got to know him as well as the milkman. One does not win back a seemingly lost cause like Norwood against a candidate like Ronald Chamberlain by sitting on a platform and making speeches.

Frances and I stalked doubtful voters like hungry lions, and we would motor right across the constituency to answer a query from some disgruntled old lady. However, during the last three days I started a bout of 'flu. I managed to keep going until the poll ended at 9 p.m. and was then put to bed with a high temperature.

At Ronald Chamberlain's eve of poll meeting in St Luke's Hall, the Chairman told the large audience at the end of the meeting: 'You have helped to put a nail into Brigadier Smyth's coffin and I call upon you to give a donation to the fighting fund as you go out to help buy the Brigadier a damned great pair of brass handles for it.' But alas for Labour hopes:

The man recovered from the bite,
The dog it was that died.

Frances went to the count where, amid scenes of tremendous enthusiasm, the result was declared at 3 a.m. on the morning of 24 February:

Brigadier Smyth	24,811
Ronald Chamberlain	22,736
Robin Fredericke	3,770
Conservative majority	2,075

Frances made the speech thanking the returning officer on my behalf and then rushed home to tell me I was a Member of Parliament. Success is a wonderful pick-me-up and I was down in the constituency next day to attend a victory meeting of my supporters. The rest of Lambeth remained strongly Labour, Brixton with a majority of 5,058 and Vauxhall with 13,370. But a little wedge of blue had appeared in this otherwise completely Labour Borough, which did form a springboard from which the Conservative Party was to win several more seats in South London.

The *Sunday Times* of 26 February noted: 'Brigadier Smyth's victory in Norwood was all the more remarkable because his Socialist opponent, Mr Ronald Chamberlain, polled 6,000 more votes than he had done five years earlier.' Ronald Chamberlain was indeed a redoubtable opponent. He never gave in. He was there to fight me again in 1951.

For me it was the greatest thrill of my life to become a Member of Parliament and to do it the hard way by winning back a Labour seat. I was told it was a unique achievement for a Regular Indian Army officer after thirty years' service.

On 1 March the Commons met, still in the Lords Chamber, as our new Chamber was not yet ready after its wartime bombing, and Colonel Clifton Brown was unanimously elected as Speaker. On 6 March came the official opening of Parliament, and I was launched on a thrilling new career which lasted sixteen years, with two ministerial appointments, a baronetcy and a privy councillorship.

I made my maiden speech in a big defence debate on 16 March. Contrary to the advice of many old hands in Parliament I didn't believe in hanging about.

The Labour Government suffered its first defeat in the House on 17 March. And on the 26 October the King opened the new House of Commons. At Winston Churchill's suggestion the archway leading from the Members' Lobby into the Chamber was allowed to stand in its scarred and battered condition. It was now generally known as 'the Churchill Arch'.

On 30 November 1950, his seventy-sixth birthday, Winston Churchill, as leader of the Opposition, made one of his greatest speeches, on the war in Korea. The Speaker called me at 5.50 p.m. and, rather surprisingly at that hour, there was a crowded attendance – particularly on the two front benches, which included both Attlee and Churchill. I was of course delighted to have such a distinguished audience, but equally cast down when the Prime Minister and Winston, with most of the two front benches, trooped out in a body. It transpired that a cable had suddenly arrived from Mr Truman, the American President, in answer to one sent by the P.M., suggesting that the latter should visit Washington immediately to discuss a proposal which had been made for the use of atomic weapons in Korea.

Mr Attlee flew off at once to Washington with his usual lack of fuss. After a week of critical talks, first in Washington and then in Canada, he returned to London. On his first day back in the Commons to make his important report he spotted me in the Members' Lobby and said : 'Oh, Smyth, I'm sorry I had to go out in the middle of your speech, but my wife stayed on in the gallery to hear it and told me it was jolly good.' No back-bencher could fail to feel flattered at such a remark, made at such a time, by the Prime Minister – particularly to one on the opposite side of the House.

I came to have a great admiration for Attlee, one of the toughest individuals, both mentally and physically, I have met in any walk of life. What a general he would have made! No one could have remained leader for so long of a party torn by so many differing interests and beliefs. He was like the conductor of an orchestra who puts his baton in his pocket and appears to allow the band to play its own tune, yet is always ready to produce his magic wand and rap the music stand at the slightest sign of discord. His attitude on the front bench, whether in Government or Opposition, was typical of the man. The front bench in the Chamber of the House of Commons is apt to be a very self-conscious making place. Some sit bolt upright and look down at their stomachs. Others fidget with their ties, their collars, their glasses or their papers; others recline languidly with their feet on the table – a position which I, being short, found somewhat difficult; but Attlee, though shorter still, managed it to perfection. He got well down with his head almost on the seat so that all I could see of him was his feet. And behind these feet he had a second line of defence in the shape of a large blotting pad, on which he doodled industriously, without seeming to be listening to the debate at all. Then suddenly he would uncoil, spring to the despatch box and reply pungently to some rudery which had appeared to float over his head.

Attlee of course was a great devotee of lawn tennis and was a regular attender at Wimbledon in the royal box. As a member of the All England Club and a regular attender myself I met him there from time to time. He always read my tennis articles in the *Sunday Times* and long after I had ceased to write them he would introduce me as 'the former Lawn Tennis Correspondent of the *Sunday Times*'!

One day, whilst I was a Parliamentary Secretary and was working in my room in the House of Commons I had a telephone call from his private secretary to say he wanted to come and see me on an urgent private matter. I wondered whatever it could be. When he came in he said :

'I'm very worried. My invitations for Wimbledon have not come and it's a week beyond the time I usually get them.'

I felt sure there had been some mistake as they always liked having anyone so distinguished and so keen and he usually came at least twice in each week. I replied : 'I'm sure there has been some mistake, I will probably be able to let you know while you wait.' I rang the Secretary and he told me that they had been delayed but were already in the post. Clem Attlee went away happy.

I was very cunning about my own Wimbledon. It was necessary for me to see at least the important matches in order to write about them in my Sunday article. So I found out all the Labour members who were keen on tennis and gave them tickets for the days I wanted to go so that I could pair with them. I remember James Callaghan was one of them.

Ever since the war ended, and indeed before that, I had interested myself in the problems of our British ex-prisoners of war and particularly the F.E.P.O.W.s – the Far Eastern ex-prisoners of the Japanese. My friend, Arthur Percival, the President of the F.E.P.O.W.s, and their Committee asked me to take up their case in Parliament : this was for some compensation for their suffering at the hands of the Japanese. No less than 10,000 of our British prisoners of the Japanese had died in captivity, which is 27 per cent of the total as compared to 4 per cent who had died in German hands.

With the coming of peace the sufferings of the F.E.P.O.W.s became forgotten. From time to time individual Members of Parliament had tried to raise their case in the House but nothing ever came of it. I therefore advised Percival that the only possibility of success was to raise it in the House on all-party lines. And this they asked me to do.

Early in 1951, with my colleague Tufton Beamish (later Lord Chelwood), Conservative M.P. for Lewes, and George Thomas, Labour M.P. for Cardiff West (later Speaker of the House of Commons), warmly supporting, I arranged an all-party meeting of M.P.s in the House at which General Percival, his deputy, Phil Toosey (later Sir Philip), and some of his colleagues, stated their case. The meeting was packed to overflowing and were 100 per cent supporting. As a result we put down a motion on the order paper on 21 March :

That this House is of the opinion that His Majesty's Government should give early consideration to the claim of the British Far Eastern Prisoners of war and the dependents of those who died in captivity, for compensation from the Japanese, through treaty or by other methods, for the brutalities, indignities and gross undernourishment to which they were subjected in flagrant contravention of the Hague Convention on similar lines to the action already taken by the United States Government, or that decided upon by the Australian Government in this connection.

The motion was put down in the names of myself, George Thomas and Joe Grimond, representing Conservative, Labour and Liberal opinion in the House. Members of all parties flocked to add their signatures and, in a short time, these had amounted to nearly 300, including 89 members of the Labour Party on the Government side of the House. In addition, I had been promised support by front-bench members on both sides. It was said to be the largest all-party motion against the Government ever put down.

I was under no illusion that there was not powerful opposition to the claim. Both the Government and the Opposition were influenced by the Chiefs of Staff, who considered it would be wrong to give any special consideration to ex-prisoners-of-war. I was advised privately from a high level that my motion was certain to be defeated, which would be a blow to my political career. Indeed, the official brief issued by the Conservative Party was against me. Although only a new Member I demanded an interview with the Chief Whip at which I pointed out that the great majority of the Party had come out openly in my support. Very wisely he quietly withdrew the brief.

The Press were wholeheartedly on our side. And from then on I and my supporters rose constantly in the House to demand time to debate the motion – and it was constantly refused. Eventually, when I rose once again on 12 April and my request was once more refused by the Leader of the House, Anthony Eden rose on our behalf and said that the Opposition would give half one of their precious Supply Days for this debate.

The big occasion came on 10 May 1951, and it was a very thrilling moment for me when I got up to move the motion at two minutes past seven, with the large public gallery of the new House of Commons full of eager F.E.P.O.W.s. I asked for a sum of ten million pounds from the Japanese and made it clear that the F.E.P.O.W.s would not be willing to take a penny from the British tax payer.

George Thomas then rose to support me in a powerful and moving speech, as did other Members on both sides of the House. My last speaker was Selwyn Lloyd who was one of the F.E.P.O.W.'s most powerful supporters. But before this, Mr Younger, the Minister of State, had intervened in the debate to announce, wisely, that the Government would not oppose the motion. He did however state there would be little chance of our getting a clause into the Peace Treaty and, even if we did, there was little likelihood of obtaining any substantial compensation for the F.E.P.O.W.s.

When the question was finally put by Mr Speaker it was carried unanimously. From then on we continued to press the Foreign Secretary, Herbert Morrison, with regard to getting a clause into the

Peace Treaty. After several months we were informed that two clauses had been included, one authorizing us to seize Japanese assets frozen in the United Kingdom and the other allowing us to have a share in those Japanese assets frozen in Allied and neutral countries. Herbert Morrison congratulated me on the success of my endeavours, but warned me that the outcome from a financial point of view would be quite insignificant.

Ten years later, on 20 April 1961, John Boyd-Carpenter, the Minister of Pensions and National Insurance at that time, informed me in writing that the total amount received for the benefit of the F.E.P.O.W.s from all sources (Article 14, Article 16 and the Burma-Siam Railway) was just short of £5 million (five million) pounds. But behind this bald statement lay years of endeavour on the part of a number of Conservative Ministers and legal authorities. Gradually, very gradually at first, through the endeavours of people like Selwyn Lloyd and John Boyd-Carpenter, the frozen assets began to melt.

The F.E.P.O.W.s had stipulated from the start (wrongly in my view) that any money received should be distributed to living ex-prisoners on a per capita basis. The result was that most of the money had been distributed in this way, giving individuals something like £80 each.

There was then a pause and suddenly another quarter of a million pounds appeared. John Boyd-Carpenter and I urged strongly that this nest egg should be put into a Trust fund established by the Government and then controlled by the F.E.P.O.W.s themselves. Percival and his Committee agreed. The Trust was established with myself as the first Government Trustee, and the F.E.P.O.W.s had a welfare fund which was the envy of all other ex-Service Associations.

In the House of Commons the Labour Government had survived precariously since February 1950 with a hopelessly inadequate majority. They had several times narrowly escaped defeat on major issues of policy. On one occasion they had only got through by one vote and there had twice been a tie, in which the Chairman's vote had been given in their favour. Five other times they had been defeated, but on less important occasions. To add to their other difficulties they had lost two of their greatest parliamentarians through ill-health – both of whom I greatly admired. First, Sir Stafford Cripps, the brilliant, austere Chancellor of the Exchequer, who had at last to resign from his office and from the Commons in October 1950; and then my own opponent in Central Wandsworth, Ernie Bevin, who, also on account of ill-health, resigned from his office as Foreign Secretary and died a month later. I remember how absolutely shocked Winston

Churchill was at Bevin's appearance on the last occasion when he took his place on the Government front bench.

In the summer of 1951 I went over to the United States to report the tennis for the *Sunday Times*. Jack Kennedy, then a young Senator, later to become President of the United States, invited me to lunch at his club. We had a most interesting talk about our respective parliamentary affairs and I liked him a lot. We would have welcomed another meeting but we both had too many engagements in the short time I had left in America. I was at a party in my constituency when a flash came through on the News reporting his assassination. I was so shocked that such a brilliant young man in such a high position should have suddenly gone out like a light that I felt I had to leave the party at once.

The general election of 25 October 1951 restored Winston Churchill to the Premiership with the Conservative Party gaining a majority of seventeen over all the other parties. I had a straight fight in Norwood, this time against Ronald Chamberlain, with no Liberal intervention. But Chamberlain's opposition was even tougher than before and the count couldn't have been more exciting: at 2.30 a.m. we were neck and neck. Finally I came out the winner by a majority of 2,949, an increase of only 874 on 1950. Chamberlain, in two successive elections, had increased the Labour vote by 7,584, yet lost both times! This was a heartbreaking experience for him and no wonder he then packed up and called it a day. The rest of Lambeth remained solid for Labour and Marcus Lipton in Brixton actually increased his majority. Of the forty-three seats in the London boroughs, twenty-nine were held by Labour and fourteen went to the Conservatives, including two gains. This was the first election when television was used to any extent. Afterwards of course it became a major factor.

When the new Parliament met for the first time on 31 October for the election of a Speaker, the nominee – W. S. Morrison, Conservative Member for Cirencester and Tewkesbury – was opposed and a vote had to take place, for the first time since 1895. This resulted in 'Shakes' Morrison being elected by a majority of sixty-seven over Major J. Milner.

In the few days' interval before the official opening on Tuesday, 6 November, Frances and I attended a number of victory celebrations in Norwood. Coming home to our flat in Dolphin Square after one of these in happy mood, we found both telephones ringing madly. Frances picked up one of them and said to me in an awed voice: 'It's 10 Downing Street wanting you urgently.'

The Prime Minister's private secretary was on the line. He said: 'The Prime Minister has been trying to speak to you all day and we have tried everywhere to get you. The Prime Minister is now at an important meeting and will ring you in the morning. On no account must you go out until he has spoken to you.'

It seemed obvious that Mr Churchill was about to offer me a position in his Government, which I had never anticipated for a moment, although my F.E.P.O.W. debate had brought me many congratulations. It could not be more than a Parliamentary Secretaryship, which was very poorly paid at that time. I was just starting to make a little money and had to think hard about what I should reply. After much discussion with Frances into the small hours I decided to refuse.

But other people have tried to refuse Winston Churchill something he was determined to have. When he came on the telephone I was submerged in a flood of oratory. He wanted me as Parliamentary Secretary to the Ministry of Pensions. I was the only person who could do it; the gallant ex-Servicemen, particularly the disabled, demanded a sympathetic Minister. I hummed and hawed, I floundered and stalled for time. At last all I could think of to gain more time was: 'What is the pay and do I have to give up my parliamentary salary?' (I was not sure about this, I had never anticipated being offered a job.) To my question Winston replied: 'You know, I haven't any idea but I will go and find out.' I smiled reassuringly at Frances – and then the P.M. was back on the line. He told me the pay was miserable, only £1500, and I should lose half my parliamentary salary.

To my astonishment I heard myself saying that in that case I would be honoured and pleased to accept. Winston was charming and appeared delighted. And I must admit that being a Minister in his Government was one of the most wonderful experiences of my life and I wouldn't have missed it for all the tea in China. Winston was always charming to me and I would have done anything in my power to serve him. Even when he got rather ancient and couldn't remember people's names, he never forgot mine. Derick Heathcoat-Amory (later 1st Viscount), aged fifty and eight years younger than me, was my Minister and we got on together very well.

My first visit to 10 Downing Street was to hear 'the gracious speech' to be delivered by the Sovereign at the official opening of Parliament. Winston and Anthony Eden liked to make this a full dress affair, with white ties and medals; but on this occasion, as he was so busy completing his Government appointments, it was held in the early evening over a glass of sherry.

The Ministry of Pensions was then located in Sanctuary Buildings, Great Smith Street, within a few hundred yards of the House of Commons and within walking distance of Dolphin Square. We were extremely fortunate in the Ministry in our two senior Civil Servants.

The Secretary was Sir Arton Wilson, and the Deputy Secretary was Dame Marjorie Cox. My own relations with these two sterling people and great public servants were of the happiest.

Our first task was a very urgent one : to give an immediate and much needed rise in war disability pensions. Fortunately we had in Rab Butler a Chancellor of the Exchequer who was sympathetic to our claim and, in his first Budget of 1952, he announced the biggest ever rise with ten shillings on the basic rate and seven shillings for war widows. It does not seem much today, but the value of money had not then been eroded.

After that, in addition to my ordinary work, I was immersed in implementing the provisions of the F.E.P.O.W. claim which I had myself initiated as a back-bencher in the previous Parliament – an almost unprecedented sequence of events. Derick Heathcoat-Amory gave me a fairly free hand in the long and intricate proceedings, which lasted several years. John Boyd-Carpenter, first as Financial Secretary to the Treasury and then as Minister of Pensions and National Insurance, was immensely helpful, and Selwyn Lloyd gave me wise advice when I had to attend a Cabinet meeting to get approval for my plan.

Our first Conservative Party Conference after the new Government was held at Scarborough from 9 to 11 October 1952. On the first morning the three subjects for discussion were defence, foreign affairs and pensions. These three debates were replied to by Field-Marshal Alexander, Anthony Eden and myself. It was Alex's first appearance as Minister of Defence. He read a prepared brief and got a great ovation – as Alex, a very popular war hero. But Winston made a mistake in bringing him into politics.

Foreign Secretary Anthony Eden, and his recently wedded wife (formerly Clarissa Churchill), who was seated next to me on the platform and was a most delightful person, got a tremendous welcome from the Conference. Anthony Eden was the *beau ideal* of a Foreign Secretary and exercised immense power behind the scenes in diplomatic circles. With a Prime Minister other than Neville Chamberlain, he might just have managed to bring in American influence earlier and so possibly have stopped the Second World War.

Winston was a great hero worshipper. Ever since Alex had been left in command of the last corps to be re-embarked at Dunkirk, and had at considerable risk to his own life walked along the whole length of the beach to see that no one had been left behind, he became one of Winston's heroes. Winston had the same feeling about the Battle of Britain pilots and the annual Battle of Britain Remembrance Service was always an important date in his calendar.

Later in the year Frances and I were holidaying at Studland Bay.

I was just going into the sea when a waiter from the hotel rushed down to the beach, coat tails flying. He shouted out: 'Brigadier Smyth, Mr Churchill wants to speak to you urgently on the telephone.' This caused a great sensation amongst the bathers. Frances wrapped me round in a towelling wrap and I ran up to the hotel. The Prime Minister meanwhile had rung off but would call again in an hour's time. I wondered what on earth it could be. I sat at the end of the telephone indulging in all sorts of day-dreams. Eventually Churchill came on the line: he had to be out of the country for the Battle of Britain Service which he had never missed and would I represent him in Westminster Abbey on 22 September. Naturally I replied that I would be proud and honoured to do so.

I had no idea it was going to be such an ordeal. I had imagined that a paragraph would appear in the paper and that I should go to the Service in the ordinary way and sit at the front. Not so. A police motor cycle escort called for us at Dolphin Square and, ensconced in a large Humber and clad in top hat, frock coat and full medals, we crashed through all the traffic lights to arrive at the Abbey with every-one else already seated. Frances was swept away from me by another church dignitary and, escorted by the Dean, I walked the whole length of the Abbey to my special pew. I could hear my shoes going clickety-clack, clickety-clack on the stone and felt heads being turned and people thinking, 'Who the hell is this?'

After the service the Dean came to collect me and we walked slowly back to the main entrance followed by Clement Attlee, Marshals of the Royal Air Force and senior officers of the other Services, lords, ladies and Members of the Houses of Parliament. My Humber was purring at the entrance, the door being held open for me. I said: 'But where is my wife?'

People rushed off to find her. The Dean said, 'Would you mind going by yourself, otherwise all these distinguished people will be kept waiting?'

I said: 'No. I came with my wife and I'm not going without her.'

At last someone rushed up to Frances and said: 'Are you the Prime Minister's wife?'

To which she most sensibly replied: 'Yes, I suppose I am.' So we were re-united and all ended happily.

The next year the Prime Minister was again out of the country and he once more asked me to represent him, this time at St Paul's as the Abbey was undergoing repairs.

Winston also had an obsession about the Victoria Cross. One evening when we were sitting together after some official dinner, I said to him: 'What a wonderful career you have had.'

He leaned towards me and said: 'Yes, but I would give it all for that one little medal you are wearing.'

I replied: 'How absurd; there have been over 1,300 V.C.s – but only one Winston Churchill.'

On 26 February 1953 the Prime Minister announced in the House two very important changes in administration. One was the amalgamation of the Ministries of Transport and Civil Aviation, and the other was the amalgamation of the Ministries of Pensions and National Insurance. The first of these proposals caused little comment; but the second met with strong and unexpected opposition from the British Legion and other ex-Service associations such as BLESMA, which were concerned with war disability pensions. Even though this amalgamation brought several important advantages to this class of pensioner, the ex-Service community were dead against it. The Ministry of Pensions had a high reputation and had done a great job and the ex-Service associations felt it was their own Ministry. On the ministerial side an additional Parliamentary Secretary was to be appointed to the new Ministry, and it had been intimated to me that I would be offered this new appointment. The Minister of the new Department was to be Osbert Peake, while Derick Heathcoat-Amory was to be offered another appointment.

Even so, the Order was only carried with a majority of fourteen. From my own point of view I was in two minds whether or not to accept the new Parliamentary Secretary appointment. I had been wholly employed on the administrative side of war pensions for two years, with few opportunities of making speeches at the despatch box, and would have liked a complete change. But I was under strong pressure from Winston and the ex-Service community, and from Dame Marjorie Cox, who would go over to the new Ministry with me; also there was still much work to be done on the implementation of the F.E.P.O.W. claim. So when, later in the year, I was formally offered by Winston the appointment of Joint Parliamentary Secretary (first with Robin Turton and then with Ernest Marples) to the new Ministry, I duly accepted. The new Ministry was located in John Adam Street, off the Strand. I remained with my office at Thames House to start with but then had to move to much more cramped and less pleasant accommodation in John Adam Street.

On 29 November 1954 I dined at 10 Downing Street for the last pre-opening of Parliament dinner during the premiership of Winston Churchill. I always enjoyed these occasions enormously. The dress was white tie and medals. The Speaker and all the Ministers were present and Winston used to start by reading the Queen's Speech, which was to be given by Her Majesty at the official opening next day. Winston's wonderful sense of history and tradition also gave great panache and drama on these occasions. The Chief Whip was ordered to guard the door before the reading started. And I always enjoyed one of those famous Churchill cigars after dinner and a word with the P.M. himself after the brandy.

It was a great privilege to have been in his Government and to have had the opportunity of getting to know his family. I would not compare Winston with Lloyd George as an orator; their methods were very different. Both of course gave great attention to an important speech. Lloyd George spoke from rough notes at which he hardly glanced and he altered his speeches as he went along in accordance with the response he got from his audience. Winston's speeches had been written and rewritten beforehand, with each sentence carefully moulded. He was really a fine writer of Engilsh prose and a great speaker of his own writing. The speech lay on the despatch box in all its perfection before he rose to his feet to deliver it. He then donned his powerful magnifying glasses and read the speech, though he knew it so well that he did not always appear to be doing so. He marked places where he expected to be interrupted and he could then continue without being, so to speak, knocked off his perch. For this reason Churchill's speeches read much better than anyone else's.

Winston was fortunate, I think, in that he was in his prime before the advent of television. He would of course have adapted himself for short set speeches and his appearance would have been fine on the box, but I do not believe it would have been his métier as the radio was.

Many stories have been told of Winston Churchill. I remember I said something to him on his eightieth birthday which pleased him. 'It was once said of a famous steeplechase jockey that he rode at the last fence as though it was not there. That is how you will approach old age.'

And one night when we were sitting late in the Commons I said to him : 'You are looking very well, sir.'

To which he replied : 'I feel very well. My wife is away and when she is away I have champagne for lunch as well as for dinner.'

During the years before his death, when I was Chairman of the V.C. and G.C. Association and he was President (a position he was still holding when he died), he took the closest interest in our doings and would send me personal telegrams from time to time about this or that. He was a tremendous personality and I had the warmest affection and respect for him.

Tuesday, 5 April 1955 was the last day of Sir Winston Churchill's premiership. Colonel Marcus Lipton, Labour Member for Brixton, tried to move the adjournment of the House to mark the importance of the occasion but his motion was disallowed by Mr Speaker. After his stroke, which was not publicized and from which he made an amazing recovery, Winston had suddenly aged, and it became essential that he should hand over the reins of office. But the House missed him enormously on the Government front bench, though he still came from time to time to sit in his old seat below the gangway; but he never spoke in the House again. With his passing from office something went out of us all because greatness elevates all who come in contact with it.

CHAPTER NINETEEN

Sir Anthony Eden Becomes Prime Minister

THE premiership of Anthony Eden was a tragedy in one very short act, lasting only twenty-one months. For part of it I was one of his Ministers and the barometer then seemed set fair. For the latter part I was a back-bencher, sitting in the third bench below the gangway with several other ex-Ministers. It was from that very close-up position that I watched, and took some part in, the last weeks of Eden's premiership, which was highlighted by the drama of the Suez crisis and then by his severe illness.

On 15 April 1955, only ten days after he became Prime Minister, Eden announced in a broadcast from Chequers, that Parliament would be dissolved on 6 May and that polling would take place on the 26th. I had a new Labour opponent in Norwood in the person of James Avery Joyce, an international lawyer, educationalist and an experienced political campaigner. Once again the Liberals decided not to put up a candidate which, in Norwood, was certainly an advantage to me. The *Birmingham Post*, in its 'Review of the Battle of London', said :

> In the still substantially suburban Norwood Brigadier J. G. Smyth cannot afford to be too casual in his campaign if he is to hold, or improve upon, his 2,949 Conservative majority of 1951. There have been no boundary changes in the three Lambeth divisions so no abnormal swings are expected by either party.

On the whole it was a quiet election as elections go. Eden paid me a visit and got a rousing welcome. My majority rose to 5,032, a swing of nearly 3 per cent, which was one of the best results in the country,

In three elections I had achieved a turnover of 7,097 votes from 2,075 against me in 1950 to 5,032 in favour, in an otherwise completely Labour borough. Marcus Lipton did wonderfully well to hold Brixton for Labour with almost as big a majority as he had in 1951. George Strauss's vote dropped in Vauxhall but he still had a majority of nearly 9,000. As there was no appreciable swing in London we were much congratulated on our result. The result of the election was that the Conservatives gained an overall majority of fifty-nine, a great send-off for Anthony Eden.

The Conservative Party Conference that year was held at Bournemouth and we stayed with Richard Pilkington, the M.P. for Poole, and his wife Rosemary. On 24 October, my sixty-second birthday, I dined at 10 Downing Street with the other Ministers on the eve of the opening of the new Parliament. It was a triumphant occasion, following as it did a rather historic election in which, for the first time in a hundred years, the party in power had gone to the country and been returned with an increased majority. Eden had come into his own at last after many years of waiting; and, as I well knew, the time of waiting and uncertainty had seemed to him sometimes to be almost intolerable.

I had now become a Freeman of the City of London and was on the Court of the Farriers Livery Company. I found myself invited to speak at many City banquets and, just before Christmas, I spoke two nights running at the Mansion House. On the first of these occasions I introduced Pat Smythe, the well-known international horsewoman, to the Farriers and she was admitted to the Honorary Freedom of the City of London in the Farriers' Livery Company. This was a rare and almost unique honour for her and for us. The admission ceremony, which was delightfully informal and yet impressive, took place at a Special Court at the Apothecaries' Hall on 28 November 1955. Frances and I stayed with Pat at her home at Miserden and also went to Windsor to watch her training with the British Olympic team.

Pat's patience and thoroughness with her horses was phenomenal and her determination and courage indomitable. She was a complete professional and a great horse master. She also had a great quality of leadership and everyone who worked for her became devoted to her. One day I heard news of a young horse in Kent which was showing great promise as a jumper. I phoned Pat, who was always on the lookout for new horses which she could buy at a reasonable prices and then school herself, and suggested that we might go down and have a look at it. The owners were thrilled at having a visit from Pat. Frances and I took her down in our car and on the way we called at her address to pick up her post. She gave me a bundle of letters to keep until we got back. I said: 'I think there is one here you would like to see now – it's from the Prime Minister.' She opened it and it was to say that he was recommending her for an O.B.E. This made our day, horse or no horse.

When we arrived at the stables they led out the horse all saddled and bridled. Pat said: 'Take him back into the stable and unsaddle him. I will tell you when I am ready.' She then went into the stable to stroke and make friends with the horse. By the time she arrived at the jumps a small crowd had gathered. Pat took the horse to the end of the field and began to school him – circle right, circle left, this way, that way – for at least half an hour, until she had got him calmed down and under perfect control. Then over the jumps, which he negotiated perfectly.

Pat said to the owner: 'Perfect little horse but how high is he?'

The owner answered: 'I would say about sixteen hands.'

Pat said: 'I would say about fifteen hands – but get your measuring rod.' And fifteen hands it was.

'You've got a lovely horse there,' Pat told him. 'But he just isn't big enough for the big spreads in the show ring. So sorry.'

On the way home we found a place where we could enjoy a picnic lunch over a bottle of wine with which we duly celebrated the O.B.E.

Before the House rose I had informed the Prime Minister that I would like to return to the back benches. I had had a hard and enjoyable four and a half years in two ministerial appointments and wanted now to be able to speak on defence, foreign affairs and education, which were my three greatest interests. Had Sir Walter Monkton not decided to stay on in the Government as Minister of Defence a higher appointment might have been offered to me. He was a sick man and nearing the end of a distinguished political career; but he stayed on for a short time and the opportunity passed. Winston was most annoyed that I had not remained in the Government, but I was awarded a baronetcy for my ministerial services.

There were quite a number of ministerial changes at this time. The most important being a change of Chief Whip. Patrick Buchan-Hepburn was relieved by Ted Heath, who had joined the House with me in 1950. Patrick Buchan-Hepburn (later Lord Hailes) had done a magnificent job as Chief Whip, though he was never popular with his own party or with Labour. He was sensitive, touchy and rather unapproachable, and his fine presence and sartorial perfection were a constant irritation to some people. But he was a strong disciplinarian, unsparing of his own or his colleagues' energies, and a very delightful person when you got to know him. He had an excellent and forward-looking intelligence. I had the greatest affection and admiration for him and he brought us brilliantly through those very difficult years of 1951–55, when we had to govern the country with a very small majority. Frances and I formed a warm friendship with Patrick and his charming wife, Diana. He was created a baron in 1957 and was Governor-General and Commander-in-Chief of the West Indies from 1957 to 1962. He died in 1974.

Ted Heath was an entirely different character. He had been in the Whip's Office since February 1951 and remained as Chief Whip until 1959, when he became Minister of Labour. Thenceforward he held various high appointments until he finally became Prime Minister. He has a very good brain, a wonderful temperament and considerable charm of manner, which hid his very strong personal ambition, and an enormous belief in his own powers. He was certainly a very successful Chief Whip, and one of the ablest politicians of his era.

No sooner did the New Year start than there began a hostile and critical Press campaign against Anthony Eden. This was difficult to explain. Perhaps there is something in the British character which rebels against perfection or success; perhaps it was that Eden was too brilliant, too good-looking, too popular, and he had married a very lovely and charming wife.

The seizure of the Suez Canal at the end of July 1956 faced the Western world – and Britain and France particularly – with a situation of the greatest gravity. *The Times* of 28 July said that M. Pineau, the French Foreign Minister, had declared on the previous day that France could not accept the nationalization of the Suez Canal Company and would take action in consultation with Great Britain in the matter. When asked whether France would take up the matter with the United Nations, M. Pineau had replied. 'That is a very slow procedure. The action I foresee will be much more rapid.'

It was obvious that the British Prime Minister, Anthony Eden, was thinking along the same lines. As he told me at the time, he had always felt that if the British and the French had taken immediate action when Hitler had invaded the Rhineland in 1936, he would have had to withdraw, and Hitler himself in his later writings acknowledged that if his bluff had been called he would have done so. It is of course easy to be wise by hindsight and Eden afterwards acknowledged that, as his relations with Foster Dulles, the American Foreign Secretary, were not at that time of the happiest, he should at this juncture have relied on the good sense and support of his old friend, Ike Eisenhower, and put through a personal call to him at the White House. Had these two men got together at this stage much damaging future misunderstanding between their two countries might have been avoided. But it must also be remembered that some time back Eden had had a by no means successful operation on his bile duct and he was in no condition physically to face the great strain of this very difficult situation. Nor was he entirely *au fait* with the limitations in the British military set-up which prohibited the quick military action which alone could have been successful if he meant to go it alone.

The Times in its leading article of 1 August 1956 said:

When the Commons take up Suez tomorrow there is one thing they can be sure of. It must be their guiding thought. If Nasser is allowed to get away with this coup, all the British and other western interests in the Middle East will crumble. If a country will not stand up for its rights, it must surely lose them. The spirit of giving in is the most fatal disease to which nations are subject, and it is apt to attack them like a cancer, when they have arrived at the meridian.

On the following day, 2 August, the matter was debated in the House of Commons. The Prime Minister restated that no arrangements for the future of the Suez Canal could be acceptable which would leave it in the unfettered control of a single power.

Hugh Gaitskell, Leader of the Opposition, followed with a most impressive and statesmanlike speech in the course of which he said: 'It is all very familiar. It is exactly the same as that we encountered from Mussolini and Hitler in those years before the war.'

Herbert Morrison was even more forthright and intimated that the use of force on our part might well be justified. *The Times* headed their account of the day's debate in big capitals 'IMPRESSIVE UNITY IN THE COMMONS'.

As it was, at the time of Nasser's seizure of the Suez Canal in 1956, the United States were in the throes of a presidential election and an approach to the United Nations, as M. Pineau had said, would have been a very lengthy business. If immediate action was to be taken therefore it could only be done by Britain and France, the two nations most affected and the only two who were capable of taking immediate military action, which their two premiers considered would be within the terms and the spirit of the U.N. Charter.

Had immediate action been instituted the Suez Canal could have been taken from Nasser's hands and then dealt with as the United Nations decided. It was because there was so much delay in the political planning, and the military action which resulted was so slow and ponderous, that world opinion went sour on Britain and France, and their closest ally, the United States, led the condemnation of their unilateral action. The Russians screamed threats, the United Nations condemned them as an aggressor, the Opposition in the House of Commons joined in and attacked Eden with mounting violence and bitterness, and, unkindest cut of all, some of his own party in the House withdrew their support from him and two of his junior Ministers resigned in protest.

On 1 November, in an emergency session of the United Nations, Mr Dulles, on behalf of the United States, described the Anglo-French action as 'a grave error, inconsistent with the principles and purposes of the Charter'. The United Nations demanded an immediate cease fire and at the same time the United States exerted such heavy pressure on sterling that Britain was forced to call an immediate halt in their military action.

At last, on 5 November, Anglo-French paratroopers landed at Port Said and on the same day the Anglo-French forces landed on Port Said beaches, three months after Nasser had seized the Canal. Almost immediately a United Nations force took over from them. This had the wholehearted support of Eden. But all this proved too much for his physical resources and, on 9 January, in view of the grave report issued by his doctors, he had no option but to resign the Premiership. It was a tragic end to the brilliant career of a man who had done so much for world peace and had for so many years been one of the finest Foreign Secretaries in British history. I felt sick at heart for him.

CHAPTER TWENTY

Harold Macmillan at the Helm

THE Conservative Party were fortunate in having two such outstanding men as R. A. (Rab) Butler and Harold Macmillan from whom to chose a Prime Minister. Rab Butler, the Lord Privy Seal, was generally regarded as the heir apparent to Anthony Eden, but in those days the Tories settled such matters by a queer form of stomach-thinking, somewhat akin to that practised by the tribes of darkest Africa : and in this curious way they often came to the right conclusion. So, in the end, and with the minimum of fuss and altercation they chose Harold Macmillan, who was summoned to Buckingham Palace on the afternoon of Thursday, 10 January 1957. I felt the deepest sympathy for Butler, whose prospects of attaining the Premiership had appeared so bright. He bore his disappointment with commendable dignity – and continued to serve the new Prime Minister with complete loyalty.

Macmillan's character was an unusual mixture. He was a man of good will, with warm emotions and genuine humanity. He had energy and courage and yet he was an intellectual as well. In some indefinable way he carried to an ever-increasing degree an aura of greatness and a quality of vision. Above all he was unflappable, sensitive to the wind of change but not blown off course by it. I liked and admired him greatly and he was, above all other Prime Ministers with whom I had dealings, the most helpful over ex-Service affairs, particularly to my V.C. and G.C. Association.

Having now ceased to be a Minister I was able to concentrate in the House on my old interests, defence and foreign affairs, and spoke in every major debate on defence matters. The Gurkha Brigade had asked me to represent their interests in the House, which I was glad to do as I had been so closely connected with them. I did my best to 'keep them on the island' when Army cuts were being contemplated.

This was only common sense as they were cheaper to maintain than British units, besides being magnificent soldiers – particularly in Eastern theatres of British interest such as Sarawak and Borneo. Also it was important for us to maintain friendly relations with Nepal, where the Gurkha soldier was the most profitable export. But of course, at a time when cuts in military expenditure were being advocated and it was a choice between cutting a British or a Gurkha regiment it was hard to maintain that the latter should have priority. However, during all the time I was representing them they had no serious cuts in establishment, either of their British officers or their Gurkha personnel, until 1963 when the whole strength of the British Army was reduced.

Being a Member of Parliament in the large Borough of Lambeth, where overcrowding, lack of housing, and inadequate school places were very pressing problems, I was naturally concerned by the growing numbers of coloured immigrants who were crowding into the borough and making all these problems more difficult. I pressed continuously that the immigrants we had accepted should be absorbed into the life of the community, but that much stronger controls should be imposed on further immigration which, if unchecked, could make life more difficult for the immigrants already here and for the life of the community as a whole.

Wrapped up with this immigration problem was that of education. Classes were far too large and schools too few, although one small area of my Norwood constituency around Tulse Hill was reported to have more schools and school children than in any other area of the same size in Britain. Nevertheless there were not enough schools or teachers in Lambeth. The language problem and the standard of intelligence of the immigrant children imposed almost insuperable difficulties. A head teacher of a primary school would say to me : 'Should I concentrate on those with the lowest standards and neglect the brighter children, or vice versa? I can't do both at the same time with the staff and facilities at my disposal.'

At that time I believed sincerely that an improved standard of education would solve many of our problems. And I thought that in the schools lay the best method of integrating the coloured section of our community, that the next generation would have made friends and been accepted by their contemporaries, and that this would cause a profound change in the general attitude with regard to race. But this also involved facilities to bring on children who had difficulties over language to an acceptable educational level, so that they could hold up their heads with everyone else.

I was strongly opposed to the Labour Party policy of concentrating on large comprehensive schools – without much more trial – and doing away with grammar schools (and the public and private schools), but in favour of using and improving all existing means of education and of giving parents some choice in selecting the school in which their children should be educated. So education became one of my first interests. Frances and I became governors of some of the local schools and were deeply interested in all of them, their staffs and their children.

I also maintained my interest in war pensions and spoke on this subject from time to time. I was particularly concerned over Servicemen who had undergone great strain, both nervous and physical, which did not necessarily entail hospital treatment or a medical record at the time, but which often resulted in severe after affects. Without any medical record it was extremely difficult for their G.P.s to make a case that their condition was attributable to their military service.

In a speech I made in the House on this subject I took as an example the sinking of the County cruiser, H.M.S. *Dorsetshire*, commanded by Captain Augustus Agar (a V.C. of the First World War), in the Indian Ocean in March 1942. Following the capture of Singapore and Rangoon a powerful Japanese task force was sweeping through the Indian Ocean towards Colombo. Their aircraft spotted the two cruisers and attacked them with dive-bombers in overwhelming numbers. Within eight minutes from the time of the first Japanese attack *Dorsetshire* took her final plunge to the bottom. Many of the crew had been killed and the wounded and the living were flung into a tropical sea infested with sharks.

There followed a ghastly ordeal which lasted throughout the remaining hours of daylight, the long night which followed and the greater part of the following day. Captain Agar went down very deep and came up with only half a lung still functioning, but with his courage as high as ever. The living made a circle round the wounded and dead bodies and fought the constant attacks of the sharks and the barracuda, who were even more vicious at the smell of either flesh or blood. The leadership of the officers was magnificent, as was the courage and cheerfulness of the men, who were black with fuel oil and coughing and retching to get it out of their systems. They even kept alive a tiny kitten which had somehow escaped from the ship!

At 6 p.m. on the second day, with only half an hour before darkness set in, a cruiser and two destroyers came on the scene and picked them up. *Dorsetshire* had left Colombo with 800 men; when the ship sank there were about 500 in the water, of whom fifteen died in the night. The unwounded sailors went back to duty immediately, as did the wounded when they had recovered. But the point I made in my speech to the House was that a lot of these men, and many more who had suffered similar ordeals, could never be the same again and might suffer for it later, as did our Far Eastern prisoners of war. When deciding therefore on attributability to war service war pensions boards should, I maintained, take note, not only of actual disabilities such as the loss of a limb, but of details of a man's war service. I think quite a lot of attention was given to this point thereafter.

Becoming a Privy Councillor in 1962 was a great help in my political speaking, as it was customary for the Speaker to give preference to Privy Councillors when calling upon Members to speak. There had previously been only five people in our history who had been both P.C.s and V.C.s. These were two Field-Marshals, Lord Roberts and Sir Redvers Buller, Sir Dighton Probyn and Lords Gowrie and De L'Isle, the latter being the only one living besides myself.

Harold Macmillan gained a great triumph in the general election of October 1959, when the Conservative Government was returned to office with an overall majority of 100 seats. It was the third successive contest in a series in which the party had gained a victory and then increased their majority, an achievement for which there was no precedent for more than a century. Taking over the leadership in January 1957, when the party's fortunes were at a low ebb after the strife and buffetings that Suez had brought them, Harold Macmillan had succeeded in giving his supporters new heart and unity, and in not only restoring but increasing public confidence at home and abroad in the Conservative Government.

Polling day, Thursday 8 October, was a thrilling one for me in Norwood. There was of course an obvious national swing to the right, so we didn't suffer quite the same anxiety as usual. Frances and I arrived at Lambeth Town Hall at 10.30 p.m. to join the other candidates at the count. The first to be announced was George Strauss, who held Vauxhall for Labour comfortably with a majority of 7,125 (a drop of 1,500). Then came Brixton, where Marcus Lipton held the seat for Labour with a drop of 3,000. My total electorate in Norwood was 57,807 as compared with 52,261 in Brixton and 45,802 in Vauxhall. My majority was 6,983, an increase of 1,951 on the previous election. This was a very good result, particularly as a Liberal took 4,744 votes, mostly from me. The final state of the parties after this election was Conservatives 365, Labour 258, Liberals 6, others 1.

When the Queen opened the new Parliament on 23 October television was used for the first time to bring to millions of people the ceremonies surrounding this colourful event.

The Army Estimates for 1963–64 were moved for the third time by John Profumo, Secretary of State for War. He told me beforehand that he would be speaking about the Gurkhas, who were my special interest. Field-Marshal Bill Slim had also told me that, at the request of the Government, he had visited Nepal to discuss the future of the Gurkha Brigade with the King of that country. Quite early in his speech Mr Profumo told the House that the strength of the British Army was being reduced to 180,000 men. In addition the Brigade of Gurkhas was being kept in being but with an establishment reduced from 14,000 to 10,000.

I was called by the Speaker at 6.07 p.m. and confined my speech almost entirely to the Gurkhas. I made it quite clear that I very much deprecated the decision to reduce the Gurkhas at that particular time as it would only mean that the Chinese would make immediate efforts to enlist them into their own army. I did however appreciate that the decision was irrevocable and urged that the reduction should be made in a way that would reduce the fighting efficiency and morale of the Gurkha Brigade as little as possible. I also expressed a hope that the Government would deal generously with those Gurkha soldiers who would become redundant. I had considerable support from both sides of the House, particularly from Mr Emanuel (Manny) Shinwell, who followed me in the debate. He had been an excellent Minister of Defence in the Labour Government and we had seen eye to eye on a number of Defence questions. He said :

> The Rt Hon. and gallant Member for Norwood (Sir J. Smyth) speaks with considerable authority on military affairs and is an expert on the Gurkhas. I beg him and those associated with him to continue their pressure on the Secretary of State for the retention of the Gurkhas. As to the Rt Hon. Gentleman's remarks about Lord Slim meeting the King of Nepal, we should not blame Lord Slim for the decision that has been taken, which is entirely the Secretary of State's.

Both the Labour and Conservative Party elected new leaders during 1963. Mr Hugh Gaitskell died on 18 January 1963 at a time when his authority over the Labour Party was absolute and his political stature was unanimously acknowledged. In October 1963, just before the Conservative Party Conference opened at Blackpool, Harold Macmillan was forced to have an immediate prostate operation which compelled him to resign the premiership. The Conference became in a sense an election forum in which several contenders for the crown were on view. The strongest candidates to start with appeared to be Rab Butler, Lord Hailsham and Reggie Maudling. Harold Macmillan conducted matters from his sick bed with Martin Redmayne, Chief Whip since 1959, 'collecting the voices'.

As a result of all this the party's choice turned out to be Alec Douglas-Home, the Earl of Home, who of course was still in the House of Lords. Although he had not been my choice when I was first consulted, as I had no idea he would consider renouncing his title, I gladly gave the appointment my fullest support. I had sat next to him on the back benches when I first became a Member of Parliament and had a high opinion of him as a sterling character and thoroughly capable parliamentarian. He at once renounced his title under the Peerage Act and was returned to the Commons as Sir Alec, after winning a by-election at Kinross and West Perthshire. Hailsham also took advantage of the Act and as Quintin Hogg fought and won a by-election at St Marylebone.

Had the procedure for choosing a Conservative leader, which Sir Alec himself introduced in 1965, been in force in 1963 I think that the members of the 1922 Committee would undoubtedly have selected Reggie Maudling. But in 1963 the Cabinet's choice was Rab Butler and it was a cruel blow for him that, for the second time running, he had just missed being appointed to the highest office in the land. To his eternal credit he at once pledged his support to Alec Douglas-Home. I was greatly disappointed in Iain Macleod, for whom I had had the highest regard, that he, as Chairman of our Party and an obvious contender for the leadership himself, did not follow Rab Butler's example.

CHAPTER TWENTY-ONE

The Tory Leadership and the End of My Sixteen Years in the House

ON 28 July 1964 the Rt Hon. Sir Winston Leonard Spencer Churchill ended his career as a Member of Parliament. It had lasted sixty-four years. Full of years and honour he entered the Chamber for the last time through the ruined Churchill Arch, wearing his favourite blue spotted bow tie, short black coat and striped trousers, just after 3 p.m. in the middle of Question Time. Rab Butler, the Foreign Secretary, was at the despatch box answering Questions. Sir Winston halted at the Bar of the House, bowed to the Speaker, and then very slowly, with rather tottery footsteps, walked across to his favourite seat on the corner of the front bench below the gangway. I was seated immediately behind him and he gave me a nod and a little smile. He stayed for a short time after Questions ended and then, supported by two M.P.s, he walked wearily to the Bar of the House, turned slowly to face the Speaker, and departed for ever from the place he had graced so much for so many years. He felt too emotional to visit the smoking room or to tarry further in the House.

Later in the day an all-Party tribute was paid to him in the House of Commons – the first time such a gesture had been made since the premiership of the Duke of Wellington. The Motion read :

That this House desires to take the opportunity of marking the forthcoming retirement of the Rt Hon. Gentleman, the Member for Woodford, by putting on record its unbounded admiration and gratitude for his services in Parliament, to the nation and to the world. Remembers above all his inspiration of the British people when they stood alone, and his leadership until victory was won.

And offers its grateful thanks to the Rt Hon. Gentleman for these outstanding services to this house and to the nation.

I have always considered that the general election of October 1964 was a triumph for Sir Alec Douglas-Home, although he was on the losing side. There was no doubt that the tide was running strongly towards Labour and they were confident of winning a substantial majority. In fact they crawled past the winning post with a majority of four. It was largely the personal popularity of Sir Alec with the electorate as a whole which so nearly turned the scale in our favour. It is true he did not present a very good image on television: his wife said to me afterwards that if he had worn the bifocal glasses he afterwards adopted he would have won – and there is many a true word spoken in jest. At that time, when he was speaking with notes, he wore his glasses on the tip of his nose and peered over them at the audience like an amiable sheep. Nevertheless people of all parties liked and trusted him and he was eminently sound, with a well-balanced temperament and great strength of character. His personal following in the country and the Party exceeded that of any other Tory politician since Sir Winston.

In Norwood there were very obvious signs of apathy among our own supporters and supreme confidence on the part of Labour, who had a new and extremely capable candidate in John Frazer. I was buoyed up by the fact that Bob Mellish, the Chairman of the London Labour Party since 1960 and a man I respected and admired, had said: 'We shall never win Norwood as long as Jackie Smyth is there.' I hoped this was true but I was well aware that, as the Duke of Wellington said about Waterloo, it was going to be a 'damned close-run thing'.

Polling day in a marginal seat, particularly with the tide flowing strongly against you and coming at the end of an exhausting three weeks' campaign, is a harrowing affair – touring the committee rooms and polling stations, being available for last minute calls, assisting in the all-important knocking up of last minute voters. And I was seventy-one! At 10.30 p.m. we go to the Town Hall, where the excitement mounts from hour to hour. In the last stages Frances and I take our seats on the platform with the Mayor and Mayoress, Frances looking as cool as a cucumber and I in a muck sweat as the piles of trays build up, each one holding 2,500 votes. At last there is a breathless hush. The piles are dead level. But one more tray is seen coming from the back of the hall. On which pile is it going? Then a terrific cheer from my supporters as it is put onto mine. But my agent rushes up to warn me that there are hardly any votes in the tray and Frazer's agent has called for a recount. Another two hours of anxiety. Then, at the stroke of 3 a.m. I am in by 451. What a cliff-hanger!

More women Members were returned in 1964 than in any previous election, but the total of twenty-eight was still remarkably low. I decided I would not contest another election but would remain as M.P. for Norwood until it came.

Early in 1965 murmurings started in the Press and within the Party with regard to Sir Alec's future as leader of the Conservative Party. On 10 February a leading article by Peregrine Worsthorne appeared in the *Sunday Telegraph* headed: 'Are Tories disloyal to their Leader?'

Uncertainty about the succession to Alec Douglas-Home's leadership of the Tory Party is beginning to assume the proportion of a public scandal. The manoeuvres of some of the contenders' supporters are becoming so brazen and reckless and the rumours about what each contender says about the others so disagreeable and vindictive that grave offence is being given to the public's sense of decency and decorum. It would be priggish and unrealistic to blame the contenders themselves. The front runners are all relatively young and whoever wins can look forward to leading the Party for an exceptionally long period and whoever loses must resign himself to abandoning the supreme political prize while still in the prime of life. So naturally the struggle is ruthless and relentless.

In view of what has occurred since this underlines how impossible it is to forecast the future!

There had been, for some time, suggestions within the Conservative Party that a better method should be evolved for the election of a leader than that which had been adopted on the resignation of Harold Macmillan. Alec Douglas-Home was himself all in favour of this idea and I wrote a letter to *The Times* on the subject which they published on 14 January 1965 under the heading 'The simplest way best', which was very much on the same lines as that put forward by Sir Alec shortly afterwards. His proposals put the final onus of the selection of leader fairly on the 1922 Committee of Conservative M.P.s in the House. The only matter which he failed to introduce was a clause by which a leader could be removed from office if the Party so wished.

Rumours and murmurings with regard to Sir Alec's leadership rumbled on and eventually, on Thursday, 23 July 1965, he decided to ask for a vote of confidence from the 1922 Committee. I felt sure he would receive that vote as the dissidents were confined more or less to a comparatively small, but well-organized and powerful group of Heath supporters. I had arranged with the *Daily Telegraph*, for whom I was writing regularly in the correspondence columns, to have a letter published on the Thursday morning of his meeting and they had a leading article in that issue as well, both giving warm support to Sir Alec. During the preceding weekend in Scotland however he had come to the conclusion that any split in the 1922 Committee would be damaging to the Party and that, in the best interests of the latter therefore, he would announce his resignation as leader immediately.

Sir Alec came down to London on the Tuesday and called a Press Conference on the Wednesday, at which he made the announcement. So he arrived at the 1922 Committee on the Thursday to bid them a fond farewell as leader. They gave him a great ovation. In a letter to me next day thanking me for my letter to the *Telegraph*, he said he could have stood all the criticism of the Press indefinitely but 'any wobble' from his own side would not have done the Party any good. He finished with the words: 'Thank you for all your loyalty and support which heal all the scars of political life.'

He never allowed those scars to show and served his successor as leader with complete loyalty and great distinction as Foreign Secretary. But I was not alone in considering that he had received very shabby treatment from the Conservative Party. He remained their most popular statesman up to the time of his retirement from the House of Commons. The machinery he had initiated was accepted for the election of a new leader and at once put into operation. The candidates were Reginald Maudling, Edward Heath and Enoch Powell. Although there was not the same blatant lobbying as had been the case over the election of the Labour leader, the campaign on behalf of Ted Heath, conducted discreetly but nonetheless effectively, was in itself enough to decide the result – as Reggie Maudling's supporters really conducted no campaign at all.

The final ballot showed Heath 150, Maudling 133 and Powell 15. Maudling then withdrew, making a second ballot unnecessary. The bad thing about the ballot was that it was not conducted secretly, as in the case of a general election, where the electorate merely put a cross on the voting paper. The Members of Parliament simply signed their names; and although only the numbers of those voting for each candidate were published, and not the names of the voters, they were well-known to those in charge of the proceedings and became known to a number of other people subsequently.

Rab Butler (later Lord Butler), in his autobiography, published in July 1971, was very critical of the pro-Heath lobby – but Rab of course was very much a Maudling man.

Maudling and Heath were both experienced and highly qualified politicians, the former having held higher office. Heath was the stronger character and had a greater sense of purpose. Maudling had an excellent brain and was a brilliant speaker. It was a difficult choice. And Heath became Prime Minister and was one of the greatest Conservative characters of my time.

On 16 December 1963 the Labour Government's proposal virtually to do away with the Territorial Army, which had been received with widespread indignation throughout the country, was debated in the House. The debate was opened by the Secretary of State for Defence, Denis Healey, and replied to by Ted Heath, the leader of the Opposition. After the Deputy Secretary for Defence, Mr Fred Mulley, had replied for the Government, I rose at 5.18 to make the first speech from the Opposition back benches. As one who had been G.S.O.1 of the 2nd London (T.A.) Division at the start of the war and had commanded a Territorial Brigade at Dunkirk, I was listened to with great attention by the House, as they always accord to anyone who speaks with personal experience. I allied myself entirely with the arguments Ted Heath had put forward and added a number of my own.

Having told the House that in 1939, on the outbreak of war, the 2nd London (T.A.) Division, was entirely deployed on anti-sabotage duties in London. I went on to say:

Does the Secretary of State think that the age of sabotage has passed and that in future emergencies none of this guarding will be necessary? If he thinks that I would say it is absolute nonsense. *The age of sabotage is just beginning. In the Vietnam war and in other conflicts we find such devices being used in suitcases and cars loaded with high explosives drawn up outside important buildings. In fact the age of sabotage is only in its infancy and anti-sabotage activity will be far more important in future emergencies than ever before. We want all the men we can get on the ground – men in uniform who will counter sabotage right at the beginning of an emergency.*

I have emphasized this part of my speech as it was very prophetic in view of the grave disturbances in Northern Ireland and the hidden bomb campaign which caused such destruction to military and civilians alike, there and in the U.K. In winding up the debate Denis Healey paid a tribute to 'my very interesting speech'.

I made my final speech in the House of Commons in the Defence Debate of 7 March 1966, only three weeks before the election. I made a final plea to the Secretary of State that at the end of the debate he would give an assurance to the Gurkha Brigade and to the Government of Nepal that the future of the Gurkhas in the British Army will be looked after.

Sir John Eden, speaking later in the debate, began by saying:

The first day of what has been called this great national debate has been marked by two valedictory addresses, one from the Hon. Member of Ashfield (Mr Warbey) and the other from my Rt Hon. and gallant friend the Member for Norwood (Sir J. Smyth), who will be greatly missed by hon. members. My Rt Hon. and gallant friend spoke, as he has done on previous occasions, on behalf of the Brigade of Gurkhas, that magnificent fighting force. He asked pointedly for a firm guarantee as to their future in the British Army. I hope that when the Secretary of State winds up the debate to-morrow he will make a special reference to the position of the Gurkhas in the future.

And when winding up on the first day of this debate on behalf of the Government, the Minister of Aviation, Frederick Mulley, said: 'I know from my experience as Minister of Defence for the Army that in the retirement of the Rt Hon. Member for Norwood (Sir J. Smyth) the Brigade of Gurkhas will lose a powerful advocate in the House.'

That night I spoke in Norwood at the adoption of my successor, Douglas Wilson, and supported him on the platform all through the election.

Polling day was 31 March. It felt very queer that I was not standing myself. The gallup polls gave Labour a lead of 8½ to 11 per cent which would have given them a majority of over 100. Frances and I voted at Westminster and then went on to Norwood. For the first time for twenty-one years we did not have to be present at the count so we went home and watched on television. In Norwood Labour had a majority of 2,273. The wheel had turned full circle from 1950, when I had won it back from Labour with almost exactly the same majority. The Conservatives have never won Norwood since (up to 1977). I had been twenty-one years as the Conservative representative in Norwood, for sixteen of which I had been their Member of Parliament.

For quite a long time I missed the House of Commons a lot but, having ceased to be a Member I made a clean cut and ceased all political activities, although of course I remained intensely interested in the passing political scene. I had served in the House with six remarkable Prime Ministers: Attlee, Churchill, Eden, Macmillan, Douglas-Home and Wilson. I had admired them all and been privileged to know some of them well. And my Chairmanship and Presidency of the Victoria Cross and George Cross Association brought me in close contact with each of them, quite apart from politics. They have certainly all been very kind to me.

I think the most astute Prime Ministers of my time in the House were Macmillan and Wilson. The way the latter stayed in the saddle with such small majorities was a miracle; and he was a great master of the all-important TV medium. Macmillan was not only astute but he had a great feeling for the important issues and future trends. He too, in a different way, was a master of TV.

I would say that the two best orators in the House in my time were Nye Bevan and Iain Macleod. At one time we had instructions not to interrupt Nye Bevan whilst he was speaking as his riposte was always so devastating. Iain Macleod however made his reputation and gained immediate ministerial rank by deliberately tackling Nye, and having got himself called in a health debate immediately after Nye, scored a decisive triumph on matters of fact on which Macleod was particularly well primed. His death soon after Ted Heath had made him Chancellor of the Exchequer was a dreadful blow to the Conservative Party. Had he not refused to serve under Alec Douglas-Home's premiership he would have been very much in line for the leadership of the Conservative Party.

As a speaker for any occasion and on any subject, political or otherwise, Enoch Powell, who joined the House of Commons with me in 1950, was in the highest class. Frances and I got to know him and his charming wife Pam very well.

Enoch had quite a large personal following in the country and might well have influenced political feeling in a negative way in at least two general elections. It is a tragedy that such high potential has not been directed into more positive and co-operative channels. But he is still only sixty-seven and who knows what the future may bring for him.

Michael Foot, speaking from the Opposition front bench below the gangway, could be a dynamic and devastating idol breaker. He was never quite so good as poacher turned gamekeeper when Labour was in power. There have not been many great women parliamentarians. The two whom I thought quite outstanding were Shirley Williams and Margaret Thatcher. They really did know their stuff, were brilliant speakers in the House and on TV and had great integrity. The difference between them, in my opinion, was that Margaret Thatcher wanted to be Prime Minister, was well qualified for this highest office, and was confident that she could carry it out, whereas Shirley Williams did not have this ambition. In addition Margaret Thatcher had great powers of leadership, and great courage.

It is idle to prophesy what the future will hold; but at the time of writing Margaret Thatcher is the elected leader of the Conservative Party and all set to be Prime Minister should there be a change of Government. She faced unprecedented difficulties over her election to the leadership, and faced them bravely and well; and she has gained in stature all the time. She had to contend with a Labour majority over the Conservatives of forty as a result of the 1974 election, a factor which the general public did not always understand. The 1974 election was a disaster for the Conservative Party.

I would not have missed my twenty-one years in politics for anything. There were times of course when the ritual and the tramping through the division lobbies in the middle of the night, and the strain of keeping a very marginal constituency warm, all at the same time, were very great. But one always felt at the hub of great events; one could get up and say what one felt; and one could occasionally, even as a backbencher, get something constructive done. The House of Commons is essentially a talking shop rather than an executive machine. Frances once said of me : 'Jackie always expects talking to be followed by action.' That was not always possible in the House, but at least I was instrumental in getting £5 million from the Japanese for the Far Eastern Prisoners of War and for getting an £100 annual tax free allowance for the V.C.s in 1959 and for the G.C.s in 1963, besides various war pensions increases, which made a lasting difference to the lives of very many worthy people.

Frances was the ideal Member of Parliament's wife. She really did know about politics and gave me the most valuable help and advice. She was immensely popular with my constituents, worked like a beaver and could make a useful speech at women's meetings, though I never allowed her, on principle, to make public political speeches. She was, however, perfectly capable of drafting one for me and often wrote briefs on White Papers and Government legislation which I found very helpful. And she had the capacity of making it all seem fun.

CHAPTER TWENTY-TWO

Sport and My Ex-Service Associations

THE First World War destroyed any chances I may have had of becoming a first-class athlete. Nevertheless, although I was twenty-five when the war ended in 1918, and had become very much 'general officer potential' from a military point of view, I achieved quite a good standard in various sports. India of course was a splendid country for sport for a penniless young captain, particularly where the horse was concerned.

I had never been brought up for 'fishin' and shootin' ', although I did a bit of deer and tiger shooting in India, but never with any enthusiasm or success. I don't really enjoy killing things for sport. The Sikhs were fine hockey players and Indian hockey was of a very high standard, particularly I think because the pitches were hard and true – very different from so many of the soft muddy hockey fields in England. Both Jack Turner and I played in the 15th Sikh team and when we became students at the Camberley Staff College in the early nineteen-twenties we were at once in great demand by the Army hockey selectors. We were both chosen to play in several international trials; after I had returned to India Jack gained his international cap for England and played centre half for the English hockey side in all their matches that year (which they won), before he too returned to India.

On my return to India I was invited to captain an Indian Army hockey team in New Zealand and then to play in the final trial for the selection of an Indian team which was to make its first tour of Europe. Alas, my staff appointment at Army Headquarters Delhi made both of these attractive invitations impossible. Also I felt I was getting a bit old for international athletics. Had I been selected for the Indian side I would probably have been the only white man.

My best game would undoubtedly have been polo. So many of the top polo players were either good riders and moderate hitters of the ball or good hitters of the ball but indifferent riders. I therefore soon became much better than the ponies I could afford and had to make the big decision whether to transfer to an Indian Cavalry regiment or not. I have described this dilemma in an earlier chapter; but I much enjoyed the carefree polo in Chitral many years later.

I also did some race-riding in India, both on the flat and over jumps and was Master and Huntsman of the Delhi Foxhounds. Colonel Gibbon, a famous oarsman and a very keen horse rider, had a somewhat exaggerated opinion of my riding and asked me to ride a horse of his in the Grand National steeplechase. I had agreed to do so but got appendicitis and had to drop out. Perhaps lucky for me – and the horse – but I would have liked to have had a go. Finally a bad fall when I was doing field master of the famous Peshawa Foxhounds in 1936 put me out of horse-riding entirely.

When I was a student at the Camberley Staff College I played a lot of cricket, was made a Free Forester and might have reached county standard if I had not been so busy from a military point of view. At Camberley I also became keen on squash rackets and was admitted to the Amateur Championships played at the Bath Club and limited to the best twenty-four players. The Prince of Wales (later King Edward VIII) was also admitted, though his squash was really not up to that standard. Squash is a game where an experienced player can make an inferior one look good by playing the ball to him. A little later on the Prince was invited to play in a Club match against an elderly colonel who was not going to give anything away and beat him all ends up. The Prince realized that people had been having him on and he never played competitive squash again. He took to golf where there can't be any make-believe : you either get the ball in the hole, or else.

In 1924 I was asked to play an exhibition squash match against the reigning British Lady Champion to open the new Camberley courts. I had never played a lady before and was very nervous about taking it on. She knew more about squash, the strokes and the tactics than I had ever dreamed of; but women can't play squash, or tennis, on equal terms against men. I set such a pace that she didn't get any games at all. She was very annoyed as a lot of people were watching. She challenged me to a replay, but by this time she was very tired and I won even more easily. It was an embarrassing episode. I was picked to play squash for the Army but had to return to India before the match.

Had it not been for the First World War I would almost certainly have been a lawn tennis player of Wimbledon standard; as it was, even though I was really too old, I represented the Army in India, the British Army at home and my county, Devon, and played a number of first-class tennis tournaments in India and in England. But as I was stationed in India my visits to England were sporadic.

After the Second World War, from 1946 onwards, I became deeply involved in the game of lawn tennis as lawn tennis correspondent of the *Sunday Times*, a member of the All England Club (from 1938) and of the International Lawn Tennis Clubs of France, America and Britain; I have been a Vice-President of the last for many years. I also did two tours of the U.S.A. for the *Sunday Times*, wrote constantly in many lawn tennis journals, and also broadcast. I wrote four books on the game and, in 1948, was invited by the All England Club to write all the articles for the Wimbledon programmes, which carried an article, three pages of photos and a cover photo, for every day of Wimbledon. I continued these for twenty-five consecutive years, until 1974 when I handed over to Peter Wilson, the famous sports writer of the *Daily Mirror* group. When I became a Minister in Winston Churchill's Government I had to give up my *Sunday Times* assignment and all other writing for the Press, but was, by special permission of Winston Churchill himself, allowed to continue my articles for the All England Club.

The Wimbledon articles had to be discussed with Christopher Lampard of Programme Publications on the one hand, and the All England Club on the other. My great friend Colonel Duncan Macauley was followed by David Mills as Secretary of the All England Club and they gave me every possible assistance. Then there was the planning of our own tickets and the small lunches we used to give to our friends each day in the Members' Enclosure.

We were generally invited to the Royal Box on finals day, following a Committee lunch, at which royalty were usually present every year. In my later years, after my eightieth birthday, I was favoured with a special car sticker which allowed me to drive into the ground right up to the entrance to the Royal Box. Wimbledon has been an important part of our lives for thirty years. I got to know a number of the leading players and had many dear friends on the Committee and among my fellow members of the All England Club. I myself sat in the same seat in the Members' box in all those years. I liked to look straight down the court and I had to get there in good time to get this particular seat. Sometimes, if I was a little late and some new member sat down in my seat, one of the other members would say, 'Excuse me, but that is Jackie's seat!' Wimbledon is the greatest Lawn Tennis Championship in the world and is the one where all the top players most like to compete.

The great landmark in the game of lawn tennis came in 1968 when, at long last, thanks mainly to the endeavours of the late Herman David, the Chairman of the All England Club, open tennis was introduced. And the hypocrisy of sham-amateurism was buried for good and all. I had warmly supported Herman both in the Committee of the Club and in my writing. But although this was what the public wanted and it was obviously for the good of the game, it did result in new problems and with increasing pressure on the clubs and tournament managers to produce bigger money prizes. The leading lawn tennis players in world tennis, male and female, have become very rich players.

The Wimbledon Centenary came in 1977 and Frances and I were invited to the Royal Box for the parade of the champions on the first day of the championships, when most of those who were still living and able to travel came to receive their commemoration medals on the Centre Court. The official Centenary magazine said:

> There are indeed a number of writers with long campaigning records who would qualify for a Wimbledon Hall of Press Fame. Among present day writers are Peter Wilson (*Daily Mirror*), Lance Tingay (*Daily Telegraph*), Sir John Smyth (*Sunday Times*), David Gray (*The Guardian*), John Oliff (*Daily Telegraph*) and Fred Perry.

It was a great fortnight, made even more memorable with victory in the Ladies' Singles going to Virginia Wade, after many years of endeavour, and above all the presence of the Queen to present her with the winner's salver.

With the coming of peace in 1946 I became interested in various ex-Service associations, with which I was to be much concerned in my ministerial appointments in the Ministry of Pensions and National Insurance. The 'Not Forgotten' Association did splendid work for the gravely war disabled of both world wars. The Royal Family had always given it their greatest support, and in March 1921 Princess Mary, later the Princess Royal, became its first Patron and gave it her devoted service for the rest of her life; King George V and Queen Mary and the Prince of Wales (later as Duke of Windsor) all took the closest interest in it.

In 1930 Sir Louis Greig became Chairman and Lady Monro Vice-Chairman. Sir Louis was a keen lawn tennis player and he and King George VI (while Duke of York) had won the R.A.F. Doubles in 1926 and played together at Wimbledon in the same year. Sir Louis became

Chairman of the All England Club in 1936 and remained in that office until 1952. He continued as Chairman of the 'Not Forgotten' until his death in March 1956.

The Second World War brought a big addition of permanently disabled men to be cared for by the 'Not Forgotten'. I had had a special responsibility as Parliamentary Secretary to the Ministry of Pensions for two of the largest hospitals in which 'Not Forgotten' men were accommodated, Roehampton and Stoke Mandeville, in the former of which I was a governor. During 1949 a further four hospitals were added to the 'Not Forgotten' list, making a total of forty-two. I deputized on occasions at their Christmas parties in the Royal Riding School for Field-Marshals Alexander and Templer and officiated myself on other occasions.

In 1961 Colonel Crosfield, himself a gravely disabled man, resigned the Chairmanship after eight memorable years and was succeeded by Major-General G. M. (Moti) Dyer, a great friend of mine from Indian Army days. He and his wife Evelyn have given invaluable service to the 'Not Forgotten' over the last seventeen years. I became a Vice-President in 1956 and in 1958 I was invited by Field-Marshal the Lord Wilson of Libya to succeed him as President of the Distinguished Conduct Medal League. The Princess Royal was also Patron of that Association; so in the last ten years of her life I saw quite a lot of her.

The D.C.M. is the highest award for gallantry in action which is confined to warrant officers, non-commissioned officers and men of the Army, Royal Air Force and Royal Marines. Many of the D.C.M.s were near misses for the Victoria Cross. The League was founded in 1931 and had branches in many parts of the country. They held a rally once a year in London and a dinner, both of which I always attended. As I was by that time Chairman of the Victoria Cross and George Cross Association, which had biennial reunions, the League decided to have their rallies biennially in the odd years so as not to clash with the V.C. and G.C. Reunions. Frances and I became very devoted to the D.C.M.s, who were lovely old soldiers of great gallantry and high repute.

The Princess Royal and I had family connections as I have explained earlier. She was always very kind to me. She seldom missed a D.C.M. rally but on one occasion Queen Elizabeth the Queen Mother took the parade on the Horse Guards. She was really superb. It rained cats and dogs from the moment she arrived. She never stopped smiling and refused to cut any part of the ceremonial, nor one word of her excellent address. She didn't even put up an umbrella. I was to see much more of her in the V.C. and G.C. Association.

Sunday 21 July 1963 was the last rally of the D.C.M. League which the Princess Royal attended. The Parade assembled at the Horse Guards at 3 p.m. and she inspected them and took the salute. A service was then held at the Cenotaph and the Parade proceeded to Wellington Barracks for a short address by the Princess, dismissal and tea. Usually the Princess and I had walked along from the Horse Guards to the Cenotaph, but knowing that she had been far from well I had arranged for her to go by car. But not a bit of it: she said, 'I will walk with you.'

The Princess was very popular and as soon as we had emerged from the Horse Guards into Whitehall a crowd of people surged round us and we all marched along the pavement together. Lord Crookshank, one of my Vice-Presidents, sidled up to me and said in shocked tones: 'Jackie, you must not allow the Princess to walk along in this crowd of people.'

I replied: 'Well what do you suppose I can do about it? You run on to the Home Office and get them to open the doors.' This he did and we stayed there until the Parade arrived and the service started.

The Princess was not in the least put out. But the amusing part was still to come. I had left the procedure from the service onwards in the hands of the Chairman. He was to go in the Princess's car, take her to a retiring room in Wellington Barracks and then on to tea in the Sergeants' Mess. I was to follow in my own car with Frances. I put the Princess into her car and was making way for the Chairman when she said, 'But where are you going?' When I told her she said: 'Oh no. I would like you to come with me. Perhaps the Chairman could go with your wife.'

So off we started to Wellington Barracks, the Chairman following with Frances. On arrival at the Barracks I suddenly realized that I didn't know what arrangements had been made about a retiring room. At that moment I saw someone signalling me on. We followed his direction and stopped. I enquired where we were and was told that it was the Corporals' Mess.

'Oh dear me, this won't do at all,' I said.

The Princess said firmly: 'The Corporals' Mess will do,' and got out of the car.

Meanwhile the Officers' Mess, where the retiring room had been arranged, was signalling wildly, but in vain. When the Parade arrived the Princess asked if I would say a few words on her behalf and then dismiss the Parade. The tea afterwards was a great success and I presented some of the members of the League and their wives to her.

I only saw the Princess once more, at the 'Not Forgotten' Christmas party in the following year. Her death was a great shock to the D.C.M. League, as it was to the 'Not Forgotten'. I attended her Memorial

Service in Westminster Abbey on 1 April 1965 as President of the D.C.M. League.

In 1966 we were greatly honoured when H.R.H. the Duke of Kent agreed to become our Patron and he and the Duchess attended several D.C.M. gatherings before, in 1970, I had to start cutting down my many ex-Service commitments and resigned from the Presidency. I had the warmest regard for the Kents, who are a delightful couple. I came in contact with them also at Wimbledon and in the V.C. and G.C. Association and the 'Not Forgotten' of which the Duchess became a most popualr Patron.

The Far Eastern Prisoners of War Federation I have already described. After General Percival's death I became the closest of friends with his successor, Phil (later Sir Philip) Toosey. Frances and I have attended their Reunions each year. I was first made an Honorary F.E.P.O.W., then an Hon. Vice-President and spoke with and for them on many occasions.

In the first week of Wimbledon a party of disabled men of the 'Not Forgotten' have always been invited by the All England Club to tea and to watch the tennis. As the Duke of Kent was President of the Club and the Duchess had succeeded the Princess Royal as Patron of the 'Not Forgotten' it became a custom that I, who was connected with both, should escort the Duchess to the 'Not Forgotten' party.

In 1970, the Jubilee year of the 'Not Forgotten', I was invited to write a short history of the Association. The Duke of Windsor, who had been very interested in the Association when he was Prince of Wales, wrote to the Chairman :

> I have read the history of the 'Not Forgotten', written by Sir John Smyth, V.C., with great interest. It brought back pleasant memories of the occasions upon which I attended the Christmas parties in the Association's earlier years. I am glad to know therefore that it is still flourishing and wish it all success in the wonderful work it has for so long performed.

On 28 August 1972 the Hon. Lady Monro, senior President of the 'Not Forgotten', died at the age of ninety-two. She had been a member of the Committee for over forty years and had given a lifetime of service to the Association. I gave the address at her Memorial Service, which was held at St James's, Piccadilly on 6 October 1972.

In the Burma Star Association I became President of the South-West London Branch. Bill Slim used to like to take me with him as a sort of A.D.C. on the Burma Star Parade to show that he valued the services of those who, like himself, had taken part in the Burma defeats of 1942, as well as all those of the victorious 14th Army. The Burma

Star Association was a very great ex-Service association, with Admiral Lord 'Dickie' Mountbatten as Patron, Bill Slim as President and General W. E. V. Abraham (now Sir William) as Chairman. On Bill's death his son, John, became President.

I became Vice-President of the Dunkirk Veterans and for several years took the parades at the annual gatherings of the London branch. I also had close connections with the British Legion and the Old Contemptibles, and attended many of their functions. But my chief ex-Service association was of course the Victoria Cross and George Cross Association which I founded, and of which I was the first Chairman for fifteen years, and then became President in succession to Winston Churchill.

The centenary of the institution of the Victoria Cross came on 26 June 1956 and there were some epoch-making celebrations in London. It had been twenty-seven years since the last (1929) reunion had taken place, with 321 V.C.s present, and during those years it had often been suggested that a Victoria Cross Association should be formed to sustain the comradeship of the holders of the Cross throughout the Commonwealth. Amongst others Field-Marshal Lord Gort, V.C., had been very keen on the idea. During the 1956 Reunion a meeting took place of a number of V.C.s (quite unbeknownst to me) who were eager, before they all separated, to set in train some machinery by which a V.C. Association could be formed. They were wholeheartedly in favour of this idea and were all agreed that I should be invited to found the Association. Why me? I think perhaps it was because for nearly five years I had been a minister in Churchill's and Eden's Governments where I had been in close touch with the ex-Service associations and was well known to take a great interest in them.

Although I realized there was considerable demand for such an association there were great difficulties. I was a busy Member of Parliament with no office and no private means. It would be very difficult to maintain contact with the overseas V.C.s and still more difficult to get them over to London for reunions. And we had no finances whatever. However a good many of my doubts were resolved when I received a telephone call from my friend, Sir Ralph Rayner, a fellow M.P. and the Chairman of the Royal Society of St George. They had always maintained a close association with the Victoria Cross, to many holders of which they had extended honorary membership. On behalf of the Royal Society, of which the Duke of Devonshire was President and Her Majesty the Queen Patron, Sir Ralph invited me – if I decided to found a V.C. Association – to base it on their St George's House and to use their board room for our meetings.

The founding of this Association, in which the holders of the equivalent decoration, the George Cross, awarded for supreme gallantry not on the field of battle, were soon added (first as associate members and then in full membership), turned out to be one of the most worthwhile things I have done in the whole of my life. It brought me into close touch with the Prime Ministers of Britain and the Commonwealth and with a number of other Ministers in both Conservative and Labour Governments, who were always ready to help the Association and its members. And all members of the Association enjoyed close contact with the Queen and many other members of the Royal Family. Above all, it enabled me to get to know hundreds of the holders of our two highest decorations and their families.

It meant a great deal of hard work for me, and for Frances, who had to give up her only spare room in our flat for an office, and do a great deal of the secretarial work until the Association got its own secretary.

The Royal Society of St George were as good as their word. They held a ball at the Royal College of Surgeons, under the patronage of H.R.H. Princess Margaret, in aid of the new Association and the proceeds, some £800, were given to us. We were on our way.

The first event of the V.C. Centenary celebrations, run by the Government, was the opening by the Prime Minister of the V.C. Exhibition at Marlborough House. This was a great success and it remained open until 7 July. On Monday 25 June, at 3 p.m., there was a thanksgiving service in Westminster Abbey, at which the address was given by the Archbishop of Canterbury. This was followed by a tea party given by the Government in the historic Westminster Hall of the Houses of Parliament. Our new Association was invited by the War Office to produce a parchment scroll containing the signatures of all the V.C.s for presentation to Her Majesty the Queen. I roped in fifty M.P.s of all parties to assist me.

The tea party was a very happy affair. I took Sir Anthony and Lady Eden round the tables, where the Prime Minister signed autographs and talked to a number of the V.C.s. Later the scroll was beautifully bound into an attractive book which I took to Buckingham Palace. I received kind assurances from the Queen that it would be placed among her most precious archives in Windsor Castle.

But the big day of the whole Centenary celebrations was Tuesday 26 June, when the Queen reviewed the V.C.s in Hyde Park under the command of the senior V.C., General Lord Freyberg. This was a moving, but most exhausting, occasion. On the same evening, in brilliant summer weather, a garden party was held at Marlborough House, which was attended by Her Majesty Queen Elizabeth the Queen Mother.

On the morning of the 27th the newly constituted Committee of the V.C. Association met under my chairmanship at St George's House. The Duke of Devonshire attended the opening of the proceedings and gave us a warm welcome. At this first meeting of the Association there were thirteen United Kingdom V.C.s selected by me and eleven Commonwealth members recommended by the High Commissioners in London.

I suggested, and the Committee agreed unanimously, that the objects of the Association should be as follows :

1. To establish a central focus and headquarters in London for Victoria Cross holders from all over the world and to provide a centre where members could meet and communicate.
2. To cement the brotherhood of the members throughout the Commonwealth and thereby, by our own unity and strength, make some contribution to the maintenance of world peace.
3. To give such help and guidance to one another as might be possible from time to time.

At our second meeting I put forward a proposal that we should invite holders of the George Cross to associate membership. This was accepted by a large majority, but it caused the withdrawal of one or two V.C. members.

On the night of 27 June the Lord Mayor held a reception for us at Guildhall. Frances and I were a little late and on our arrival the Lord Mayor said to me : 'I am glad you have arrived. Never have I seen so much champagne drunk by so few in such a short time!' The Guildhall was packed and many distinguished people had assembled to do honour to the holders of our premier decoration. Then the V.C.s dispersed once more, some of them to the ends of the earth, but not, thanks to the V.C. Association, any longer out of sight and out of mind.

The first reunion of the V.C. and G.C. Association was held at the Café Royal on 24 July 1958. By this time the holders of the George Cross had been admitted to associate membership and four G.C.s had been invited to join the Executive Committee. The first dinner was a great success. Our guest of honour was H.R.H. the Duke of Gloucester and our other guests included Duncan Sandys, then Minister of Defence; Field-Marshal Earl Alexander of Tunis; the High Commissioners and senior officers of all three Services; ninety V.C.s and thirty-nine G.C.s attended the dinner.

It was a momentous occasion for the Association as in his speech Duncan Sandys gave a pledge on behalf of the Government that never again would any U.K. holder of either of the two decorations be prevented from attending the dinner by reason of expense. This pledge has been honoured by all subsequent Governments and was broadened to include overseas members, allowing them to be brought over from the Dominions by Commonwealth Air Forces.

It had always been one of the objects of the Association to establish in London a central focus and headquarters. This object was fulfilled through the kindness of the Royal Society of St George, who put at our disposal, fully furnished, a room on the ground floor of St George's House. On the morning of Friday 10 July 1959 this room was officially opened by Prime Minister Harold Macmillan in the presence of the High Commissioners, representing our overseas members. The room, though small, was very attractive and was more than anything a symbol of the comradeship which bound our members together throughout the Commonwealth. It contained portraits of our Royal Patron, Her Majesty the Queen, and of Sir Winston Churchill, who became our first President in January 1959 and remained so until his death.

Some years later, when the Royal Society of St George had to give up their premises, Dr Noble Frankland, the Director of the Imperial War Museum, offered us a V.C. and G.C. room in the Museum, which has been a great benefit to us and at the same time allowed the public to see the V.C. and G.C. relics – photos, medal bars and so on. The Imperial War Museum has become a second home for our members.

The progress of the Association far exceeded our expectations and already firm links of friendship had been forged between our U.K. members and those in the Commonwealth and we received heart-warming letters from different parts of the world. In the office, which continued in my flat in Dolphin Square throughout all the fifteen years of my Chairmanship, we had established a most up-to-date card index system of V.C.s and G.C.s that had ever existed. Six or seven meetings of the Executive Committee were held annually in the board room of the Royal Society of St George. After each of these meetings the Committee and their wives, with one or two special guests, lunched in a private room in the House of Commons. This continued all the years I was a Member of Parliament, after which we had our lunches in the R.A.F. Club, which was most convenient and agreeable.

The Association was much indebted in those early years to Frances. After I left the Chairmanship they showed their appreciation to her by inviting her each year to the reunion dinner, not normally attended by members' wives.

The Association owed much to its first Secretary, the late Miss Betty Melrose, and to my own private secretaries who always lent a hand when necessary. Jean Gomme-Duncan, M.B.E., now Mrs David

Inglefield, succeeded Betty Melrose as V.C. and G.C. secretary in 1962 and was a tower of strength for many years. The Association Christmas card, with its special photo of the Queen, became a splendid means of keeping the members in touch with one another.

Prince Philip was Guest of Honour at our second reunion dinner in 1960 and made a most witty speech. The photograph of him being welcomed by me at the Café Royal was included in the Christmas card for that year and a copy of the message sent to me by the Vice-Chairman of the British Legion, which ran as follows: 'There is no doubt that you have forged yet another of those intangible but most effective links of gossamer which are yet as steel holding us all together in a changing world.'

In May 1961 the Association was renamed 'The Victoria Cross and George Cross Association'. My Vice-Chairman at that time was the Rev. Harold Woolley, V.C.; the Overseas Vice-Chairman was Major-General the Hon. George Pearkes, V.C. (Canada); the Hon. Treasurer was Jock Christie, V.C., and the Hon. Secretary was Cyril Martin, G.C. There were fourteen U.K. members of the Committee and eleven overseas members, representing Canada, Australia, New Zealand, South Africa, India and Pakistan.

The 1962 reunion on 17 and 18 July was particularly memorable in that the Queen and the Duke of Edinburgh invited the members of the Association to a Garden Party at Buckingham Palace, at which each member was allowed to bring two relatives. In view of the Queen's invitation I sought the assistance of the Ministries of Defence (our parent Ministry) and Commonwealth Relations, the High Commissioners in London, the Governments of the Commonwealth countries and the Royal Air Force to get some of our overseas members to London. Thenceforward the Air Forces of Britain, Canada and Australia were increasingly helpful in this respect. Latterly the R.A.F. have taken the burden previously carried by the Australian Air Force. The Minister of Defence provided travel warrants and subsistence allowances for those who needed them and the British Legion gave us their usual generous and efficient support with regard to the provision of accommodation to suit all pockets.

Philip Moore (later Sir Philip) the Queen's Assistant Private Secretary (who had been a boy at the Dragon School), consulted me about the procedure at the Garden Party. The previous one at which I had been present was in 1920. I explained how it had been managed, with the King and Queen standing on the lower steps of the Palace and each V.C. being announced by loudspeaker and coming forward to shake hands with Their Majesties. All the relatives were in chairs at the back. I understood that this same procedure would be adopted.

However, about four days before the event Philip Moore telephoned me to say that the Queen had decided on something more informal. She would do a 'walkabout' with me. I myself was to present the members and their relatives to her. I said with some alarm, 'Some of them I may not have met for years and I shall never remember their names.'

Philip Moore replied, 'The Queen said, "Tell Sir John we shall manage".' And we did, because the Queen has such a wonderful way with people and gets them talking to her. This informal procedure was very much appreciated by everybody because each V.C. and G.C. had his relatives with him and they were all in much closer touch with the Queen: but it was hard work for her. These Garden Parties lasted anything up to two and a half hours and I marvelled at her charm and wonderful concentration and endurance. She generally managed to shake hands with almost every member and their relatives, a *tour de force*. Prince Philip was escorted by my Vice-Chairman. It was a memorable occasion.

Among our members was the oldest-ever living V.C., General Sir Lewis Halliday, aged ninety-two, who won his Cross with the Royal Marine Light Infantry in China in 1900. All four of the living women holders of the George Cross were present – Miss Townsend (aged eighty-three); Miss Daphne Pearson (who came over from Australia); Miss Dorothy Thomas and Mrs Odette Hallowes. The dress for the occasion for the men, as at all our reunion functions, was lounge suit and medals.

That evening the members of the Association assembled at the Mansion House for the Lord Mayor's banquet, which was also a great occasion, carried out with all the ceremony and tradition of the Corporation of London. The ceremony of the Loving Cup was a completely new and delightful experience for most of our members. The Lady Mayoress, the wives of the two sheriffs, our three women G.C.s (without Miss Townsend this time) and our two Association secretaries, were the only women present. The Toast of the Victoria and George Cross Association was proposed by the Lord Mayor and replied to by me as Chairman. This was in fact the first time this toast had ever been proposed as the Association had only just been renamed to admit the George Cross to equal membership.

Next day, 18 July, our own reunion at the Café Royal started with tea and was followed by our Biennial General Meeting, which was packed with members. The Earl Mountbatten was Guest of Honour at the dinner which followed and the principal guests included the High Commissioners. Mr Duncan Sandys, Secretary of State for Commonwealth Relations and the Colonies; Mr Peter Thorneycroft, Minister of Defence; Mr John Profumo, Secretary of State for War;

and the Duke of Devonshire, Under-Secretary of State for Common-wealth Relations; the Chiefs of Staff of the three Services; General Sir Roy Bucher and Lord Carew of the British Legion.

After this reunion Brigadier the Hon. Milton Gregg of Canada and our first overseas Vice-Chairman, wrote to me: 'I think you have steered a course that has commended itself to practically all your colleagues. A simple, effective, loosely-knit association, with no grous-ing, no resolutions, no delegations, no lobbying and no propaganda.' As I told him, it sounded like a paradise for politicians. It was my seventh year as Chairman.

At the 1964 Reunion we introduced a Service of Remembrance at St Martin-in-the-Fields, where the vicar, the Rev. Austen Williams, was an old friend of both Frances and myself. We, and the V.C. and G.C. Association, the Burma Star Association, the Far Eastern P.O.W.s and other ex-Service organizations, came to regard St Martin's as our home church, and a very lovely one it is. I have read the lesson and given the address in that church on so many occasions. Austen Williams was a delightful person and a most distinguished vicar. On this first occasion my friend, Leonard Wilson, Bishop of Birmingham (formerly Bishop of Singapore at the time of the surrender on 15 February 1942), gave the address. He had been terribly tortured by the Japanese and it was a miracle that he had survived.

At this 1964 Reunion the Prime Minister, Sir Alec Douglas-Home, gave a cocktail party for our members at 10 Downing Street. Just before the party started Sir Alec was called away and his wife asked me to receive the guests with her. A lot of my V.C.s and G.C.s were not accustomed to drinking dry martinis and were quaffing them down like water. I wisely terminated the party rather early but even so, some of the members were marching hilariously along Downing Street arm in arm with some very understanding policemen. It was certainly a very good party!

Our Guest of Honour at the dinner next evening was Her Majesty Queen Elizabeth the Queen Mother. I much enjoyed sitting next to her and replying to her speech. Among our guests were Harold Macmillan and Denis Healey.

On Sunday 24 January 1965 our beloved President, Winston Churchill, died. I attended the most impressive funeral Service at St Paul's on 31 January as Chairman of the Association, taking with me Harold Woolley, V.C., the Vice-Chairman, and the Hon. Secretary, Cyril Martin, G.C. And on 24 September of that year we celebrated the Jubilee of the George Cross with various appropriate ceremonies, including a lunch at the Café Royal with Lady Spencer Churchill as our Guest of Honour. At the 1966 Reunion I was elected to succeed

Winston Churchill as life President and agreed to continue as Chairman for the time being in addition. Our Guest of Honour at the dinner was Prime Minister Harold Wilson.

The 1968 reunion was a very thrilling one for me and Frances as the Australian V.C.s and G.Cs were bringing over from Canberra my son, Julian, and his wife Phyllis, whom we had neither of us met. The R.A.F. had given us a Comet aircraft which was to start in New Zealand and pick up our members and their relatives from Australia, India, Pakistan and other places on the way. Also the Queen and Prince Philip had generously agreed to give us another reception at Buckingham Palace.

It was always a thrill to meet the buses arriving from the airport at the Royal Commonwealth Society in Northumberland Avenue on the first Sunday morning of a reunion week, with their excited crowd of mixed races and colours. By this time they had been several days on the aircraft and had got to know one another quite well and by the time the reunion was over they were bosom pals and some of them made lasting friendships. And no sooner was one reunion over than there was another to look forward to.

Julian and Phyllis were both wonderful mixers and Julian, a great, husky, red-headed young man, was very popular on the flight as there were several rather elderly and crippled V.C.s on board who needed help getting around the plane, which Julian gave. Phyllis is a gem of a girl, bubbling over with enthusiasm and gaiety, a trained nurse and midwife, and a wonderful wife for Julian and mother to their seven splendid children. The week flew by, what with the reunion entertainments, visits to relatives and sightseeing, and my daughter Jill's wedding on 20 July to David Firth. The wedding at Friend's House in the Euston Road was my first experience of a Quaker wedding. It was a very happy event and we all liked David immensely.

Before going by bus to the Queen's Reception the V.C.s and G.C.s lunched at Chelsea Barracks by kind permission of London District. It was an excellent means of getting the whole party together and gave me an opportunity to talk to them all. Once more I had the privilege of taking the Queen round. This time the reception was indoors in the Banqueting Hall, which had many advantages and meant we were not so dependent on the weather. This made it easier for the Queen and Prince Philip and I think they shook hands with every single person. Throughout the two and a half hours the Queen never lost interest for a moment. The last person I presented to her was my own son, Julian, and she talked to him just as though he was the first.

At the dinner at the Café Royal our Guests of Honour were the

Duke and Duchess of Kent. They stayed on to the end of the dinner and then walked round all the tables with me. It had been a memorable reunion; but when I saw Julian and Phyllis off at the end of it I little thought that it was the last time I should ever see him.

In 1970 the V.C. and G.C. reunion was held earlier than usual as the Queen was to open the V.C. and G.C. Exhibition at the Imperial War Museum. The late Admiral Sir Deric Holland-Martin, the Director, Dr Noble Frankland, and all their very efficient staff had taken a great deal of trouble in organizing the exhibition, which was to remain open for a year, after which a V.C. and G.C. corner was to be established in the Museum which would remain as a permanent memorial.

On 10 June the Museum was packed with our members and their relatives and distinguished guests as the Queen and Prince Philip entered the hall and took their places on the platform. In opening the exhibition the Queen made the following speech, copies of which were issued to all our members.

The gathering of holders of the Victoria Cross and George Cross in London this week is the seventh since 1956 and it gives me the greatest possible pleasure to welcome you all again.

Your Association deserves every credit for arranging these reunions and one man in particular has played a most important part. Sir John Smyth is retiring as Chairman of the Association at the end of this year, having devoted an immense amount of time and energy to its affairs. I am glad to say that he is to continue as President in succession to the late Sir Winston Churchill.

The purpose of this occasion is to open the special exhibition arranged by the Imperial War Museum, which is to be succeeded by a permanent Victoria Cross and George Cross Memorial Corner. In March and April this year I saw the Memorial Corners in Dunedin and Canberra. Together these Corners will commemorate the gallantry of individuals and as a network stretching across the Commonwealth they will link all those who have fought for this brotherhood of free and independent nations.

When Queen Victoria introduced the Victoria Cross it was exceptional in that it could be awarded to anyone who served in the Armed Forces of the Crown whatever their rank or race. At that time it was rare for civilian populations to take a direct share in military activities. The last war brought our homeland directly under enemy attack and at once it became clear that at home civilians as well as servicemen were performing similar feats of valour to those of the Services in the face of the enemy. It was to recognise their courage that my father introduced the George Cross, which has rightly taken its place beside the Victoria Cross.

Memories of battles long ago and distant wars quickly fade. This special exhibition will remind us all of half forgotten stories of the heights of action to which human beings can rise in the service of their fellow men.

I congratulate the Imperial War Museum on having arranged this exhibition and it gives me great pleasure to declare the exhibition open.

Before touring the exhibition Her Majesty invited me to present all our overseas V.C. and G.C. members. She also invited me to present to her Admiral Godfrey Place, V.C., who was succeeding me as Chairman of the Association. As I had some forty V.C.s and G.C.s to present to her I had made out a little plan showing exactly where they were all to stand. This had been shown to them beforehand. When I started off with the Canadians by introducing Lieutenant-Colonel Dave Currie, V.C., the overseas Vice-Chairman, I was horrified to see that the place next to him, which should have been occupied by Brigadier the Hon. Milton Gregg, V.C., was empty. The Queen, who doesn't miss much, said: 'Who should be here?' When I told her, she said: 'Well I've already seen him in the Museum. I would like to know why he isn't here.' I think she thought he might have been taken ill, as he was one of our older members. I said I would find out and let her know.

When it was all over Milton Gregg, a very dear friend of mine, came along almost in tears. About half an hour before the presentation he had paid a visit to the upstairs lavatory – and got locked in. He rattled the door, yelled and shouted, but everyone had gone down to the exhibition. It was not until some time later that he had been released. I dropped a line to the Queen's Private Secretary accordingly. Her Majesty was much amused. Milton Gregg died on 13 March 1978, to our great sorrow, in his eighty-sixth year.

The Queen had also very kindly conveyed a message to me that she would like me to present my two grandsons, Timothy and Christopher. But thereby hangs rather a sad tale. I had been swimming with Christopher before breakfast in the Dolphin Square pool when he, in diving into the pool, ricked his neck. This was so painful that he had to retire to bed. So he missed the thrill of his life, which was accorded to Tim, when the Queen said a few words to him in the Museum. However, Christopher was somewhat comforted when the Queen deputed her Private Secretary to telephone to ask how he was getting on. The Queen is a very kind and thoughtful person. (Christopher returned in 1978 with a wife, Frances, and my two first great-grandsons.)

The Lord Mayor had then invited our members to a most enjoyable reception at the Mansion House. Our Guest of Honour at the dinner on Friday 18 June, which in this year (1970) was held in the Connaught Rooms, was Her Royal Highness Princess Alexandra. She was accompanied by her husband, the Hon. Angus Ogilvy. It was the last time I was to speak at the dinner as Chairman.

In February 1972 I handed over the Chairmanship to my good friend, Rear Admiral Godfrey Place, V.C. The Association gave a farewell lunch to me as Chairman, and Frances, at the R.A.F. Club on 16 February and made a presentation of a casket and a picture of the Queen with Sir Winston Churchill on her right and myself on her left. The inscription on the accompanying plaque reads:

The originals of these three pictures now hang in the Imperial War Museum, London, and formed part of the Victoria Cross and George Cross Exhibition opened by Her Majesty, the Queen on 10th July 1970. The photograph of Her Majesty, Patron of the Victoria Cross and George Cross Association from 1957, and that of Sir Winston Churchill, President of the Association 1959–65, were displayed originally in the Victoria Cross and George Cross room in St George's House, which was opened by the Rt Hon. Harold Macmillan, M.P., on 10th July 1960 in the presence of Sir John Smyth, founder of the Association and its first Chairman from 1956–1971, and members of the United Kingdom Committee of the Association. These copies were presented to Sir John Smyth on relinquishing the Chairmanship in February 1971, by all the members of the Association as a token of their affection and appreciation of his unique service.

The casket contained two beautiful glass goblets both engraved with the V.C. and G.C.:

Presented to Sir John and Lady Smyth by all the members of the Victoria Cross and George Cross Association who wish to express their affection and gratitude for the devoted service they have given to the Association since it was founded by Sir John Smyth in 1956.

On 22 October 1972 Prime Minister Edward Heath announced in the House of Commons that the living holders of the Albert and Edward Medals were authorized to exchange their medals for the George Cross. As President of the Association I at once wrote a letter, which was published in the *Daily Telegraph*, warmly welcoming these new members whom the Queen had been pleased to honour with our highest civil decoration, to our Association. And Godfrey Place, as Chairman, wrote to all of them in the same cordial vein. The new G.C.s amounted to some 122 in all, about equally divided between the Albert Medals and the Edwards Medals. It did of course involve a considerable amount of readjustment of our small Association but Godfrey Place and his Committee coped with this most efficiently.

For the 1972 reunion two more of my grandchildren, Margaret and John Smyth, arrived from Canberra with the Australian party. We had a lovely time with them. The first function of the reunion week was my President's Party on Tuesday 11 July, which was graced by Her Majesty the Queen Mother; and Princess Anne was our Guest of Honour at the reunion dinner.

Towards the end of 1973 the Association was making preparations for the 1974 reunion and Frances and I were in close correspondence with Canberra whence members of my family would be coming over. I very much wanted to see Clare, my second eldest granddaughter. We had been told that the Queen would be giving another reception for us, for which the age limit had been raised from fourteen to fifteen. This just allowed Clare to attend. But she would obviously have to have some older member of the family to travel with her. It would have to be either Julian or Phyllis as Timothy was in the throes of medical exams, Margaret was at university and Christopher had just got married. Phyllis would naturally find it difficult to leave the younger children, so Julian it was to be. We planned to get Robin over from Washington too so that my three living children could all be together. Julian was looking forward to a second visit with the greatest anticipation.

On the evening of Wednesday 23 January 1974 the telephone rang and Frances answered it. Suddenly there was a heavy silence, somehow fraught with disaster. Frances said : 'It's Phyllis from Canberra. Julian is dying from inoperable cancer of the stomach.'

The doctors could give no idea how long he would last – perhaps two or three months. My daughter Jill at once flew to Canberra and returned on 2 February. Julian was facing death with immense courage and for the moment was not in much pain. He most emphatically wanted Clare to come over for the reunion and for Tim to bring her. From time to time Frances and I talked to Julian on the telephone. Always he was thinking of us and his family and never murmured a word of complaint or dismay about his own impending death. Phyllis and Julian went off on a short holiday together but by April he had little time left. He was conscious almost to the end and had all the children in one by one to say goodbye. On 29 April he died, mourned by a host of friends.

On 18 May (the anniversary of my V.C. in 1915) we were meeting Tim and Clare at the Royal Commonwealth Society in London, with two coach loads of V.C.s and G.C.s and their relatives. The R.A.F. plane that had brought them had started from Darwin on 14 May and had flown via Auckland, Sydney, Perth, Gan, Delhi, Akrotiri and Brise Norton. Tim was now twenty-one, the head of the family and heir to my baronetcy, and altogether a very responsible and fine young man. Clare was a darling and at once declared that I was her favourite grandfather (in fact I was her only one) but I was by that time a great-grandfather as Chris had produced a son, Matthew.

The reunion week, which flew by far too quickly, was the best antidote to the great sorrow we all felt at Julian's death. On the first Monday was my President's Party, with Princess Anne and Captain Mark Phillips as Guests of Honour.

As the funds of the Association increased more financial help was able to be given to any member in particular need.

Victoria Crosses fetch increasingly fantastic prices at auction sales. At the time of writing the record price for one bit of old Russian cannon is £7,500 – which is naturally more than a regiment can afford. We do not of course encourage the sale of V.C.s and it is almost unheard of for a man to sell his own Cross; but it is rather hard for a poor family, whose grandfather perhaps won the V.C. many years ago, to keep it lying on the mantelpiece when they can get such large sums for it.

We have from time to time had impostor V.C.s. Sometimes it is a hallucination where a man thinks : 'Well I *ought* to have got the V.C.'; later perhaps he thinks : 'Yes, I *did* get the V.C.', and then, 'Yes, I'm sure I did get the V.C. but what I did with it I'm danged if I know'.

Sometimes it is done quite deliberately and the man concerned gets away with it. It is however not nearly so easy since the V.C. and G.C. Association was formed and each holder receives the £100 annuity. Not only do we know the names and addresses of all the living holders but the Government does too, which was not the case before 1956. On the other hand fake V.C.s are now made which are hard to tell from the authentic ones.

One day I had a letter from a boy in Australia who said he was going to put his father's medals into the Canberra V.C. Memorial Corner and as the V.C. ribbon was rather frayed he wondered if I could get him another. I had to tell him, very sadly, that his father never won the V.C. Another case was of a man who, from the age of about twenty-five, had impersonated a posthumous V.C. from the

First World War. Soon after the V.C. Association had been formed he emigrated to one of the dominions and eventually died and was buried with full military honours. Had his widow not written to me to ask if any money or pension was due to him the impersonation would never have been discovered. The War Office replied that the V.C. in question had died in Mesopotamia when winning his V.C. in 1916.

One day the Matron of St George's Hospital rang me and said: 'I think I ought to tell you that one of your V.C.s, Commander Cameron, is seriously ill.' He was one of the midget submarine V.C.s. So I rang his 'buddy', Admiral Godfrey Place. There was a pause. Then he said: 'But he is here, sitting beside me.'

I rang the Matron and said: 'I'm sorry that your Commander Cameron is so ill – but he is not a V.C.'

A little later I had a letter from the author of a biography of another of the midget submarine V.C.s. He had completed the book and wanted to know where he could get a photo of him as he was at the time. I told him to try the Imperial War Museum. Shortly afterwards he wrote rather angrily: 'Your V.C. is an imposter. The photo they gave me is of a small, insignificant man. The real V.C. I have written about is a tall, upstanding man with an anchor tattooed on his arm.'

I told him: 'Tall, upstanding men were not accepted for the midget subs – the height limit was about 5 ft 7 in.' I heard no more about the matter – or of the book.

Our Royal Patron, the Queen, gave the reunion a magnificent focal point by inviting us to a reception at Windsor Castle on her fiftieth birthday, Wednesday 21 April 1976. I was told that when it was pointed out to her that she had invited us on her birthday, she replied: 'I can't think of a nicer thing to do on my birthday.'

The Remembrance Service that year was held, as usual, at St Martin-in-the-Fields on the afternoon of 20 April and this was followed the same evening by my President's Party at the National Army Museum. This was a splendid setting and the Museum staff had taken infinite trouble over the arrangements. My Guest of Honour was Princess Margaret, who couldn't have been a more interested and delightful guest. In former years this party had been quite a small gathering of about one hundred people for the overseas members and their relatives to meet members of the Committee and their wives. This time we invited all the V.C.s and G.C.s attending the reunion, each with one relative. In addition I had about twenty personal guests who included Field-Marshal Sir Gerald Templer, Viscount Slim (son of the Field-Marshal) and members of my own family. This made a party of over three hundred.

The next day we all foregathered at Windsor Castle – a party of

512, as members were allowed to bring two guests. Unfortunately, just as the Queen and Prince Philip arrived and I was about to present my Chairman, Godfrey Place, and the two Vice-Chairmen, General Foote (U.K.) and Colonel Dave Currie (Overseas), the Queen was informed that Princess Anne had had a bad riding accident and was unconscious; and at that point they had no idea how bad the accident was. Nevertheless, the Queen and Prince Philip went their walkabout for about two hours, shaking hands and talking to all present, and never showed for a moment how anxious they must have been.

At the end of the proceedings I made a little speech and presented the Queen with a glass bowl on which was engraved her royal insignia and the emblems of the V.C. and G.C. against a background of Windsor Castle. Whereupon, to the Queen's obvious surprise and delight our members, well primed beforehand, burst into 'Happy Birthday to You'. It was a great occasion for us.

It is impossible for me to speak adequately about the Queen and what she means to us. Our regard for her goes far beyond the ordinary feelings of loyalty and affection that her subjects have for their Sovereign. She has made each one of us in the Association feel that we matter to her and our loyalty and devotion to her are beyond measure.

On the following day (23 April) we held our Biennial General Meeting at the Café Royal, followed by the reunion dinner, at which our Guest of Honour was H.R.H. Prince Philip, who received all the members and distinguished guests and proposed the Toast of the Association, to which Godfrey Place replied. Though I was not on the Toast list I was called upon to make a short speech at the end.

On the Saturday of the same week Aileen Slim had invited Frances and me to attend in the Crypt of St Paul's, with her family, at the unveiling of a plaque to her late husband, Field-Marshal Viscount Slim, and then to take part in the service in the Cathedral. The members of the Burma Star Association filled the church. It was a simple, moving and dignified Service.

The eleventh biennial reunion of the V.C. and G.C. Association was held in the second week of May 1978. We had a remarkable attendance despite difficulties over air transport and the increasing age of our members. On Monday the 8th a cocktail party was held at the R.A.F. Club for the Committee and their wives to meet the overseas members. The next day we held our usual Service of Remembrance at St Martin-in-the-Fields, which was followed by my President's Party. This time, by invitation of the Lord Mayor, it was a tea party at the Mansion House with Princess Alexandra and her husband as Guests of Honour. Godfrey Place had done an excellent thing in inviting thirty widows, a gesture which was much appreciated. This made a total of nearly 400, all of whom I received with the Lord Mayor and Lady Mayoress. I then presented my personal guests to the Princess. It was a splendid occasion.

Various other pleasurable entertainments had been arranged, including a delightful day at Penshurst by invitation of Lord de L'Isle, V.C. After the Biennial General Meeting the dinner took place at the Café Royal. In the absence of any member of the Royal Family, only the second occasion this had happened, and with the Prime Minister prevented from attending, I was invited to be Guest of Honour. Although I much appreciated the kindness of the members in wanting me, I felt rather diffident, in my eighty-sixth year, of coming out of my retirement and making the main speech. However, I had Frances sitting next to me and I managed to rise to the occasion, so much so that the whole gathering gave me a standing ovation. It was a most heart-warming occasion, and maybe my last, as no man can live for ever. I was very gratified at the warmth of affection our members showed to Frances, who had done more for them over the years than most of them realized. Altogether it had been a memorable week, one of the best we had ever had.

The Secretary of State for Defence, the Rt Hon. Fred Mulley, wrote to the Chairman, following the dinner : 'Your Association is a valuable and irreplaceable way of maintaining links among a unique group of people and I know that I and my colleagues here, both Service and civilian, are immensely grateful for anything the Association does.'

Our membership is of course shrinking sadly. With the death of George Cartwright (Australia) aged 83, in February; Milton Gregg (Canada) aged 85, in April; and Philip Neame, 89, the First World War V.C.s have dwindled to thirty and the total of living V.C.s has dropped to under 100 and the G.C.s to 158.

I felt that the wheel had turned full circle and that this was a chapter in my life which was closing – a noble chapter which I had been privileged to share and enjoy with some of the bravest, and yet the humblest, of our British and Commonwealth men and women, of all races, all creeds and all colours.

CHAPTER TWENTY-THREE

On Books and Book Writing

I LOVE writing and am utterly happy in the doing of it. I didn't start writing until the end of the Second World War, when I was fifty-one, and during the next thirty-one years I have published thirty books and two plays. I would like to have written on a more settled basis, getting down to it after breakfast each day and I am sure I would have written more and better books if I could have done so. But I had so many other things on my plate that I had to write when and where I could. Also I would like to have had a good agent which I never really acquired. Nevertheless I had books published by some of the best publishers in the land and my relations with them were extremely good.

Although I can dictate correspondence I have never been able to dictate a book and, like many other and more distinguished writers, I write always in longhand with a biro pen, with very few corrections. As long as I can write and publishers are prepared to publish what I write I shall continue to do so.

My first book, *Defence Is Our Business*, was published by Hutchinson in 1944. In 1950 I was invited by Alan Wingate to arrange, edit and introduce *The Western Defences*, described by Paul Henri Spaak, who wrote the foreword, as 'a book of burning topicality'.

After the Second World War lawn tennis became an important part of my life, as I have described in an earlier chapter, and I wrote four books on the subject – *Lawn Tennis, a History of the Game* (Batsford, 1953); *The Game's the Same* (Cassell, 1957); *Behind the Scenes at Wimbledon*, with Colonel Macaulay (Collins, 1965); and *Jean Borotra* (Stanley Paul, 1974).

Before the Dawn, published by Cassell in 1957, described my own experiences as commander of 127 Infantry Brigade at Dunkirk and of the 17th Indian Division, which bore the full brunt of the first Japanese invasion of Burma. This book was selected by Sir Edwin McAlpine as his presentation book at his Christmas lunch at the Dorchester and he ordered 600 copies. This gave it a very good start and it soon went into a second edition.

The first of my three children's books, *Paradise Island*, was published by Max Parrish in 1952. I had always rather enjoyed telling bedtime stories to children and several people suggested I should write a book for them. My heroine of this first book, Ann Sheldon, aged thirteen, tells the story of her adventures on a European island in her own words. When Derek Hart interviewed me about this book on television he appeared astonished that, as a middle-aged brigadier, I should put myself into the mind of a thirteen-year-old girl! Max Parrish invited me to write a sequel, which I called *Trouble In Paradise*, and then a third, *Ann Goes Hunting*, by which time Ann was getting rather too grown up and one small reader wrote and suggested that she should now get married. Max Parrish hoped that I would go on writing books for children – one every year if I liked – but there were so many other books I wanted to write and I felt three was enough, though I much enjoyed writing them, partly because children who read them wrote me such delightful letters.

In 1959 I wrote *The Only Enemy* (Hutchinson), and that was followed in 1961 by *Sandhurst* (Weidenfeld and Nicolson), the history of the Royal Military Academy Woolwich, the Royal Military College Sandhurst and the Royal Military Academy Sandhurst 1941–61. This book was warmly sponsored by the Chief of the Imperial General Staff, Field-Marshal Sir Francis Festing; Field-Marshal Viscount Montgomery of Alamein very kindly offered to write the foreword and took the greatest interest in the book. I enjoyed writing it. The Roll of Honour in the Sandhurst Chapel contains the name of my son John. I was tremendously impressed with this beautiful new Memorial Chapel and ended my book with a quotation from its brochure.

In 1962 Frederick Muller published my *Story of the Victoria Cross*, a magnum opus, with a foreword by Field-Marshal Earl Alexander of Tunis. A number of books had been written about the Victoria Cross but this was the first book which recorded every V.C. since the decoration was first instituted in 1856, and made retrospective to cover the Crimean War. The great merit of the book was that I had arranged the V.C.s in the order in which they had been won, instead of by the dates of the Gazettes, which often bore no relation historically to the battles in which they had been gained. Every detail of the book was checked by my friend and one-time Staff College pupil Brigadier William Underhill, who was the chief expert on the subject at the War Office. The book was at once accepted as the 'bible' of the V.C. and has remained so ever since. Mullers published a second edition but then, owing to financial difficulties, allowed it to go out of print. It is still in constant demand. Much against my will I was persuaded to publish a 'Cadet' edition, largely for schools. This was produced in a hard-back edition and then in a 'limp' cover. The Cadet editions sold quite well but they did not contain more than a small proportion of the V.C. awards, which disappointed a number of readers.

I promised my friends of the George Cross that I would write their book in due course and, in 1968, it was published by Arthur Barker as *The Story of the George Cross*, with the following dedication :

DEDICATION

To all those gallant men and women who have won the George Cross – in admiration and comradeship.

The Steady heart that seldom slurs its beat
The Soul unbroken when the body tires
These are the things our weary world requires.

After the war Frances and I became great Siamese cat lovers and we always had at least two Siamese cats in our flat, and later two Burmese. Our cats became important people in our lives. I officiated on several occasions for Sir Compton Mackenzie, President of the Siamese Cat Club, at their annual show, and I wrote extensively about the Siamese in journals of various sorts. The first of my three cat books, *Beloved Cats*, was published by Frederick Muller in 1963 and was followed by *Blue Magnolia* in 1964. An American edition, combining both these books under one cover, was published by the Citadel Press, New York in 1965. Our cats became quite famous in the cat world and indeed to many people outside it. In addition to my first two books about them, they were included in Rank's film, *The Price of Valour*, which was one of their 'Look at Life' series of documentaries. The film was actually about the Victoria Cross, but when the camera men came to take shots of me in my study as Chairman of the V.C. Association, they became quite entranced by our four cats – Pooni, Blue Magnolia, Leo and Tomkin – who were themselves intrigued by all the photographic apparatus and basked in the warmth of the camera lights. The film was beautifully made and was a great success. Rank's people reckoned it had been seen by some ten million people in the Rank circuit alone, before it went into general release. A copy of the film was to have been presented to Sir Winston Churchill, President of the V.C. and G.C. Association, but he died before the presentation could be made, so they gave it to me instead.

The cats were such a success in *The Price of Valour* that Ranks decided to make another film entirely devoted to cats. But when the camera men came to take our four cats, Tomkin and Leo had both died suddenly of a virus infection and there were only two females remaining, Pooni and Blue Magnolia, and they were too miserable to care how they looked before the camera and were pining for their dead comrades. However, they realized that the show must go on and did their best. The new film was called *Cool Cats*.

As a result of my two cat books and the two films our cats became familiar to a wide public and we had many messages of sympathy for our two dead pets. My third cat book, *Ming – The Story of a Cat Family* (Muller, 1966), was dedicated to Sir Winston Churchill, 'The greatest and most beloved cat lover of all time'. Through the kindness of Lady Churchill I was able to obtain a historic and not previously published frontispiece photo (by Mrs Anthea Sieveking). This photo was taken at his grandson's wedding on 15 July 1964 – six months before his death and shows Sir Winston with his last cat sitting on his knee. He had expressed a wish to have a ginger kitten and the R.S.P.C.A. made a search for one all over London. Eventually one was found and was presented to him by his Personal Assistant, Sir John Colville. It was his constant companion to the day of his death.

In 1966 I was invited by the late Lady Whistler to write the life of her husband, General Sir Lashmer Whistler, commonly known in the Army as 'Bolo', who died of cancer on 4 July 1963 at the age of sixty-four. The most flattering remark about this book was made by one of his greatest admirers, who said: 'You must have known him very well.' In fact, though our ways had sometimes run along similar lines, particularly at Dunkirk, we had never met. Bolo was a born leader, a great character and a very warm and human personality. No less a person than Field-Marshal Montgomery had referred to him as 'about the best infantry brigade commander I knew and later a superb divisional commander'. Field-Marshal Sir Gerald Templer told me that 'Bolo Whistler was the finest type of British soldier it had ever been my good fortune to know'. All his padrés loved him and thought the world of him. The Rev. J. R. Youens (later Chaplain General to the Army) had the greatest admiration for him and gave the address at his Memorial Service in Chichester Cathedral. But perhaps the person who knew him best and had the greatest affection for him was the late Duke of Norfolk, who had served under him in the Royal Sussex Regiment. Major Norfolk, as he was to the Regiment, and 'Bernard Norfolk' as he was to Bolo and Esmé Whistler, was a great person in the Royal Sussex Regiment, as his father had been before him.

I invited both Monty and the Duke to write forewords to the book. Monty was pleased to accept and took the greatest trouble about his foreword. I asked the Duke to come and have a talk on my dictaphone. 'You will never get Bernard to do that,' said Esmé. But he came and we had a great talk.

I enjoyed writing the Bolo book enormously, not least because, as a result, Frances and I made many dear friends, including Esmé Whistler and her family and John and Pam Youens. *Bolo Whistler – The Life of Sir Lashmer Whistler* was published by Frederick Muller in 1967 (Esmé died in 1978). I felt very honoured (and considerably surprised) when a little later John Youens asked me to write the story of the Army Chaplains.

The Story of the Army Chaplains, which ran to 365 pages, was published under the title *In This Sign Conquer* (Mowbray, 1968), which is the motto of the Army Chaplains. It was dedicated to 'All Army Chaplains who throughout our history – in the day of battle and in time of peace – have served the British soldier and in proud remembrance of those who joined so many of their comrades in the supreme sacrifice'. The foreword was written by Field-Marshal Sir Richard Hull, Chief of the Defence Staff, who wrote:

I am honoured and delighted to have been asked by the Chaplain General to write a foreword to this book. As the author, Brigadier Jackie Smyth, points out, it is far more than just the story of the Chaplains' Department. It is, in fact, an abridged history, and a very good one too, of our nation. From the middle of the seventeenth century the Church, State and Army are inextricably interwoven, and the pages that follow make fascinating reading from Master Bowles to Archdeacon Youens.

It is significant that our great commanders of history, Marlborough, Sir John Moore, Wellington, Lord Roberts and in our own time the Lords Haig, Wavell, Montgomery and Slim, all put so much emphasis and importance on the spiritual well-being of their armies and their own relationship with their chaplains.

I received the greatest possible assistance in writing the book from the Chaplains' Department, particularly from John Youens and his Deputy, the Rev. D. H. Whiteford. The Staff at the Departmental Centre at Bagshot also gave me and Frances their utmost co-operation and kindest hospitality. Many people wrote to me and came to see me, from field-marshals to former chaplain-generals and padrés of all denominations. Alexander wrote an excellent review of the book and put me in touch with the chaplain whom he considered to be the best

As President of the Distinguished Conduct Medal League greeting our Patron, the Princess Royal, at her last parade before her death in 1965

With Bill Slim during one of his last appearances as President of the Burma Star Association

At a Burma Star Parade on the Horse Guards

My daughter Jill, now
Mrs David Firth

My second son Julian, aged
eighteen

My first wife Margaret,
the devoted mother of my
four wonderful children

My third son Robin, now Foreign
Correspondent of the *Observer*
newspaper in Paris

As President of the Victoria Cross and George Cross Association with Bhanbhagta Gurung, V.C., 2nd Gurkha Rifles (right) and Rambahadur Limbu, V.C., 10th Gurkha Rifles

With Sir Charles Forte at the eleventh Reunion Dinner of the V.C. and G.C. Association at the Café Royal, 11 May 1978

he had ever met : the Rt Rev. Abbot J. R. Brookes, then the representative of the English Benedictines in Rome, who was Alex's Chaplain in the Irish Guards and was generally known as 'Dolly'.

There have been many famous general–chaplain relationships, of which perhaps the best known was that of Field-Marshal Montgomery and the Rev. F. L. Hughes (later Dean of Ripon) in the 8th Army in North Africa and in the 21st Army Group in Europe. In my knowledge no other General has attached so much importance to spiritual stamina in war as Monty. He once said at one of his briefing conferences before battle : 'The most important people in the Army are the Nursing Sisters and the Padrés – the Sisters because they tell the men they matter to us – and the Padrés because they tell them they matter to God. And it is the men who matter.'

When Monty heard that I was writing this book he insisted I should go and stay with the Dean of Ripon and with his customary thoroughness arranged the visit himself. Frances and I had a delightful two days with the Dean and his wife in January 1967 and we sat enthralled while he talked of his times with the Field-Marshal. The Dean had a great sense of humour and when he became Senior Chaplain to the 21st Army Group in December 1943 he found he was confronted with a colossal amount of paper, nearly all marked 'Top Secret'. He asked Monty if it would be in order if he marked his files 'Top Sacred'! Alas, the Dean died soon after our visit. We attended his Memorial Service in the Guards Chapel, at which Montgomery read the lesson.

The picture on the frontispiece (by Terence Cuneo) of *In This Sign Conquer* showed King George V presenting the Victoria Cross in France to the Rev. Theodore Bayley Hardy, who won it in April 1918. The original picture is hung in the Royal Army Chaplains' Museum at Bagshot. On Palm Sunday, 7 April 1968, the Queen and the Duke of Edinburgh visited the Royal Army Chaplains' Centre. After a short Service the Queen was shown the picture and Terence Cuneo and I were presented to Her Majesty. 'Whatever is the Queen talking about to your husband?' someone said to Frances, seeing us deep in conversation. She was in fact asking me about another occasion when her grandfather had presented me with my V.C. at an investiture at Buckingham Palace in July 1915.

My next book, *The Valiant* (Mowbray, 1970), was dedicated to my eldest son, John, and contained an account of the action at Kohima in May 1944 in which he was killed, together with a number of other valiant occasions in our history.

The Will to Live (Cassell) was published in the same year. This was the story of a very gallant nursing sister, Margot Turner, who had a miraculous escape from death when her ship was torpedoed by the

Japanese in the Java Sea. Only her intense will to live enabled her to survive and endure years in a Japanese prison camp. She was one of the comparatively few ex-prisoners of the Japanese who returned to their pre-war professions, and she rose to the top by becoming Matron-in-Chief of the Royal Army Nursing Service. The foreword was written by Brigadier Barbara Gordon, who succeeded her as Matron-in-Chief. Here again we made some lifelong friends in Margot and Barbara and the Army Nursing Sisters.

Percival and the Tragedy of Singapore (Macdonald) followed in 1971. I wrote this book to set the record straight and counter the unworthy calumnies which had been put around regarding General Percival (and his troops), who, like others of our earlier commanders, had to carry the can for the sins of successive British Governments who were unwilling to pay the price in peacetime to ensure against another war. And in 1974 B.B.C. Radio put on an hour's programme entitled *The Guns of Singapore,* in which I was able to put across these truths with regard to Singapore once more, to a wider audience. The programme was repeated the following year.

In 1972 I wrote the life story of the late Brigadier P. J. D. Toosey (later Sir Philip), the very gallant President of the Far Eastern Prisoner of War Federation, which he had printed for private circulation only. He was in fact very near to death at the time but made a marvellous recovery and lived several more years. In this book I was able to highlight some of the awful sufferings of the Far Eastern prisoners and the wonderful courage which was shown in their survival.

Then came two recent books, *Leadership in War 1939–45* and *Leadership in Battle 1914–18* (David and Charles). I had originally planned these as one book, but the length of it made the cost of publication too prohibitive in these inflation-ridden days.

In July 1977 my thirty-first book appeared, *Great Stories of the Victoria Cross* (Arthur Barker). This book was dedicated, with her kind permission, to Her Majesty the Queen, the only book she had ever allowed to be dedicated to her. It was a Queen's Jubilee book.

In 1974 I took on a new interest, reviewing books for that excellent publication, *Books and Bookmen.* And in that year Frances and I took part in the B.B.C. Radio programme, *The Raj,* repeated the following year and later made into a book called *Plain Tales from the Raj* (Deutsch, 1975), which went into the best-selling list and was a great tribute to Charles Allen, who had done the interviewing of so many people who had known India in the days of the British Raj. Frances also appeared with Charles Allen in *Nationwide* in a review of the book.

I marvel every day that, having survived two grave illnesses, two world wars and seven frontier campaigns, I have now reached the middle eighties. Frances and I are so exceedingly lucky that we like the same things; and she makes a massive contribution to our family life in that she types and sub-edits all my books, in addition to all the ordinary secretarial work, which she has tackled single-handed since I gave up the Chairmanship of the V.C. and G.C. Association. This togetherness in itself makes for a really happy marriage. As Derek Hart said when interviewing me on television once: 'In fact you are a happy man.' Yes, I am a happy man; happy in my life with Frances, in my children and my grandchildren, and in my friends. I remain as I began – an incurable optimist.

Index